God and the Rhetoric of Sexuality

OVERTURES TO BIBLICAL THEOLOGY

Editors

WALTER BRUEGGEMANN, Professor of Old Testament at Eden Theological Seminary, St. Louis, Missouri

JOHN R. DONAHUE, S.J., Professor of New Testament at the Jesuit School of Theology, Berkeley, California

GOD

AND
THE RHETORIC
OF
SEXUALITY

PHYLLIS TRIBLE

 FORTRESS PRESS   Philadelphia

Fourth printing 1985

Library of Congress Cataloging in Publication Data

Trible, Phyllis.
God and the rhetoric of sexuality.

(Overtures to Biblical theology)
Includes index.
1. Bible. O.T.—Criticism, interpretation, etc.
2. God—Biblical teaching. 3. Bible. O.T.—Hermeneutics.
4. Image of God—Biblical teaching. 5. Sex
(Theology)—Biblical teaching. I. Title. II. Series.
BS1171.2.T74   221.6   77-78647
ISBN 0-8006-0464-4

in memoriam
JAMES MUILENBURG

Contents

Series Foreword

Biblical theology has been a significant part of modern study of the Jewish and Christian Scriptures. Prior to the ascendancy of historical criticism of the Bible in the nineteenth century, biblical theology was subordinated to the dogmatic concerns of the churches, and the Bible too often provided a storehouse of rigid proof texts. When biblical theology was cut loose from its moorings to dogmatic theology to become an enterprise seeking its own methods and categories, attention was directed to what the Bible itself had to say. A dogmatic concern was replaced by an historical one so that biblical theology was understood as an investigation of what was believed by different communities in different situations. By the end of the nineteenth century biblical theology was virtually equated with the history of the religion of the authors who produced biblical documents or of the communities which used them.

While these earlier perspectives have become more refined and sophisticated, they still describe the parameters of what is done in the name of biblical theology—moving somewhere between the normative statements of dogmatic theology and the descriptive concerns of the history of religions. Th. Vriezen, in his *An Outline of Old Testament Theology* (Dutch, 1949; ET, 1958), sought to combine these concerns by devoting the first half of his book to historical considerations and the second half to theological themes. But even that effort did not break out of the stalemate of categories. In more recent times Old Testament theology has been dominated by two paradigmatic works. In his *Theology of the Old Testament* (German, 1933–39; ET, 1967) W. Eichrodt has provided a comprehensive statement around fixed categories which reflect classical dogmatic interests, although the centrality

ix

of covenant in his work reflects the Bible's own categories. By contrast, G. von Rad in his *Old Testament Theology* (German, 1960; ET, 1965) has presented a study of theological traditions with a primary concern for the historical dynamism of the traditions. In the case of New Testament theology, historical and theological concerns are rather roughly juxtaposed in the work of A. Richardson, *An Introduction to the Theology of the New Testament*. As in the case of the Old Testament there are two major options or presentations which dominate in New Testament studies. The history-of-religion school has left its mark on the magisterial work of R. Bultmann, who proceeds from an explanation of the expressions of faith of the earliest communities and their theologians to a statement of how their understanding of existence under faith speaks to us today. The works of O. Cullmann and W. G. Kümmel are clear New Testament statements of *Heilsgeschichte* under the aegis of the tension between promise and fulfillment—categories reminiscent of von Rad.

As recently as 1962, K. Stendahl again underscored the tension between historical description and normative meaning by assigning to the biblical theologian the task of describing what the Bible *meant*, not what it *means* or *how* it can have meaning. However, this objectivity of historical description is too often found to be a mirror of the observer's hidden preunderstanding, and the adequacy of historical description is contingent on one generation's discoveries and postulates. Also, the yearning and expectation of believers and would-be believers will not let biblical theology rest with the descriptive task alone. The growing strength of Evangelical Protestantism and the expanding phenomenon of charismatic Catholicism are but vocal reminders that people seek in the Bible a source of alternative value systems. By its own character and by the place it occupies in our culture the Bible will not rest easy as merely an historical artifact.

Thus it seems a fitting time to make "overtures" concerning biblical theology. It is not a time for massive tomes which claim too much. It appears not even to be a time for firm conclusions which are too comprehensive. It is a time for pursuit of fresh hints, for exploration of new intuitions which may reach beyond old conclusions, set categories, and conventional methods. The books in this series are concerned not only with what is seen and heard, with what the Bible said, but also with what the Bible says and the ways in which seeing and hearing are done.

In putting forth these *Overtures* much remains unsettled. The certainties of the older biblical theology *in service* of dogmatics, as well as of the more recent biblical theology movement *in lieu* of dogmatics, are no longer present. Nor is there on the scene anyone of the stature of a von Rad or a Bultmann to offer a synthesis which commands the theological engagement of a generation and summons the church to a new restatement of the biblical message. In a period characterized by an information explosion the relation of analytic study to attempts at synthesis is unsettled. Also unsettled is the question whether the scholarly canon of the university or the passion of the confessing community provides a language and idiom of discourse, and equally unsettled—and unsettling—is the question whether biblical theology is simply one more specialization in an already fragmented study of scripture or whether it is finally the point of it all.

But much remains clear. Not simply must the community of biblical scholars address fresh issues and articulate new categories for the well-being of our common professional task; equally urgent is the fact that the dominant intellectual tradition of the West seems now to carry less conviction and to satisfy only weakly the new measures of knowing which are among us. We do not know exactly what role the Bible will play in new theological statements or religious postures, nor what questions the Bible can and will address, but *Overtures* will provide a locus where soundings may be taken.

We not only intend that *Overtures* should make contact with people professionally involved in biblical studies, but hope that the series will speak to all who care about the heritage of the biblical tradition. We hope that the volumes will represent the best in a literary and historical study of biblical traditions without canonizing historical archaism. We hope also that the studies will be relevant without losing the mystery of biblical religion's historical distance, and that the studies touch on significant themes, motifs, and symbols of the Bible without losing the rich diversity of the biblical tradition. It is a time for normative literature which is not heavy-handed, but which seriously challenges not only our conclusions but also the shape of our questions.

The present volume by Phyllis Trible makes a major contribution to a most urgent issue in scripture study. The problem of sexist presuppositions and methods is widely recognized and may be addressed at various levels in different ways. But for all the recent attention to the problem, little substantive work has been done.

Trible's treatment is a peculiarly helpful one precisely because she is able to hold together and in tension a variety of agendas. In one way, her study concerns the problem of language. She suggests that the language crisis will be best solved if we pay attention to the texts' own concern for language and for speech. But Trible obviously understands that the language issue concerns the tone and texture of interpretation and is not a matter of just changing some words. Her discussion, then, is a formidable exercise in hermeneutics. She is fully conversant with the newer literary criticism and effectively understands the power of metaphor as a means for interpreting scripture. Thus her method by way of metaphor is consistent with the substance of her argument, for in method as well as in substance her work represents an important break with the procedure and epistemology that seem linked with sexism.

Trible's book is indeed an "overture," a hint of a quite fresh way of doing exegesis. But it is not simply an exercise in method, nor is it a special pleading for a cause. It is an offering of serious substantive theology that requires a rethinking of some most central aspects of biblical faith. The book will be an important one because it challenges some most familiar assumptions about texts and alerts us to resources in texts that have appeared marginal and safely neglected. The book meets our expectation for the series because it addresses a problem of scripture on its own terms, but with inescapable implications for our situation of faith and life.

Overtures originated in 1973 at a Chicago meeting of the present editors, other colleagues from biblical studies, and representatives of Fortress Press. The formulation of the project as well as its basic goals and aims owes much to the conversations at this meeting and especially to the proddings and insights of Norman Habel, then of Concordia Theological Seminary, now at the University of Adelaide, Australia. The continuance and success of the project will demand the same kind of dialogue and communal quest.

WALTER BRUEGGEMANN
JOHN R. DONAHUE, S.J.

Abbreviations

AB	*The Anchor Bible*
CBQ	*Catholic Biblical Quarterly*
Int.	*Interpretation*
JAAR	*Journal of the American Academy of Religion*
JB	*The Jerusalem Bible*
JBL	*Journal of Biblical Literature*
KJV	King James Version
NAB	*New American Bible*
NEB	*New English Bible*
RSV	Revised Standard Version
VT	*Vetus Testamentum*

The Foreword

According to Brevard S. Childs, 1963 was a pivotal date for biblical studies. With the publication in that year of J. A. T. Robinson's *Honest to God,* the Biblical Theology Movement ended as a major force in American theology. Since that time, scholars, including Childs himself, have been seeking to re-shape the discipline (Brevard S. Childs, *Biblical Theology in Crisis* [Philadelphia: Westminster Press, 1970]). The volumes in this Fortress Press series approach that same goal.

If 1963 was an important date for biblical theologians, it was a much more momentous year for society at large. Certain events of that period continue to haunt me: the assassination of John F. Kennedy; the bombing of a black church on "Birmingham Sunday," resulting in the deaths of four little girls; the publication in America of Betty Friedan's *The Feminine Mystique;* and the publication in England of Sylvia Plath's *The Bell Jar,* followed closely by her suicide. Clearly, life was turning upside down in 1963, not just in the discipline of theology but also in the broader human community, afflicted by cries of suffering and injustice and by violent acts that threatened a reign of chaos.

Meanwhile, in that same year, my own world was undergoing decisive changes. James Muilenburg retired as Davenport Professor of Hebrew and Cognate Languages at Union Theological Seminary. Concurrently, I completed doctoral studies at Union and began teaching at Wake Forest University. Very soon I realized that the theology which informed my life was inadequate for addressing the concerns of students; nor was it still wholly satisfying for me. Ironically, the mighty acts of God in history proved wanting, and the ensuing years have heightened that deficiency.

In ways that I do not fully understand, the convergence of crises in 1963 has led to this study of God and the rhetoric of sexuality. To be sure, I have not been working on the book all that time, but the book has indeed been working on me. The first opportunity for sustained reflection came in 1974–75. A Younger Humanist Fellowship from the National Endowment for the Humanities made research possible in Jerusalem; the Albright Institute for Archaeological Research was home for the school year. After that, I traveled to Japan, a land that had nourished me once before. Seinan Gakuin University in Fukuoka provided a congenial environment for writing. While sojourning later in the ancient capital of Nippon, I contemplated what Kyoto has to do with Jerusalem and what either of these cities has to do with Boston, where the issue of feminism and biblical faith is ever present. Suffice it to say that these faraway places encouraged my meditations, yielding the early drafts of a manuscript. Appropriately, a sabbatical leave from Andover Newton Theological School in the spring of 1977 permitted completion of the study in Boston.

Briefly sketched, this is the story of how the book came to be. Focusing on texts in the Hebrew scriptures, I have sought a theological vision for new occasions. But I do not propose thereby to offer a comprehensive program for doing biblical theology. Nor do I claim that the perspectives given here dominate the scriptures. Instead, I have accented what I consider neglected themes and counterliterature. Using feminist hermeneutics, I have tried to recover old treasures and discover new ones in the household of faith. Though some of these treasures are small, they are nonetheless valuable in a tradition that is often compelled to live by the remnant. This understanding has guided my vision since events symbolized by 1963 muted the proclamation of the mighty acts of God in history. Thus, I dare not despise the day of little things (see Zech. 4:10).

Among the blessings of this day has been a developing interest, on my part, in interdisciplinary study. This interest expresses itself in various ways throughout the manuscript: literary criticism flavors the text from beginning to end; psychoanalytic terminology appears in one section; and existentialism, philosophical hermeneutics, structuralism, and Zen Buddhism figure here and there. Though these idioms are not the language of

Zion, I welcome their contributions to my understanding, even as I remember the beneficial presence of Ruth the Moabite in the faith of Israel.

Moreover, I continue to ponder the language of Zion itself. Two hermeneutical considerations are paramount. First, I want to show how stylistic and rhetorical features of the language illuminate its interpretations. Thus, I have often been more interested in preserving Hebrew syntax than in presenting felicitous translations. Second, wherever possible, I want to use inclusive, rather than sexist, language in translation. This task has proved precarious and formidable, with ramifications that exceed the limits of the study. Thus, my efforts here have been halting and tentative, though my commitment to the issue is steady and firm.

These and other considerations have resulted in the use of a variety of translations. Frequently I have followed the Revised Standard Version of the Bible, but more frequently I have altered this text. Passages thus altered are designated by an asterisk after the abbreviation RSV (RSV*). Other published translations, such as the *New American Bible* and the *Anchor Bible*, are cited with their appropriate abbreviations. Private translations of others are credited in the notes; my own translations are left unmarked.

Over the years many people have shared in this story of hermeneutical wanderings. To name four is to recall others: Kay Coughlin has made available numerous secretarial services; Gail Hamilton has changed the manuscript to typescript through countless drafts. Emily King has read and encouraged the writing along the way. Dr. Mary Ann Tolbert has participated graciously in the entire project, from conception to completion, providing ideas, critical judgments, and counsel. Indeed, her help has been extensive and steadfast. Each of these women knows the measure of my debt to her. Through them I tender thanks to many, especially to those students whose interest has often sustained my work over the years.

Finally, the silence surrounding the dedication speaks what words cannot.

PHYLLIS TRIBLE

CHAPTER 1

Clues in a Text

The Bible is a pilgrim wandering through history to merge past and present. Composed of diverse traditions that span centuries, it embraces claims and counterclaims in witness to the complexities and ambiguities of existence. Similarly, it engages struggles and perplexities outside itself to generate varied applications throughout the ages. These private and public journeys of scripture yield three clues for our study of God and the rhetoric of sexuality: hermeneutical, methodological, and topical. By exploring these clues we join the peregrinations of a text from an ancient to a contemporary setting.

THE HERMENEUTICAL CLUE

1. THE CLUE WITHIN THE TEXT

To illustrate the hermeneutics functioning within scripture, I have chosen the pilgrimage of an ancient portrait of God.[1] Early one morning, Moses, in obedience to a divine imperative, climbed Mount Sinai to stand before Yahweh. In the meeting these words were proclaimed:[2]

> Yahweh, Yahweh, a God merciful and gracious, slow to anger, and abounding in loyalty and faithfulness, keeping loyalty for thousands, forgiving iniquity and transgression and sin, but who will by no means clear the guilty, visiting the iniquity of the ancestors upon the children and the children's children, to the third and the fourth generation (Exod. 34:6–7, RSV*).

This description held in tension God the lover and God the punisher.[3] The merciful one who forgave sin also inflicted the iniquity of the parents upon their children for several generations. Such punishment assumed the corporate personality of a

1

household that bound all members in the solidarity of transgression.[4]

Another narrative about the wilderness period depicted Moses repeating this portrait of God in a prayer, though he omitted a few of the phrases (Num. 14:18). Centuries later Jeremiah quoted a greatly condensed version of it, also in a prayer to Yahweh (Jer. 32:18). Applicable to different settings, the same proclamation was altered by compression. Yet from earliest times to the eve of the Exile, a particular text that retained a balanced stress upon God the lover and God the punisher persisted in the memories of Israel.

Meanwhile, other formulations of the passage appeared with different accents. Reversing the order of emphasis, the Deuteronomic decalogue appropriated the text to distinguish between those who hate and those who love the deity (Deut. 5:9–10; also Exod. 20:5–6). The former received punishment; the latter, mercy. Although this version affirmed solidarity in sin, that teaching was mitigated in a context which offered the covenant relationship anew to every generation: "Not with our ancestors did Yahweh make this covenant, but with us, who are all of us here alive this day" (Deut. 5:3, RSV*). Moreover, in another Deuteronomic statement reference to the solidarity of generations shifted from iniquity to loyalty: "Yahweh . . . the faithful God who keeps covenant and loyalty with those who love him and keep his commandments, to a thousand generations, and requites to their face those who hate him, by destroying them . . ." (Deut. 7:9–10, RSV*).

This interpretive process continued as the text acquired more settings and duties. To introduce his poetic diatribe against Nineveh, for example, the prophet Nahum employed a highly truncated form of the passage that omitted altogether any reference to the mercy of Yahweh. The phrase "slow to anger," which in other places had paralleled the abundance of divine love, received here the opposite meaning of judgment and destruction:

> Yahweh is a jealous God and avenging,
> ....
> Yahweh is slow to anger and of great might,
> and Yahweh will by no means clear the guilty.
> (Nah. 1:2–3, RSV*)

In the prophecy of Joel the dynamics of this portrait were reversed again. All references to the wrath of Yahweh disappeared, and another phrase, "repents of evil," joined the list of gracious attributes. Thus, in a poetic invitation to repentance, the forgiving deity alone was emphasized:

> Return to Yahweh, your God,
>   for he[5] is gracious and merciful,
> slow to anger, and abounding in loyalty,
>   and repents of evil.
>   (Joel 2:13, RSV*)

The prophetic narrative of Jonah gave an ironic twist to these words of Joel. In a prayer motivated by anger against Yahweh, Jonah accused the deity of being "a God gracious and merciful, slow to anger, and abounding in loyalty, and repents of evil" (Jon. 4:2b, RSV*). Although in vocabulary this description matched precisely the quotation from Joel, in function it corresponded to the version of Nahum. Since Jonah himself willed the destruction of Nineveh, the merciful God was for him not redemption but wrath. Reciting words of love, Jonah convicted God. In the two passages from Joel and Jonah, then, a single text, with not one word changed, has yielded contradictory meanings. At the same time, the two very different descriptions of God given in Nahum and Jonah resulted in similar meanings.[6] Context altered text.

Our proclamation traveled also among the psalmists, who repeated and paraphrased it in hymns (Ps. 111:4; 112:4; 145:8), in a song of thanksgiving (Ps. 103:8), and in an individual lament (Ps. 86:5, 15). From selfless praise of God to a request for deliverance from enemies, the poets appropriated the text. Each use was an interpretation fitted to particular occasions and experiences.

In post-exilic Israel, the passage engaged the despair and sorrow of a defeated people. Understandably, it became there a message of comfort, with no allusions to the punishing God. Weeping, mourning, and fasting, Nehemiah confessed the sins of his people and sought their redemption when he prayed to Yahweh God "who keeps covenant and loyalty with those who love him and keep his commandments" (Neh. 1:5, RSV*). In a recital of the history of Israel, Ezra recalled the disobedience of his ancestors in the wilderness period. Yet he maintained that even when they made a molten calf Yahweh did not forsake them because "thou art a God ready to forgive, gracious and merciful, slow to anger and abounding in loyalty" (Neh. 9:17b, RSV*). According to Ezra, the God of the wanderings was solely compassionate, sustaining the people even when they were guilty of iniquity (see also Neh. 9:19, 27, 28, 31).

With a radically altered perspective, these words of Ezra have returned to the setting that began the sojourn of this portrait. In the meeting of Moses and God at Mount Sinai, the depiction of the merciful Yahweh balanced the description of the punishing Yahweh, "who will by no means clear the guilty, visiting the iniquity of the ancestors upon the children and the children's children, to the third and the fourth generation" (Exod. 34:6–7, RSV*). Centuries later, recalling that ancient event for his own situation, Ezra changed the tradition to omit any threat of a wrathful deity. The past moved into the present both to interpret and to be interpreted.

These two biblical understandings of God, one in Exodus and the other in Nehemiah, are located in the same period of Israel's memories, the time of the wanderings. They employ the same text, "the merciful God slow to anger and abounding in loyalty," but in different versions. Juxtaposed, these passages illustrate the hermeneutics at work within the Bible. And the other travels of this portrait reinforce the thesis. A single text appears in different versions with different functions in different contexts. Through application it confesses, challenges, comforts, and condemns. What it says on one occasion, it denies on another. Thus, scripture in itself yields multiple interpretations of itself.[7]

Furthermore, this hermeneutics does not employ a single set of principles to achieve meanings. As our proclamation wandered through the centuries, it provided no map of its peregrinations. Seldom did it disclose precisely how it got from one time to another, from one setting to another, or from one meaning to another. Yet it did provide glimpses of numerous methodologies, such as compression, displacement, additions, omissions, and irony. Interpretation, then, eschews systematizing. It invites participation in the movement of the text, and it requires risk on the way to application.[8] Though mute, a text speaks to attentive hearers in particular contexts. In turn, these hearers construe the text variously, be they a vindictive Nahum, an angry Jonah, a repentant community, a selfless worshiper, or an obedient Moses leading a disobedient people. Involving the totality of interpretation, this inner hermeneutics of scripture is a clue to the pilgrimage of the Bible in the world. And this clue is a process of understanding rather than a method of control. Using it, we turn to the contemporary scene.[9]

2. THE CLUE BETWEEN THE TEXT AND THE WORLD

With increasing emphasis, current discussions of the Bible journey outside its traditional setting in a community of faith to engage the world as their province. The interpreters may or may not be biblical scholars. They may be sympathetic to the text, dispassionate about it, or even hostile to it. They may or may not stand within a religious context. In various ways, with different values and unequal results, these readers understand scripture from the perspective of contemporary issues; or, conversely, they view present interests in light of the Bible. To illustrate this hermeneutics, I shall cite only a few instances, most of which overlap. My purpose is not to examine these interpretations but simply to acknowledge them as participants in a pilgrimage of understanding that is application—and thereby to introduce the particular focus of this study.[10]

For some commentators, interactions between the Bible and the black experience are paramount. The motif of slavery and liberation, as exemplified in the traditions of the Exodus, speaks forcefully to the search for human rights.[11] This theme joins others to embrace all protests against oppression. For instance, in its treatment of masters and slaves the Old Testament moves toward a revolution in overcoming class struggle.[12] Similarly, the teachings of Jesus about justice and restitution undercut claims to ownership through coercion and violence. When set in a context of the poor and the powerless, the Bible critiques every culture of injustice to proclaim the good news of liberation.[13]

In these journeys against oppression, scripture engages various ideologies. Heard from a Marxist perspective, Jeremiah 28 offers a way in our time to differentiate ideology from truth,

Logos from *Praxis.*[14] Moreover, a Marxist view of Jesus gives the Gospels afresh both to Christians and to atheists and so provides each group with new insights of itself and the other.[15] Such readings contribute responsibly and beneficially to global issues. Conversations between the Bible and American ideology are likewise illuminating. According to one interpretation, contradictory themes within scripture resonate with opposing traditions within American politics.[16] The "zealous nationalism" of Daniel, Maccabees, and Revelation vies with the "prophetic realism" of Hosea, Isaiah, Jeremiah, and Jesus. In secularized versions, the former emphasis has influenced the concept of "manifest destiny," movements such as the Ku Klux Klan and the New Left, characters in our comic books, like Captain America, and the national crises of Vietnam and Watergate. On the other hand, "prophetic realism" has guided the vision of Abraham Lincoln, the political writings of Reinhold Niebuhr, and the nonviolent perspective of Martin Luther King, Jr. Hence, this analysis sees diversity within the Bible affecting tensions and dichotomies in American ideology.[17]

The psychological idioms of our age also participate in this hermeneutical venture. In expounding their orientations, Freud reflected upon Moses, and Jung contemplated Job.[18] More recently, a Jewish philosopher has viewed Paul through the lens of Freudian thought.[19] A Christian teacher has employed a psychoanalytic approach to the Gospel stories for the purpose of evoking human change.[20] Still others have read the parables from Freudian and Jungian perspectives.[21] And a psychiatrist has meditated upon innumerable biblical sayings in his existential quest for wholeness and enlightenment.[22] Thus, within this one area the interpretive journey again follows different paths.

Ecology is yet another topic. Ancient prophets, for example, condemned the destruction of the environment through human negligence and willfulness. In an oracle of judgment Hosea saw the death of the land as a consequence of disobedience (Hos. 4:1–3).[23] With his own nuances Jeremiah echoed this understanding (Jer. 2:7). If these and similar prophecies (e.g., Amos 8:8; Joel 1:10–12) see pollution resulting from sin, other passages come across ambiguously. Specifically, dominion over all the earth, which is granted to humankind in Genesis 1:28 and

Psalm 8:6–8, has become a text of contention. Is it a license for the exploitation of nature by technology and thus a culprit in the present crisis?[24] Or does the phrase mean responsibility to maintain the order and goodness of creation so that it prohibits destruction?[25] Whatever the answers, the questions demonstrate interactions between the Bible and a contemporary problem.[26]

Diverse voices of scripture also engage the broad topic of human sexuality.[27] Recent interest in this conversation has occasioned discussions of the sexuality of Jesus and of the historical basis for the Virgin Birth.[28] Similarly, concern for the institution of the family,[29] as well as for the status of single people, has led to corresponding reconsiderations of biblical perspectives. The gay movement has sparked debate about the few passages that comment on homosexuality.[30] And finally, issues such as child abuse and the treatment of the elderly in society call for studies of youth and age in scripture.

Feminism is my concluding illustration of involvement between the world and the Bible. By feminism I do not mean a narrow focus upon women, but rather a critique of culture in light of misogyny. This critique affects the issues of race and class, psychology, ecology, and human sexuality.[31] For some people today the Bible supports female slavery and male dominance in culture,[32] while for others it offers freedom from sexism.[33] Central in this discussion are such passages as the creation accounts in Genesis, certain laws in Leviticus, the Song of Songs, the wisdom literature, various Gospel stories about Jesus and the powerless, and particular admonitions of Paul and his successors. Out of these materials a biblical hermeneutics of feminism is emerging.

All these contemporary interactions between the Bible and the world mirror the inner dynamics of scripture itself. The interpretive clue within the text is also the clue between the text and existence. Hence, the private and the public journeys of the pilgrim named scripture converge to yield the integrity of its life. As the Bible interprets itself to complement or to contradict, to confirm or to challenge, so likewise we construe these traditions for our time, recognizing an affinity between then and now.[34] In other words, hermeneutics encompasses explication, understanding, and application from past to present. Subject to the experiences of the reader, this process is always compelling and never ending. New occasions teach new duties. In pursuing the task here, I am specifically interested in feminism as a critique of culture. My plan is to read selected biblical texts from this perspective. But such interpretation requires first the articulation of a methodology, since methodology is one major criterion for evaluating the legitimacy of any interpretation.

THE METHODOLOGICAL CLUE

As the total process of understanding, hermeneutics employs many acceptable methodologies, though a particular interpreter may prefer one over another. My choice is rhetorical criticism,[35] a discipline I place under the general rubric of literary criticism.[36] According to this discipline, the major clue to interpretation is the text itself. Thus, I view the text as a literary creation with an interlocking structure of words and motifs.[37] Proper analysis of form yields proper articulation of meaning.

To study the Bible as literature is to recognize, not prove, that it is in fact literature.[38] I do not argue for its literary status any more than I would argue for the literary character of the *Iliad*, the *Odyssey*, the *Bhagavad Gita*, the *Divine Comedy*, or Shakespearean plays. Instead, I explore the literature to discover its vitality. This artistic pursuit is neither isolated from nor opposed to a religious interest, neither superior nor subordinate. Although aesthetic and religious modes of experience can surely be distinguished "at their more obvious levels," nevertheless, "they discover in their depths unexpected resonances and harmonies out of which a common music may be made."[39] In the totality of interpretation, their visions fuse. Thus, the Bible as literature is the Bible as scripture, regardless of one's attitude toward its authority. And conversely, the Bible as scripture is the Bible as literature, regardless of one's evaluation of its quality.[40]

A literary approach to hermeneutics concentrates primarily on the text rather than on extrinsic factors such as historical background, archaeological data, compositional history, authorial intention, sociological setting, or theological motivation and result. To be sure, these external concerns supplement one's understanding so that the critic never divorces herself or himself from them;[41] yet at the same time stress falls upon interpreting the literature in terms of itself. "The text is like a musical score and the reader like the orchestra conductor who obeys the instructions of the notation."[42] Focus upon an intrinsic reading is, then, one hallmark of rhetorical methodology.[43]

The organic unity of the text is a related emphasis. Form and content are inseparable.[44] On the one hand, the text is not a container from which ideas or substance can be abstracted to live an independent life. On the other hand, the text is not a subject matter from which stylistic and structural wrappings can be removed to exist autonomously. How the text speaks and what it says belong together in the discovery of what it is. To convey content is to employ form; to convey form is to employ content. Though these two phenomena can be distinguished for analytical purposes, their inseparability is the very life of literature.

Exploration of organic unity involves levels of analysis. First, a text can be defined in different ways: e.g., the entire Bible; a major division, such as the Pentateuch or the Pauline corpus; a single book, such as Joshua or James; a part of a book, such as the Holiness Code in Leviticus or the Sermon on the Mount in Matthew; a smaller section, such as Psalm 100, the parable of the prodigal son, or even a single riddle, proverb, or doxology; finally, an episode within a story.[45] Basic to all these definitions is the concept of a literary unit, be it large or small. The critic determines this unit by employing the criterion of form and content. Second, a text can be studied from different perspectives. The critic may trace general design and plot movement[46] or offer an exegesis of selected portions.[47] He or she may follow the unfolding of a single motif, a key work, or a particular stylistic device.[48] Again, the interpreter may pursue a close reading of the whole, examining in detail its interconnections.[49] On whatever level analysis takes place, form and content yield the clue essential for interpretation.

A text is both typical and unique, both custom and innovation. Its conventional character is the genre to which it belongs, for every text is a sample of a class or family whose members resemble each other. The genre of fairy tales, for example, embraces certain kinds of narratives.[50] Introduced by the phrase "once upon a time," these stories live in fantasy and imagination. Ironically, time is not their essence, since what occurred in the past continues to recur in an imperishable world untouched even by aging. Though brief, these tales are all-inclusive. The natural, human, and supernatural worlds intermingle so easily that miracles are a matter of course. As types rather than individuals, the characters are known through their actions. Stylistically, these stories build on repetition with a precision that leaves no room for ambiguity. Their plots move from danger to redemption, often to conclude with the familiar phrase "and they lived happily ever after." Thus, an entire set of conventions, which includes elements of form and content, classifies innumerable stories as fairy tales. To locate a single text within this genre is to begin interpreting it. In general, to know the literary type to which a text belongs is to possess a clue for reading it.

At the same time, the typical enhances the unique. While all fairy tales exhibit common characteristics, each story has its own individuality. Its life is not interchangeable with any other tale, no matter how similar. Hence, the particular wicked stepmother of "Hansel and Gretel" belongs there and not in "Cinderella." The beauty of Snow White stands apart from that of Sleeping Beauty. Moreover, deliverance by a handsome prince occurs differently in these two stories, and neither of these rescues duplicates the comparable motif in "Cinderella." Every story is unique, as the variants of a single tale illustrate further. The Grimm brothers did not retell "Sleeping Beauty" precisely as they heard it, nor did others who narrated it. The story appears in several versions, each of which is a particular creation. Thus, a single text is "an indissoluable whole, an artistic and creative unity, a unique formulation."[51] To articulate the uniqueness of its form and content is to pursue a clue for interpreting it.

The clue as text, then, involves both the typical and the unique. Within biblical studies, form criticism explores the typical.[52] Along with other emphases, it seeks to identify traditions under such narrative headings as legend, saga, folktale, letter, and exemplary story, and under such poetic designations as oracle, hymn, proverb, lament, and love song. According to this discipline, each genre has its own settings, content, and functions as well as a characteristic structure. The hymn is a song of praise, for instance, that usually consists of a call to praise, a recital of

Yahweh's acts or attributes, and a conclusion of praise, blessings, or petitions.[53] On various occasions, this typical structure is fashioned in different ways so that many kinds of hymns result: e.g., victory songs to celebrate success in battle; pilgrim songs to accompany the journey to holy places; and royal psalms to commemorate the enthronement of a king. Altogether, the common elements of the hymn become a key for understanding a single specimen. Thus, form criticism identifies types of literature as they correspond to typical human situations.[54] This emphasis upon genre relates it to literary criticism, which, as we have seen, likewise explores the typical as a major clue for interpreting a single text.[55]

Yet the clue as text is also unique. Within biblical studies, rhetorical criticism focuses on this dimension. Conceived originally as a supplement to form criticism, rhetorical criticism investigates the individual characteristics of a literary unit.[56] While it is true, for example, that all hymns share common elements, a single hymn differs from all the others. The kinds of words used and the ways they are put together make every unit a new creation.[57] In great variety, language plays with imagery, sounds, style, and viewpoints to yield particular distinctions, subtleties, and nuances. Analysis of such literary and stylistic features is the study of form and content as a key to meaning. In general, the practice of rhetorical criticism relates to literary criticism by accenting the unique as a major clue for interpreting a text.[58]

Although it employs learned procedures, principles, and controls, this methodological approach resides in the realm of art.[59] It uses critical tools but is not determined by them. Indeed, it welcomes intuition, guess, and surprise.[60] Moreover, since all methodologies are subject to the guiding interests of individual users, the application of a single one may result in multiple interpretations of a particular passage. Specifically, not all rhetorical studies yield the same results. And while multiple readings are not per se mutually exclusive, not all interpretations are thereby equal.[61] The text, as form and content, limits constructions of itself and does, in fact, stand as a potential witness against all readings.[62] Yet the interpretive task is as compelling as it is inevitable, and rhetorical criticism is one methodology at work in this total process. By using it, I participate in a hermeneutical journey in which the clue is the text. Conversely, a specific text is the clue to my subject matter.

THE TOPICAL CLUE

Genesis 1:27 is the text. It gives the first scriptural clue for the subject of God and the rhetoric of sexuality:

> And God created humankind in his image;
> in the image of God created he him;
> male and female created he them.

1. THE CONTEXT OF THE TEXT

This poem belongs to a liturgy of creation that moves in orderly fashion from chaos to cosmos (Gen. 1:1—2:4a).[63] The phrase "the heavens and the earth" functions rhetorically as an inclusion that delineates the entire liturgy.[64] As part of a circumstantial clause, it introduces the unit: "When God began to create the heavens and the earth . . ." (1:1). As part of a summary declaration, it concludes the composition: "These are the generations of the heavens and the earth when they were created" (2:4a, RSV). Between this beginning and end, creation happens in seven days, the last of which, the day of rest (2:2–3), differs from all the others.[65]

The distinctiveness of the seventh day directs us by contrast to the similarities of the preceding six (1:3–31). Each of these six episodes opens with the words "And God said." Each concludes with a similar refrain that identifies its particular day: e.g., "And there was evening and there was morning, a third day" (1:13, RSV). Furthermore, an overall symmetrical design arranges these units into two parts. On the first three days God creates the skeleton of the universe and, correspondingly, on the last three the deity fills it out:[66]

The first day:
Light is separated from darkness (1:3–5).

The second day:
The firmament separates the waters (1:6–8).

The fourth day:
The greater and lesser lights separate day and night (1:14–19).

The fifth day:
Aquatic and aerial animals appear (1:20–23).

The third day:	The sixth day:
The earth appears.	Land animals appear.
The earth puts forth	Humankind is made.
vegetation. (1:9–13)	(1:24–30)

Throughout this liturgy, specific words, phrases, and themes recur to unite the entire cosmos in harmony.[67] For instance, separation, differentiation, and responsibility characterize all levels of creation. Blessing and fertility also abound in a schema that uses the word *good* seven times (1:4, 10, 12, 18, 21, 25, 31), indeed, on the seventh, "very good." Within this unity, however, the separate acts of God are reported in great variety. Furthermore, even within this variety the last event, the creation of humankind, is unique. To it our text belongs.

On the sixth day, God creates both the land animals and humankind (1:24–31). Corresponding to the work of the third day, these creatures are to fill the earth and share its vegetation. The description of the creation of the land animals (1:24–25) follows a literary pattern established elsewhere in the liturgy (1:11–12). While reflecting this pattern in part, the report of the creation of humankind presents a distinctive picture. It falls into three main sections, which are delineated by movements from direct discourse (1:26) to narrated discourse (1:27) to direct discourse (1:28–30). God is the subject of each section, and humankind is the object. Speaking first in a plural of deliberation, God proposes to create humankind. This proposal contains key words, phrases, and motifs that are expanded later in the account:

> And God said:
> "Let us make humankind in our image, after our likeness;
> and let them have dominion
>   over the fish of the sea,
>   over the birds of the heavens,
>   over the domestic animals,
>   over all the earth,
>   and over every creeping thing that creeps upon the earth."
> (1:26)

In the narrated discourse that follows this section, the first line of the proposal is accomplished:

> And God created humankind in his image,
> in the image of God created he him;
> male and female created he them.
>
> (1:27)

Later we shall return to this text for a close reading; meanwhile, let us continue to place it in context.

Having first proposed the creation of humankind and then having made them male and female, God now speaks to them with blessing. By a repetition of words and motifs (cf. 1:26), the direct discourse of the deity resumes to develop the themes of fertility (cf. 1:22) and dominion:

> And God blessed them,
> and God said to them:
> "Be fruitful and multiply,
> and fill the earth;
> subdue it and have dominion
> over the fish of the sea,
> over the birds of the heavens,
> and over every living thing that moves upon the earth."
>
> (1:28, RSV*)

This address to the human creatures continues as God speaks in the first-person singular. To fertility and dominion the deity adds the blessing of food:

> And God said,
> "Behold, I have given to you
> every plant yielding seed which is upon the face of all the earth
> and every tree with seed in its fruit.
> To you they shall be for food.
> And to every beast of the earth
> and to every bird of the heavens
> and to everything that creeps upon the earth,
> which has the breath of life,
> [I have given] every green plant for food."
> And it was so.
>
> (1:29–30, RSV*)

Concluding the activities of the sixth day, this address to humankind reaches back to embrace the animals also (cf. 1:24–25). With the human creatures, they partake of time and table.

Both were created on the same day; both eat the same food. Moreover, these closing words allude to the corresponding creation on the third day of both the earth and the plants (1:9–12). Thereby, they complete the symmetry of the overall design.

Although this account of the making of humankind shares vocabulary and themes with the rest of creation, its unique features are most striking. To begin with, (1) it is longer (1:26–30) than any other comparable section of the liturgy. Further, (2) the divine deliberation "let us make humankind in our image" (1:26, RSV*), deviates from the literary patterns that commence the other events (cf. 1:3, 6, 9, 14, 20, 24). (3) Alone in creation, the human creatures only are made in the image of God (1:27), and (4) they are made without reference to any natural context or substance. By contrast, the waters bring forth the fish and the great sea monsters (1:20–21) and the earth brings forth domestic animals, creeping things, and the beasts of the field (1:24) (5) Whereas the sea, air, and land animals are broken down into various species, each "according to their kinds" (RSV), no comparable divisions are indicated for the human creatures. (6) Yet only for them, not for any of the animals, is sexuality designated as male and female (1:27). Moreover, this specific reference pertains not to procreation but to the image of God. Procreation is shared by humankind with the animal world (1:22, 28); sexuality is not. Hence, in this liturgy the phrase "male and female" holds a distinctive meaning. (7) Only to humankind does God grant dominion over all the earth (1:26, 28), and (8) only to humankind does God speak directly in the first person (1:29–30). Clearly, in form, content, and context, this report of the creation of male and female is unique. As it moves from direct discourse to narrated discourse and back to direct discourse, the entire account climaxes the divine work of six days. Of primary concern for us is the uniqueness of the narrated discourse. This text gives the first clue in scripture for studying God and the rhetoric of sexuality.

2. The Text in Context

A sensitivity to poetic language is basic to an interpretation of Genesis 1:27. Such language is open to nuances, suggestions, hints, and guesses. Rather than limiting a subject, it seeks fullness with a connotative, not a denotative, emphasis. To appropriate the metaphor of a Zen sutra, poetry is "like a finger pointing to the moon."[68] It is a way to see the light that shines in darkness, a way to participate in transcendent truth and to embrace reality. To equate the finger with the moon or to acknowledge the finger and not perceive the moon is to miss the point. Poetry invites, but does not compel, insight. In just such a way, Genesis 1:27 witnesses to its subject matter.

This verse has a vocabulary of only seven words. By repetition the vocabulary expands to form a poem of three lines, with four words each:

> And-created God humankind in-his-image;
> in-the-image-of God created-he him;
> male and-female created-he them.

So small a unit evinces a sophisticated structure, with a correspondence in meaning. In form, two kinds of parallelism are joined by the center line. Inverted parallelism characterizes lines one and two; straight parallelism, lines two and three. What the former emphasizes, the latter amplifies.

In lines one and two, a chiasmus of repeated words focuses on the phrase "in his/the image":

>   a   b   c
> And created God humankind in his image;
>   c'   b'   a'
> in the image of God created he him.

At the center of the inversion, the phrase "in his/the image" is locked in by the creative work of God. The chiasm accents this phrase while rendering its meaning inaccessible. Yet the sense of the poem itself does not remain hidden, because its third line introduces a new phrase that parallels "in the image of God." Thus, the straight parallelism of lines two and three amplifies the emphasis of the inverted parallelism of lines one and two:

> in the image of God created he him;
> male and female created he them.

Clearly, "male and female" correspond structurally to "the image of God," and this formal parallelism indicates a semantic correspondence. Likewise, the switch from the singular pronoun "him" to the plural pronoun "them" at the end of these two parallel lines provides a key for interpreting humankind *(hā-'ādām)* in the first line. The plural form reinforces sexual differentiation within the unity of humanity. Altogether, the third line, in straight parallelism to the second, opens up meanings that are highlighted yet hidden by the inverted parallelism of lines one and two. Let us turn next to an exploration of these meanings.

Metaphor describes best the poetic mode of Genesis 1:27. As the language of semantic motion, metaphor moves from the better known to the lesser known, from the concrete to the abstract, from the standard to the figurative.[69] Through comparison it extends meaning to express the similarity of difference. This semantic process involves the cooperation of two elements, a vehicle and a tenor. The vehicle is the base of metaphor, the better known element, while the tenor is its underlying (or overarching) subject, the lesser known element. The sense of the metaphor results from the interaction of vehicle and tenor, an interaction that varies with different metaphors. For instance, vehicle and tenor may call attention to each other equally, or one may highlight the other. Nevertheless, both are essential for the comparison; neither is an embellishment. Together they produce new meanings that are not available through the individual elements. Though clearly distinguishable, vehicle and tenor constitute the unit that is itself a metaphor. In Genesis 1:27 the formal parallelism between the phrases "in the image of God" and "male and female" indicates a semantic correspondence between a lesser known element and a better known element. In other words, this parallelism yields a metaphor. "Male and female" is its vehicle; "the image of God," its tenor.

The vehicle of this metaphor belongs to the vocabulary of humanity in the poem. This vocabulary includes three nouns and two pronouns. The nouns are humankind *(hā-'ādām)* and male and female *(zākār ûn^eqēbâ)*. Their corresponding pronouns are him *('ōtô)* and them *('ōtām)*. All five words are objects of the verb *create* with God as its subject. Given the parallel usage of this vocabulary, interactions among the five words elucidate their shared and particular meanings.

First, the shift from singular to plural pronouns shows clearly that *hā-'ādām* is not one single creature who is both male and female but rather two creatures, one male and one female. This emphasis is reinforced in the proposal of God that immediately precedes verse 27. There a plural verb form, "let them have dominion," refers back to the singular word *'ādām:* "And God said, "Let us make humankind ['*ādām*] in our image, after our likeness; and let them have dominion . . ." (Gen. 1:26, RSV*). These shifts from singular to plural disallow an androgynous interpretation of *hā-'ādām*. From the beginning humankind exists as two creatures, not as one creature with double sex. Genesis 5:1b–2 provides an external witness to this point:

> When God created humankind ['*ādām*],
>   in the likeness of God made he him;
> male and female created he them
>   and blessed them and called their name humankind ['*ādām*],
> when they were created.

Second, the singular word *hā-'ādām*, with its singular pronoun *'ōtô*, shows that male and female are not opposite but rather harmonious sexes. *Hā-'ādām* is not an original unity that is subsequently split apart by sexual division.[70] Instead, it is the original unity that is at the same time the original differentiation. From the beginning, the word *humankind* is synonymous with the phrase "male and female," though the components of this phrase are not synonymous with each other. Unity embraces sexual differentiation; it does not impose sexual identicalness. Thus, the vocabulary of humanity in the poem disallows interpretations of the sexes as either antonyms or synonyms. It recognizes distinction within harmony.

Third, the parallelism between *hā-'ādām* and "male and female" shows further that sexual differentiation does not mean hierarchy but rather equality. Created simultaneously, male and female are not superior and subordinate. Neither has power over the other; in fact, both are given equal power. Though the parallelism within the poem alone suggests this latter point, the context substantiates it. As we have seen in the verse immediately preceding, God proposes, by using a plural verb form, that *'ādām* be given dominion over all the earth: "let *them* have dominion" (1:26, RSV). Moreover, in the verses that follow our poem God blesses male and female, using the plural "them," and the deity consistently speaks "to them" with plural verb forms (1:28–29). Specifically, God reaffirms the power which they both have over the earth: "And God said to *them* . . . have dominion" (RSV). Throughout this section, then, male and female are treated equally. In plural pronouns and verbs, both are present and both have equal power over the earth. At the same time, neither is given dominion over the other.[71]

Fourth, by virtue of what they do not say, these references to humanity in Genesis 1:27 allow freedom in the interpretation of male and female. The human creation poeticized in this verse is not delineated by sexual relationships, roles, characteristics, attitudes, or emotions. To be sure, the context itself identifies two responsibilities for humankind, procreation (1:28a) and dominion over the earth (1:26, 28b), but it does not differentiate between the sexes in assigning this work. Since the first of these responsibilities, procreation, parallels the divine command given to the fish of the sea and the birds of the heavens, who are not themselves explicitly designated male and female (1:22), the use of the phrase "male and female" in 1:27 does not itself signify the potential for human fertility but rather indicates, along with other items, the uniqueness of humankind in creation. Thus, in relation to the context, this phrase is not in the liturgy to define the specific sexual functions of man and woman in procreating. On the other hand, a definite link does exist between the phrase "male and female" and the responsibility to have dominion over the earth, since both of these descriptions manifest the uniqueness of humankind. The link adds another dimension to the freedom that is allowed within the text for interpreting male and female. This freedom comes in two ways: by what the text does say about human dominion over all the earth and by what it does not say about sexual stereotypes. Although an argument from silence is never conclusive and often dangerous, this particular one may caution against assigning "masculine" and "feminine" attributes to the words *male* and *female* in this poem.[72] Open to varied meanings, these words eschew sexual clichés.

As the most basic way to know humankind in its fullness, "male and female" is the vehicle of a metaphor whose tenor is "the image of God." This vehicle suggests to the responsive imagination the integrity, the pluralism, the dominion, and the freedom of the image of God. At this level, then, metaphor compares likenesses, for by describing the vehicle, we can perceive similarities in the tenor. But we do not describe the tenor itself. After all, semantic movement from the human world to the divine world involves the disparity of the two realms.[73] Moreover, this very disparity envelops the metaphor in a comparison of unlikenesses. The phrase "the image of God" speaks mystery and otherness, an aura not arising from the phrase "male and female." And unlike the vehicle, the tenor of this metaphor is not surrounded in the poem by a vocabulary that can aid its exegesis. Nevertheless, through comparison, "male and female" affirms not only the similarity but also the otherness of the divine image. Hence, the vehicle controls the mode in which the tenor forms and thereby directs the way to interpretation. Both these components are essential for the metaphor, although they do not interact equally. The vehicle contributes explicit meanings; the tenor exists through hints and guesses. In other words, "male and female" is the finger pointing to the "image of God."

Yet this tenor itself, "the image of God," is also a pointing finger:

> And created God humankind in his image;
> in the image of God created he him.

By distinguishing between "God" and the "image of God," the poem sets up another comparison in which "the image of God" becomes the better known element, the vehicle, and "God," the lesser known element, the tenor. This tenor underlies the entire poem: it (or its pronoun) occurs in all three lines as subject of the verb *create*. Although no description of God appears and no clues are offered about the way in which the deity creates, nonetheless some hint of the Creator is allowed through the phrase "the image of God." The identity of vocabulary, *God* and "the image of *God,*" establishes a similarity in meaning at the same time that the word *the-image-of* stresses the difference between Creator and created. Moreover, the lack of any formal parallelism between these two elements of the poem suggests further their semantic disparity. This difference between "God" and "the image of God" witnesses to the transcendence and freedom of the deity. If "male and female" gives the clue for interpreting "the image of God," the phrase "image of God" gives the clue for understanding "God." In both instances, the tenor is not defined by the vehicle. It is the moon that can be seen but not possessed.

The context of Genesis 1:27 supports further emphases of this second metaphor which moves from the image of God to God. In proposing to make humankind, God used plural pronouns to refer to deity: "And God said, 'Let *us* make humankind in *our* image, after *our* likeness" (1:26).[74] Once the creative act is narrated (1:27), God speaks to humankind, this time using the first-person singular to refer to deity: "And God said, 'Behold *I* have given you . . .'" (1:29, RSV). The switch from plural to singular pronouns signifies variety, freedom, and fullness within God. Moreover, it recalls the comparable shift from singular to plural pronouns in the description of humankind, male and female. Unity embraces plurality in both the human and the divine realms.

But sexual differentiation of humankind is not thereby a description of God. Indeed, the metaphorical language of Genesis 1:27 preserves with exceeding care the otherness of God. If it depicts male and female in freedom and uniqueness, how much more does it uphold the transcendence of the deity. God is neither male nor female, nor a combination of the two. And yet, detecting divine transcendence in human reality requires human clues. Unique among them, according to our poem, is sexuality. God creates, in the image of God, male and female. To describe male and female, then, is to perceive the image of God; to perceive the image of God is to glimpse the transcendence of God.

3. THE TEXT AS CLUE

It is the first of these two metaphors, the image of God male and female, that provides the topical clue for our study of God and the rhetoric of sexuality. In this metaphor the vehicle contributes explicit meanings, while the tenor exists through hints and guesses. The vehicle connotes humankind in its fullness, a fullness that affirms both its likeness and unlikeness to God. Accordingly, I shall focus primarily upon the vehicle, which in various ways will itself suggest, but not denote, the tenor. By receiving attention, "male and female" call attention to "the image of God."

As a clue for interpreting scripture, this metaphor can function in two ways.[75] First, it can direct attention to partial metaphors of "male and female" by placing them within an encompassing network.[76] For instance, metaphors such as God the father (Ps. 103:13), the husband (Hos. 2:16), the king (Ps. 98:6), and the warrior (Exod. 15:3) are diverse and partial expressions of the image of God male. By the same token, metaphors such as God the pregnant woman (Isa. 42:14), the mother (Isa. 66:13), the midwife (Ps. 22:9), and the mistress (Ps. 123:2) are diverse and partial expressions of the image of God female. All these partial metaphors involve societal roles and relationships which the basic metaphor organizes without necessarily promoting.[77] In fact, the basic metaphor contrasts with the imbalance of these partial metaphors. It presents an equality in the image of God male *and* female, although the Bible overwhelmingly favors male metaphors for deity.[78] In contrast to the dominant language of scripture, then, this equal stress upon the image of God male *and* female provides a hermeneutical impetus to investigate female metaphors for God—a task which we shall pursue in the next two chapters of this study.

A second way in which our metaphor can function is to direct attention to traditions of the Old Testament that embody male and female within a comparable context. This context is the goodness of creation that dispels chaos, the goodness that is ultimately fulfilling and life-enhancing. Seven times in Genesis 1:1—2:4a the narrator reports that creation is "good." Indeed, at the conclusion of the sixth day on which God created male and female in his image, "God saw everything that he had made, and behold, it was very good" (Gen. 1:31, RSV). Thus, our metaphor can uncover diverse traditions in the Old Testament about male and female that reflect, in whatever ways, fulfillment in life. By amplifying the range of "the image of God," these traditions yield a rhetoric of sexuality that shows, for instance, male and female in creation and disobedience (Gen. 2—3); in the joys of eroticism (Song of Songs); and in the crises of mundane existence (the book of Ruth). These three portraits we shall explore in the latter half of this study.[79]

Within scripture, my topical clue is a text: the image of God male and female. To interpret this topic, my methodological clue is rhetorical criticism. Outside scripture, my hermeneutical clue is an issue: feminism as a critique of culture. These clues meet now as the Bible again wanders through history to merge past and present. Using them, let us trace first the journey of a single metaphor in the traditions of Israel, a metaphor that highlights female imagery for God.

NOTES

1. For a history of this confession, see Josef Scharbert, "Formsgeschichte und Exegese von Ex 34, 6f. und seiner Parallelen," *Biblica* 38 (1957): 130–50; cf. R. C. Dentan, "The Literary Affinities of Exodus XXIV 6f.," *VT* 13 (1963): 34–51.

2. Hebrew syntax allows for either Moses or Yahweh as the subject of the verb *proclaim*. Cf. Scharbert, "Formsgeschichte," p. 130; Martin Noth, *Exodus* (Philadelphia: Westminster Press, 1962), p. 261; Brevard S. Childs, *The Book of Exodus* (Philadelphia: Westminster Press, 1974), pp. 603–4.

3. David Noel Freedman, "God Compassionate and Gracious," *Western Watch* 6 (1955): 6–24.

4. H. Wheeler Robinson, *Corporate Personality in Ancient Israel* (Philadelphia: Fortress Press, 1967).

5. Hebrew grammar employs masculine pronouns for God. Though grammatical gender decides neither sexuality nor theology, these distinctions are difficult, if not impossible, to maintain in our hearing and understanding. Consequently, masculine pronouns reinforce a male image of God, an image that obscures, even obliterates, female metaphors for deity. The effect is detrimental for faith and its participants. In my own writing, I avoid pronouns for deity; an occasional resulting awkwardness of style is a small price to pay for a valuable theological statement. As yet, however, I do not know how to resolve the dilemma posed by grammatical gender for deity in the scriptures themselves, since translation must answer to both grammatical accuracy and interpretive validity. Illumination on this issue is a pressing need in contemporary hermeneutics.

24   *GOD AND THE RHETORIC OF SEXUALITY*

6. Cf. Elias Bickerman, *Four Strange Books of the Bible* (New York: Schocken Books, 1967), pp. 40–43.

7. J. A. Sanders, "Hermeneutics," *The Interpreter's Dictionary of the Bible, Supplementary Volume* (hereafter, *IDBS*) (Nashville: Abingdon Press, 1977), esp. pp. 404–5.

8. Richard E. Palmer, *Hermeneutics* (Evanston: Northwestern University Press, 1969), pp. 162–253; Hans-Georg Gadamer, *Truth and Method* (New York: Seabury Press, 1975), pp. 274–78; Paul Ricoeur, *The Conflict of Interpretations* (Evanston: Northwestern University Press, 1974), pp. 3–24; idem, *Interpretation Theory* (Fort Worth: Texas Christian University Press, 1976), pp. 71–88. Cf. L. E. Keck and G. M. Tucker, "Exegesis," *IDBS*, pp. 296–303.

9. I jump here from the ancient world to the contemporary scene without even a nod to the history of interpretation that intervenes. For a different approach, see Brevard S. Childs, *Biblical Theology in Crisis* (Philadelphia: Westminster Press, 1970), pp. 139–47; idem, *The Book of Exodus*, pp. xv–xvi and passim. Cf. Robert M. Grant, *A Short History of Interpretation of the Bible* (New York: Macmillan Company, 1963); Beryl Smalley, *The Study of the Bible in the Middle Ages* (Notre Dame: University of Notre Dame Press, 1964); Hans W. Frei, *The Eclipse of Biblical Narrative* (New Haven: Yale University Press, 1974).

10. Though the quality and/or validity of these illustrations varies, each demonstrates the thesis of interaction between the Bible and the world. This interaction does not mean that the Bible has an "answer" for every contemporary issue or even speaks specifically to it. Nor does the fact of interaction per se legitimate an interpretation. Not all interpretations are valid, and not all valid interpretations are equally so. Methodology is one major criterion for evaluation; see below.

11. James H. Cone, *God of the Oppressed* (New York: Seabury Press, 1975), pp. 63–72; idem, "Biblical Revelation and Social Existence," *Int.* 28 (1974): 422–40; cf. Peter C. Hodgson, *Children of Freedom* (Philadelphia: Fortress Press, 1974), pp. 51–62; Major J. Jones, *Christian Ethics for Black Theology* (Nashville: Abingdon Press, 1974), pp. 41–65.

12. Hans Walter Wolff, "Masters and Slaves," *Int.* 27 (1973): 259–72.

13. José Porfirio Miranda, *Marx and the Bible* (Maryknoll, N.Y.: Orbis Books, 1974); Gustavo Gutiérrez, *A Theology of Liberation* (Maryknoll, N.Y.: Orbis Books, 1973); Ernesto Cardenal, *The Gospel in Solentiname* (Maryknoll, N.Y.: Orbis Books, 1976); Robert McAfee Brown, "The View from Below: Theology in a New Key," *A.D.* 32 (September 1977): 28–31; idem, "Theology in a New Key: Resolving a Diminished Seventh," *Union Seminary Quarterly Review,* Fall 1977, pp. 23–34. Cf. also the report of Roman Catholic priests showing Brazilian "peasants and Indians how to apply Biblical concepts of justice and equality to their own lives" in the *Boston Evening Globe,* June 10, 1977.

14. Henri Mottu, "Jeremiah vs. Hananiah: Ideology and Truth in Old Testament Prophecy," *Radical Religion* 2, nos. 2 and 3 (1975): 58–67.

15. Milan Machovec, *A Marxist Looks at Jesus* (Philadelphia: Fortress Press, 1976).

16. Robert Jewett, *The Captain America Complex* (Philadelphia: Westminster Press, 1973).

17. Cf. Frederick Herzog, "Liberation Hermeneutic as Ideology Critique?" *Int.* 28 (1974): 387–403.

18. Sigmund Freud, *Moses and Monotheism* (New York: Random House, 1939); C. G. Jung, *Answer to Job* (New York: World Publishing Co., 1954).

19. Richard L. Rubenstein, *My Brother Paul* (New York: Harper & Row, 1972); see also David Cox, *Jung and St. Paul* (London: Longmans, Green and Company, 1959); but cf. Krister Stendahl, "The Apostle Paul and the Introspective Conscience of the West," *Harvard Theological Review* 56 (1963): 199–215.

20. Walter Wink, *The Bible in Human Transformation* (Philadelphia: Fortress Press, 1973).

21. E.g., Mary Ann Tolbert, "The Prodigal Son: An Essay in Literary Criticism from a Psychoanalytic Perspective," *Semeia* 9 (Missoula: Scholars Press, 1977), pp. 1–20; and Dan O. Via, Jr., "The Prodigal Son: A Jungian Reading," ibid., pp. 21–43.

22. Thomas Hora, *Existential Metapsychiatry* (New York: Seabury Press, 1977), passim; and idem, *Dialogues in Metapsychiatry* (New York: Seabury Press, 1977).

23. For a Japanese perspective, see Nobuko Kawano, "Modern Technology and the Disorder of Nature Through the Image of Hosea 4:1–3," *Jido Kyoiku Gaku Ronshyu*, March 1975.

24. Lynn White, Jr., "The Historical Roots of Our Ecologic Crisis," *Science* 155 (1967): 1203–7.

25. Walter Brueggemann, "King in the Kingdom of Things," *The Christian Century*, September 10, 1969, pp. 1165–66; Phyllis Trible, "Ancient Priests and Modern Polluters," *Andover Newton Quarterly* 12 (1971): 74–79; Bernhard W. Anderson, "Human Dominion Over Nature," in *Biblical Studies in Contemporary Thought*, ed. Miriam Ward (Somerville, Mass.: Greeno, Hadden, 1975), pp. 27–45.

26. See also David Crownfield, "The Curse of Abel," *The North American Review*, Summer 1973, pp. 58–63.

27. *Human Sexuality: A Preliminary Study* (New York: United Church Press, 1977).

28. William E. Phipps, *The Sexuality of Jesus* (New York: Harper & Row, 1973); Raymond E. Brown, *The Virginal Conception and Bodily Resurrection of Jesus* (New York: Paulist Press, 1973), pp. 1–68.

29. Walter Brueggemann, "The Covenanted Family: A Zone for Humanness," *Journal of Current Social Issues* 14 (1977): 18–23.

30. Robert L. Treese, "Homosexuality: A Contemporary View of the Biblical Perspective," in *Loving Women / Loving Men: Gay Liberation and the Church*, ed. Sally Gerhart and William R. Johnson (San Francisco: Glide Publications, 1974), pp. 23–58; John J. McNeil, *The Church and the Homosexual* (Kansas City: Sheed Andrews and McMeel, 1976), pp. 37–66.

31. On the wide spectrum of feminism, see, e.g., Sheila Rowbotham, *Women, Resistance and Revolution* (New York: Vintage Books, 1974); Sheila D. Collins, *A Different Heaven and Earth* (Valley Forge: Judson

Press, 1974); Rosemary Radford Ruether, *New Woman/New Earth* (New York: Seabury Press, 1975); *Radical Religion* 3 (1977), entitled "Feminism and Socialism"; Carol P. Christ, "The New Feminist Theology: A Review of the Literature," *Religious Studies Review* 3 (1977): 203–12.

32. E.g., Elizabeth Gould Davis, *The First Sex* (Baltimore: Penguin Books, 1972), pp. 140–44 and passim; Mary Daly, *The Church and the Second Sex*, with a new feminist post-Christian introduction by the author (New York: Harper & Row, 1975), pp. 21–22, 74–84; cf. Vern L. Bullough, *The Subordinate Sex* (Baltimore: Penguin Books, 1974), pp. 40–49, 79–120.

33. E.g., Dorothy D. Burlage, "Judaeo-Christian Influences on Female Sexuality," in *Sexist Religion and Women in the Church*, ed. Alice L. Hageman (New York: Association Press, 1974), pp. 93–116; Phyllis Bird, "Images of Women in the Old Testament," in *Religion and Sexism*, ed. Rosemary Radford Ruether (New York: Simon & Schuster, 1974); Katharine D. Sakenfeld, "The Bible and Women: Bane or Blessing?" *Theology Today* 32 (1975): 222–33.

34. Norman K. Gottwald and Antoinette C. Wire, "Introduction," *The Bible and Liberation: Political and Social Hermeneutics*, A *Radical Religion* Reader (Berkeley: Community for Religious Research and Education, 1976), pp. 2–6. See also the essays in ibid.; cf. Carl A. Raschke, "Hermeneutics as Historical Process: Discourse, Text, and the Revolution of Symbols," *JAAR* 15/1 Supplement (1977): 171–95.

35. This discussion does not cover the rich history of the terms "rhetoric" and "rhetorical criticism"; see, e.g., Lloyd F. Bitzer and Edwin Black, *The Prospect of Rhetoric* (Englewood Cliffs, N.J.: Prentice-Hall, 1971); Northrop Frye, *Anatomy of Criticism* (Princeton: Princeton University Press, 1957), pp. 243–337; Kenneth Burke, *A Rhetoric of Motives* (Englewood Cliffs, N.J.: Prentice-Hall, 1950), pp. 49–180. I focus on rhetorical criticism as it has been recently proposed for biblical studies by James Muilenburg, "Form Criticism and Beyond," *JBL* 88 (1969): 1–18.

36. By literary criticism I do not mean source criticism. Unfortunately, the two terms have been confused in biblical scholarship (e.g., Norman Habel, *Literary Criticism of the Old Testament* [Philadelphia: Fortress Press, 1971]). On this confusion, see the review by Edwin M. Good of Habel's book (*JBL* 92 [1973]: 287–89); Amos Wilder, *Early Christian Rhetoric: The Language of the Gospel* (Cambridge: Harvard University Press, 1971), p. xxii; Robert W. Funk, "Foreword," *Semeia* 8: *Literary Critical Studies of Biblical Texts* (Missoula: Scholars Press, 1977). On literary criticism, see Wilbur S. Scott, *Five Approaches of Literary Criticism* (New York: Collier Books, 1962).

37. My use of the word *structure* bears no relation to structuralism (e.g., cf. Susan Wittig, ed., *Structuralism: An Interdisciplinary Study* [Pittsburgh: Pickwick Press, 1975]). Throughout this study I am concerned with the surface structures of literary compositions and not the deep structures.

38. Cf. Frye, *Anatomy of Criticism*, pp. 315–26.

39. Roger Hazelton, "Transcendence and Creativity," The Russell

Lecture, Tufts University, October 17, 1972; also idem, *Ascending Flame, Descending Dove* (Philadelphia: Westminster Press, 1975), pp. 50–59.

40. The convergence of the aesthetic and the religious disavows the dualism of literature versus scripture that has appeared in two recent discussions: John A. Miles, Jr., "The Debut of the Bible as a Pagan Classic," *Bulletin of the Council on the Study of Religion* 7 (1976): 1, 3–6; and David Robertson, *The Old Testament and the Literary Critic* (Philadelphia: Fortress Press, 1977), pp. 1–15, 84–85. Since the word *scripture* itself means writing, it is difficult to set it over against literature. Basically, the word designates the sacred writings of a particular tradition (e.g., the *Iliad*, the Bible, the *Vedas*, the Koran). Secondly, the word identifies authoritative literature for a particular community of faith. Thus, scripture always means religious literature; in specific contexts, this literature is also normative. In pleading for the Bible as literature, rather than as scripture, Miles and Robertson oppose the authority, not the phenomenon, of scripture. Conversely, James Barr distinguishes, though not absolutely, between "literary appreciation" and "theological use" of the Bible to find the former inadequate for the latter; see James Barr, *The Bible in the Modern World* (New York: Harper & Row, 1973), pp. 53–74; cf. idem, "Reading the Bible as Literature," *Bulletin of the John Rylands Library* 56 (1973): 10–33. For yet a different view, see Robert Alter, "A Literary Approach to the Bible," *Commentary* 60 (December 1975): 72.

41. *Contra* D. Robertson, who would allow "no extraliterary hypotheses" to supplement "the new literary criticism of the Bible" ("Literature, The Bible as," *IDBS*, p. 548). Barr has warned that such a restricted approach may have "a reactionary effect towards the whole structure of historical biblical criticism" (*The Bible in the Modern World*, pp. 65, 73). On the truth of his prophecy, see, e.g., Lelan Ryken, "Literary Criticism of the Bible: Some Fallacies," in *Literary Interpretations of Biblical Narratives*, ed. Kenneth R. R. Gros Louis (Nashville: Abingdon Press, 1974), p. 33.

42. Ricoeur, *Interpretation Theory*, p. 75.

43. For a classic statement of the intrinsic approach, see René Wellek and Austin Warren, *Theory of Literature* (New York: Harcourt Brace and World, 1956), esp. pp. 139–269; in biblical studies, cf. J. P. Fokkelman, *Narrative Art in Genesis* (Amsterdam: Van Gorcum, Assen, 1975), pp. 1–8.

44. On the history of this insight, see René Wellek, *Concepts of Criticism* (New Haven: Yale University Press, 1963), pp. 54–68; cf. Roman Ingarden, *The Literary Work of Art* (Evanston: Northwestern University Press, 1973), p. 33.

45. E.g., Muilenburg's analysis of Judg. 5:19–21 in "Form Criticism and Beyond," p. 11.

46. E.g., Toni Craven, "Artistry and Faith in the Book of Judith," *Semeia* 8 (1977):75–101; Dan O. Via, Jr., *The Parables: Their Literary and Existential Dimension* (Philadelphia: Fortress Press, 1967), pp. 110–76; cf. Edwin M. Good, "The Composition of Hosea," *Svensk Exegetisk Arsbok* 31 (1966): 21–63, 315–26. See my Chapters 5 and 6, below.

47. E.g., William L. Holladay, *The Architecture of Jeremiah 1—20*

(Lewisburg, Pa.: Bucknell University Press, 1976). Cf. also my Chapter 3, below.

48. E.g., Walter Brueggemann traces the motif of land in "Israel's Sense of Place in Jeremiah," in *Rhetorical Criticism*, ed. Jared J. Jackson and Martin Kessler (Pittsburgh: Pickwick Press, 1974), pp. 149-65. George Ridout accents the phenomenon of repetition in "The Rape of Tamar: A Rhetorical Analysis of 2 Sam. 13:1-22," in *Rhetorical Criticism*, pp. 75-84. See also my Chapter 2, below.

49. E.g., Isaac M. Kikawada, "The Shape of Genesis 11:1-9," in *Rhetorical Criticism*, pp. 18-32; Edwin M. Good, "Hosea 5:8—6:6: An Alternative to Alt," *JBL* 85 (1966): 273-86; Mary Ann Tolbert, *Perspectives on the Parables* (Philadelphia: Fortress Press, 1979), chs. 4, 5. See also my Chapter 4, below.

50. Max Lüthi, *Once Upon a Time: On the Nature of Fairy Tales* (Bloomington: Indiana University Press, 1970).

51. Muilenburg, "Form Criticism and Beyond," p. 9.

52. Gene M. Tucker, *Form Criticism of the Old Testament* (Philadelphia: Fortress Press, 1971); also idem, "Form Criticism, OT," *IDBS*, pp. 342-45; John H. Hayes, ed., *Old Testament Form Criticism* (San Antonio: Trinity University Press, 1974). I am not suggesting that form criticism is a biblical variety of literary criticism; in fact, many of its emphases are historical and sociological. See Barr, *The Bible in the Modern World*, p. 64, n. 7.

53. Erhard Gerstenberger, "Psalms," in *Old Testament Form Criticism*, pp. 207-18.

54. For recent assessments of form criticism, see two reviews of *Old Testament Form Criticism:* Walter Brueggemann in *Religious Studies Review* 1 (1975): 8-13; Robert R. Wilson, "A Progress Report or an Obituary?" *Int.* 30 (1976): 71-74. Cf. also the articles in *Int.* 27 (1973).

55. Robertson, *The Old Testament and the Literary Critic*, pp. 8-10.

56. Muilenburg, "Form Criticism and Beyond," pp. 1-18; cf. David Greenwood, "Rhetorical Criticism and Formgeschichte: Some Methodological Considerations," *JBL* 89 (1970): 418-26; Martin Kessler, "A Methodological Setting for Rhetorical Criticism," *Semitics* 4 (1974): 22-36.

57. Cf. Fokkelman, *Narrative Art in Genesis*, p. 8: "Every text requires its own hermeneutics and the annoying thing is that the outlines cannot be drawn until after the event."

58. Without necessarily utilizing the rubric "rhetorical criticism," other critics have studied biblical traditions from literary perspectives; see, e.g., Luis Alonso-Schökel, *Estudios de Poetica Hebrea* (Barcelona: Juan Flors, 1963); cf. also idem, *The Inspired Word* (New York: Herder and Herder, 1972); Erich Auerbach, "Odysseus' Scar," *Mimesis* (Princeton: Princeton University Press, 1953), pp. 3-23; Fokkelman, *Narrative Art in Genesis;* Alter, "A Literary Approach to the Bible"; also idem, "Biblical Narrative," *Commentary* 61 (May 1976): 61-67.

59. Cf. Frye, *Anatomy of Criticism*, pp. 7-8, 15-20; Robertson, *The Old Testament and the Literary Critic*, p. 6.

60. Cf. Giles Gunn, "Threading the Eye of the Needle: The Place of the Literary Critic in Religious Studies," *JAAR* 43 (1975): 183-84.

61. Ricoeur, *Interpretation Theory*, p. 79.

62. James Barr, *Old and New in Interpretation* (New York: Harper & Row, 1966), p. 137; Tolbert, *Perspectives on the Parables*, ch. 4.

63. Whether we can continue to regard Gen. 1:1—2:4a as a priestly document is a moot point; see, e.g., George M. Landes, "Creation Tradition in Proverbs 8:22–31 and Genesis 1," in *A Light Unto My Path: Old Testament Studies in Honor of Jacob M. Myers*, ed. Howard N. Bream, et al. (Philadelphia: Temple University Press, 1974), p. 289; P. A. H. deBoer, *Fatherhood and Motherhood in Israelite and Judean Piety* (Leiden: E. J. Brill, 1974), p. 49.

64. On inclusion, see M. Dahood, "Poetry, Hebrew," *IDBS*, pp. 670–71.

65. Another rhetorical use of the phrase "the heavens and the earth" sets the seventh day apart from the six days (2:1). While they consist of the creative work of God, the seventh is the creative rest.

66. Karl Barth, *Church Dogmatics*, vol. 3, pt. 1 (Edinburgh: T. & T. Clark, 1961), pp. 98–228); Claus Westermann, *The Genesis Accounts of Creation* (Philadelphia: Fortress Press, 1964), pp. 12–22; Bruce Vawter, *On Genesis: A New Reading* (New York: Doubleday, 1977), pp. 15–63.

67. Trible, "Ancient Priests and Modern Polluters," pp. 76–78.

68. Philip Kapleau, *Three Pillars of Zen* (Boston: Beacon Press, 1965), pp. 167, 174.

69. I. A. Richards, *The Philosophy of Rhetoric* (London: Oxford University Press, 1936), pp. 89–138; Philip Wheelwright, *Metaphor and Reality* (Bloomington: Indiana University Press, 1962), pp. 70–91.

70. *Contra* Sigmund Freud, *Beyond the Pleasure Principle* (New York: W. W. Norton & Co., 1961), pp. 51–52, and Norman O. Brown, *Life Against Death* (Middletown, Conn.: Wesleyan University Press, 1959), pp. 132–34.

71. Hora, *Existential Metapsychiatry*, p. 35.

72. *Contra* Eric Doyle, "God and the Feminine," *Clergy Review* 44 (1971): 873; on the dangers of the words *masculine* and *feminine*, see Casey Miller and Kate Swift, *Words and Women* (Garden City, N.Y.: Anchor Press/Doubleday, 1976), pp. 69–70, 160.

73. Richards, *The Philosophy of Rhetoric*, pp. 120–27.

74. For a survey of views on this verse, see Barth, *Church Dogmatics*, vol. 3, pt. 1, pp. 191–206; on the terms "image" and "likeness," see J. Maxwell Miller, "In the 'Image' and 'Likeness' of God," *JBL* 91 (1972): 289–304, and the bibliography cited there; also John F. A. Sawyer, "The Meaning of בְּצֶלֶם אֱלֹהִים ('In the Image of God') in Genesis I–XI," *Journal of Theological Studies* 25, pt. 2 (1974): 418–26. Cf. Hans Walter Wolff, *Anthropology of the Old Testament* (Philadelphia: Fortress Press, 1974), pp. 159–65.

75. I propose no historical, philological, literary, or intentional links between Gen. 1:27 and the rest of scripture; rather, I have chosen this verse as my interpretive clue.

76. Cf. the discussion of root metaphors in Ricoeur, *Interpretation Theory*, p. 64.

77. Partial metaphors not encompassed by the image of God male and

female would include, e.g., inanimate comparisons, such as God the rock, the fortress, the shield, and the horn (cf. Ps. 18:2).
   78. Paul D. Hanson, "Masculine Metaphors for God and Sex-Discrimination in the Old Testament," *The Ecumenical Review* 27 (1975): 316–24.
   79. These three portraits are not the only traditions that fall within the second function of our metaphor. Others might include, e.g., sections of the Abraham and Sarah stories (Gen. 12:10–20; 18:1–15; 21:1–21); Judah and Tamar (Gen. 38); Hannah and Elkanah (1 Sam. 1—2); Elijah and the widow of Zarephath (1 Kings 17:8–24).

CHAPTER 2

Journey of

a Metaphor

BY WAY OF A STORY

Once upon a time two women stood before a king, both claiming ownership of the same child. They were harlots, an identification (not a judgment) which accounts for their unusual situation. After introducing them, the narrator does little more than provide transitions for their speeches. They tell their own story, speaking directly to the king without intermediaries (1 Kings 3:16–28).

The two harlots lived alone in the same house. Within three days of each other, they gave birth to sons. There were no witnesses to these natal events. No midwives were present to assist and no men appeared to claim paternity: just two women and two infants alone in one house. By night death came to one of the babies; by night deceit came to one of the women. The agent of both death and deceit was that woman who in sleep lay upon her own son and then later exchanged him for the living child while the other harlot slept. Day revealed the deeds of night. Rising to nurse her child, one woman discovered death in her bed. The light of morning showed further that the child was not her own.

When the wronged woman reports this grave injustice to the king, she is locked in a power struggle to recover her child. Claim and counterclaim precede the decision of the monarch: "No, the living child is mine, and the dead child is yours," says one woman. "No, the dead child is yours, and the living child is mine," says the other (v. 22, RSV). The chiastic structure of this exchange shows the cross-purposes for which these harlots strive. By this inversion of words (living child, dead child; dead child, living child) the women imprison themselves so that their

end is their beginning. There is no movement beyond this dilemma and no possibility of solution within it.

The king does not judge between the two women. He does not
take sides in their interpersonal struggle for possession. Instead,
he recites their impasse to show that no solution is possible at
that level:

> Then the king said, "The one says, 'This is my son that is alive, and
> your son is dead'; and the other says, 'No; but your son is dead, and
> my son is the living one' " (v. 23, RSV).

Next the king moves to break this egotistic and dualistic
thinking—mine versus yours—by showing its inevitable
absurdity:

> And the king said, "Divide the living child in two, and give half to
> the one, and half to the other" (v. 25, RSV).

This order provides an occasion for truth to disclose itself
beyond interpersonal claims and counterclaims. As they respond
to the command, the women judge themselves:

> Then the woman whose son was alive said to the king . . . , "Oh, my
> lord, give her the living child, and by no means slay it." But the
> other said, "It shall be neither mine nor yours; divide it" (v. 26,
> RSV).

Having allowed the women to reveal who they are and hence to
decide their own case, the monarch need only report the
verdict:[1]

> Then the king answered and said, "Give the living child to the first
> woman, and by no means slay it; she is its mother" (v. 27, RSV).

We have observed already that this story builds on the words
of its participants. With one exception, the storyteller shows
great restraint, limiting his or her contributions to brief introductory and transitional statements. The exception is singular in
importance, for it supplies the motivation of the woman who
offers to relinquish her child in order that the child may live. She
offers "because her *raḥᵃmîm* [*compassion*] grew warm, grew ten-

der, or yearned [*kmr*] for her son" (v. 26). Motivated by compassion (*rahᵃmîm*), this woman is willing to forfeit even justice for the sake of life. By exposing the absurdity and insolubility of the power struggle between the two women, the king has occasioned in one of them a transcendent love which brings truth and life. And only after this development does the word *mother* appear in the story.[2] Throughout, the two females have been called harlots, women, or this one and the other. Finally, when their own words identify them, the king is able to call one a mother (v. 27). According to the story, the presence of a love that knows not the demands of ego, of possessiveness, or even of justice reveals motherhood.

For us this ancient story becomes a paradigm for understanding a particular biblical metaphor. The motivational clause, "because her *rahᵃmîm* [*compassion*] yearned for her son" (v. 26), provides the key word. Difficult to translate in the fullness of its imagery, the Hebrew noun *rahᵃmîm* connotes simultaneously both a mode of being and the locus of that mode. In its singular form the noun *rehem* means "womb" or "uterus." In the plural, *rahᵃmîm*, this concrete meaning expands to the abstractions of compassion, mercy, and love. Further, these abstractions occur in a verb, *rhm*, "to show mercy," and in an adjective, *rahûm*, "merciful."[3] Accordingly, our metaphor lies in the semantic movement from a physical organ of the female body to a psychic mode of being.[4] It journeys from the concrete to the abstract. "Womb" is the vehicle; "compassion," the tenor. To the responsive imagination, this metaphor suggests the meaning of love as selfless participation in life. The womb protects and nourishes but does not possess and control. It yields its treasure in order that wholeness and well-being may happen.[5] Truly, it is the way of compassion.

Although the vehicle womb is an organ unique to women, men also participate in the journey of this biblical metaphor. For example, in a scene ladened with emotion, Joseph sees for the first time "his brother Benjamin, the son of his mother." Overcome, he seeks a place to weep, "because his *rahᵃmîm* yearned [*kmr*] for his brother" (Gen. 43:30). This phrase parallels exactly the motivation of the harlot; yet here it embraces a fraternal relationship. One subtlety in the narrative merits further comment. Benjamin is described not just as the brother of Joseph but also as "the son of his mother," a felicitous identification in the presence of the metaphor *raḥᵃmîm*. In Psalm 103:13 the metaphor extends to a father to parallel paternal and divine love:

> As a father shows compassion [*kᵉraḥēm*]
> upon his children,
> So Yahweh shows compassion [*riḥam*]
> upon those who fear him.

This appearance of divine compassion signals another semantic movement for our metaphor: the journey from the wombs of women to the compassion of God. Let us next explore the contours of this movement.

FROM THE WOMBS OF WOMEN

1. IN NARRATIVE

In the Hebrew scriptures the wombs of women belong to God. Three stories make this point. Genesis 20:1–18 (E) tells of the patriarch Abraham betraying his wife Sarah. In order to save his own life, Abraham passes her off as a sister and so permits King Abimelech to take her into his harem. Immediately God acts to save Sarah from male abuse by informing and threatening the king. A person of integrity, Abimelech releases Sarah to Abraham, the prophet turned pander. Sarah is vindicated, Abraham prays, and fertility comes to the household of Abimelech. A concluding line explains the significance of this happy ending: "For Yahweh had closed every womb [*kol-reḥem*] of the house of Abimelech because of Sarah, Abraham's wife." But now, with the liberation of Sarah, divine blessing comes to the other females. Yahweh, who has closed wombs in judgment for sin, opens them for fertility.

A second narrative shows Yahweh intervening on behalf of another mistreated woman. Having been used by her father, Laban, to trick Jacob, Leah is now hated by Jacob her husband (Gen. 29:31–35[J]). Therefore, "when Yahweh saw that Leah was hated, he opened her womb [*raḥmah*]." She bears four children, praising Yahweh, the God who has shown compassion to her. Significantly, this pericope does not contrast the favor of

God for Leah with disfavor for Rachel. It says only that "Rachel was barren," not that Yahweh had closed her womb. In other words, Yahweh is not punishing Rachel but rather blessing Leah, the rejected wife. Indeed, later, "God remembers Rachel," harkens to her, and "opens her womb [*raḥmah*]" (Gen. 30:22 [E]).[6] By opening the wombs of Leah and Rachel, the deity blesses first the woman hated and then the woman loved by their shared husband, Jacob.

As a preface to opening the womb, the phrase "God remembers" occurs also in the third story (1 Sam. 1:1–20). Unlike Leah, Hannah is loved by her husband. Yet she herself is sad because "Yahweh had closed her womb [*raḥmah*]" (vv. 5, 6). Although in the tale of Sarah closed wombs meant judgment for sin, in this narrative no reason is given for God's action. Divine freedom and mystery remain intact. But Hannah suffers, taunted by her female rival who has borne children. Not even the assurances of her husband Elkanah can erase the barrenness of her womb and the sadness of her heart. At the temple she prays directly to God, asking that her affliction be removed, and she enlists the support of Eli the priest. In time "Elkanah knew Hannah his wife and Yahweh remembered her" (v. 19cd, RSV*); she conceived and bore a son. By the remembrance of Yahweh the womb of Hannah opened.[7]

In these three stories, the noun *womb* (*reḥem*) is a physical object upon which the deity acts. Control of it belongs neither to women nor to their husbands, neither to the fetus nor to society. Only God closes and opens wombs in judgment, in blessing, and in mystery.

2. IN POETRY

Associations of God with the uterus expand in the poetic literature of Israel. Not only does Yahweh control fertility by closing and opening the womb, but also this deity works in the organ itself to mold individual life. In Jeremiah this divine activity is both the forming (*yṣr*) of body[8] and the shaping of purpose. Thus Yahweh speaks:

> Before I formed you in the womb [*beṭen*] I knew you,
> and before you came forth from the womb [*reḥem*]
> I set you apart. (Jer. 1:5)

As the place of God's creativity, the womb embraces origin and destiny for Jeremiah (cf. Ps. 139:13–16).[9]

Echoing this understanding, Job broadens it to include other people. He reasons:

> If I have rejected the cause of my manservant or my maidservant,
>   when they brought a complaint against me;
> what then shall I do when God rises up?
>   When he makes inquiry, what shall I answer him?
> Did not he who made me in the womb [beṭen] make him?
>   And did not one fashion us in the womb [reḥem]?
>
> (Job 31:13–15, RSV)

For Job, God molds in the womb all human beings, not just special ones. This organ is the place of human equality, an equality based in the creative work of a God who also governs life outside the womb. Social status and sexual differences (manservant and maidservant) mean nothing in the perspective of creation, and this perspective determines ethical norms and behavior. In choosing how he treats himself and other human creatures, Job must answer to the God of the womb of equality. Thus, the female organ becomes a moral and theological event.

These two poets, Jeremiah and Job, who know so keenly the formative power of God in the uterus, wish most fervently to make the womb a tomb. Jeremiah laments:[10]

> Cursed be the day
>   on which I was born!
> The day when my mother bore me,
>   let it not be blessed!
> Cursed be the man
>   who brought the news to my father,
> "A son is born to you,"
>   making him very glad.
> Let that man be like the cities
>   which Yahweh overthrew without pity;
> let him hear a cry in the morning
>   and an alarm at noon,
> because he did not kill me in the womb [mērāḥem];
>   so that my mother would have been my grave,
>   and her womb [weraḥmah] forever great.
> Why did I come forth from the womb [mēreḥem]
>   to see toil and sorrow,
>   and spend my days in shame?
>
> (Jer. 20:14–18, RSV*)

In a soliloquy, Job sounds the same theme, even repeating some of the words of Jeremiah:[11]

> After this Job opened his mouth and cursed the day of his birth. And Job said:
> "Let the day perish wherein I was born,
>   and the night which said,
>   'A man-child is conceived.'
> ....
> Why did I not die from the womb [*mērehem*],
>   come forth from the womb [*mibbeten*] and expire?"
>   (Job 3:1–3, 11, RSV*)

Later Job addresses this death wish directly to God:

> Why didst thou bring me forth from the womb [*rehem*]?
>   Would that I had died before any eye had seen me,
> and were as though I had not been,
>   carried from the womb [*beten*] to the grave.
>   (Job 10:18–19, RSV)

In these complaints neither Jeremiah nor Job proposes that Yahweh might have killed him in the womb. Jeremiah wishes that the messenger who brought to his father news of his birth might have instead murdered the baby before birth. And Job does not specify an agent for his desired uterine death, even though he berates the deity for giving him life. Such self-pitying complaints falter; Yahweh alone decides the meaning of the womb.[12]

Relinquishing life for the sake of life is the last act of the uterus. God does this too. The deity prepares the organ for birth, does the birthing, and then receives the infant out of the mother. In spite of the pleas of Jeremiah and Job that they might have died either in the womb or just after expulsion from it, Yahweh brought them to life.[13] Although they protested, a psalmist, on the other hand, speaks lovingly of this divine activity:[14]

> Yet thou art he who took me from the womb [*beten*];
>   thou didst keep me safe upon my mother's breasts.
> Upon thee was I cast from the womb [*rehem*];
>   from the womb [*beten*] of my mother my God thou art.
>   (Ps. 22:9–10 [10–11], RSV*)

In this poetry the divine and the maternal intertwine. Yahweh takes the baby from the womb and places it upon the breasts of the mother. In turn, the tranquillity of the breasts becomes a symbol of divine care. To be cast from the womb upon God thus completes the deity's involvement with the functions of the uterus.[15]

And yet, Second Isaiah extends these functions to include the entire span of life. Yahweh speaks:

> Hearken to me, O house of Jacob,
>   all the remnant of the house of Israel,
> who have been borne by me from the womb [beṭen],
>   carried by me from the womb [rāḥam];
> even to your old age I am he,
>   and to gray hairs I will carry you.
> I have made, and I will bear;
>   I will carry and I will save.
>
>   (Isa. 46:3–4, RSV*)

The imagery of this poetry stops just short of saying that God possesses a womb. Clearly, however, Yahweh bears Israel from its conception to its old age.

God conceives in the womb; God fashions in the womb; God judges in the womb; God destines in the womb; God brings forth from the womb; God receives out of the womb; and God carries from the womb to gray hairs. From this uterine perspective, then, Yahweh molds life for individuals and for the nation Israel. Accordingly, in biblical traditions an organ unique to the female becomes a vehicle pointing to the compassion of God. Let us follow its direction as we move now to the tenor of the metaphor.

TO THE COMPASSION OF GOD

1. THE ADJECTIVE Raḥûm

As we have already observed,[16] the phrase "Yahweh merciful [raḥûm] and gracious" repeatedly describes God in the Hebrew scriptures. The two adjectival forms, "merciful" and "gracious," are used only for the Creator, never for creatures.[17] Although it is a fixed formula, this divine portrait belongs to no one historical period, literary stratum, or religious viewpoint. Indeed, it appears in all three sections of the canon within a variety of settings, literary forms, and religious expressions, all of which expand and enhance its meaning. "Yahweh merciful and gracious" belongs to recitals of the saving acts of God in history, acts freely given for individual and corporate liberation (Ps. 111:4; 145:8; Neh. 9:17). It is also found in individual petitions for deliverance (Ps. 86:16). It is motivation for national and divine repentance (Joel 2:13; 2 Chron. 30:9; Jon. 4:2) as well as for the unmerited forgiveness of sins, even in the presence of deceit, apostasy, rebellion, and hypocrisy (Ps. 78:38; 103:8). Again, the merciful God restores after national defeat (Deut. 4:31) and sends blessings upon the righteous person (Ps. 112:4). In many and various ways, then, the maternal metaphor *raḥûm* witnesses to God as compassionate, merciful, and loving.[18]

2. THE VERB AND NOUN *Rḥm*

In addition to the adjective *raḥûm*, an abundance of verb and noun forms demonstrates the tenor of our metaphor. To develop this point we turn to the prophets. Rich in familial imagery, the prophecy of Hosea speaks often of Israel as child and Yahweh as parent. For instance, Hosea 1 recounts the birth of two boys and a girl to the woman Gomer. As Yahweh commands, Hosea gives each child a name that indicts Israel for sin. Of the three names, the second belongs to our discussion. Appropriately, the female child is called *lō' ruḥāmā*, "Not Loved" (or "Not Pitied"). The explanation for this name comes in the motivational clause that follows: "for I shall no more show compassion [*lō'* . . . *'araḥēm*] on the house of Israel, to forgive them at all" (Hos. 1:6). Withdrawing love from the baby girl, Yahweh closes the womb of compassion. This motif of judgment continues in the succeeding oracle where all the children lie outside the mercy of God (Hos. 2:4). Finally, however, the indictment resolves in a divine promise to restore love freely to them at a future time:

And in that day, says Yahweh,
....
I will have compassion [*wᵉriḥamti*] upon Not Loved [*lō' ruḥāmâ*].
(Hos. 2:21, 23 [23, 25]; cf. 2:1 [3])

Although she came from the womb of harlotry, this little girl will return to the womb of mercy. The compassionate God prevails.

What Hosea indicates by his use of the root *rḥm*, Jeremiah intensifies in a poem replete with female imagery. To appreciate the power of our metaphor here, let us examine in detail the entire composition.[19] Jeremiah 31:15–22 is a drama of voices.[20] These voices organize structure, fill content, and mold vision to create a new thing in the land (cf. v. 22b), and this new thing is the poem itself. Five strophes form a chiasmus with the voice of Ephraim at the center (vv. 18–19). Surrounding this center are the voice of Rachel (v. 15) and the voice of Yahweh (vv. 16–17), on the one side; the voice of Yahweh (v. 20) and the voice of Jeremiah (vv. 21–22), on the other. This encircling pattern mirrors the relationship between female and male throughout the poem, providing a vision of both the parts and the whole.

The first strophe (v. 15) announces the weeping of the ancestral mother Rachel. Long ago when Yahweh first opened her womb, she bore a son, whose name, Joseph, expressed her wish for another son (Gen. 30:22–24). But at the birth of the second child, death closed forever the womb of this woman. Ben-oni was the son of her sorrow (Gen. 35:16–20). Now, centuries later, from her grave Rachel laments the subsequent death of her children:

> A voice on a height![21]
>   Lamentation can be heard,
>   weeping most bitter.
> Rachel is weeping for her sons,
>   refusing to be consoled for her sons:
>   "Oh, not one here!"[22]

This structure shows a mother embracing her children with tears and with words. Her tears are profuse: lamentation; most bitter weeping; Rachel weeping, refusing to be consoled. By contrast, her words are few: only two (*kî 'ênennû*) before speech fades into the silence of desolation. Yet this fading speech belongs to an enduring voice. Directed to no one in particular, and hence to all who may hear, the voice of Rachel travels across the land and through the ages to permeate existence with a suffering that not even death can relieve (cf. Matt. 2:18).

More specifically, Rachel's voice carries into strophe two (vv. 16–17). The second word, *voice (qôl)*, repeats the first word of strophe one; likewise, the weeping (*mibbekî*) of this voice persists (*b^ekî; m^ebakkâ*). Hence, to Rachel Yahweh now responds, using the feminine-singular imperative:

> Keep your voice from weeping
> and your eyes from tears.[23]

Promise motivates and sustains this divine imperative. From a general assurance it moves to a specific pledge, with the formula "oracle of Yahweh" (*ne'um Yahweh*) intervening to reinforce the promise:[24]

> for [*kî*] there is a reward for your work—
> oracle of Yahweh—
> they shall return from the land of the enemy.

The next line repeats this pattern and posture:

> and there is a hope for your future—
> oracle of Yahweh—
> sons shall return to their borders.

In both instances the verb *return (šûb)* marks God's pledge. Repetition stresses its importance.

As the opening imperative indicates, strophe two focuses upon Rachel. Speaking to console her, Yahweh never draws attention to the divine self. No first-person pronouns occur. Conversely, at least once in every line, possessive pronouns address Rachel: your voice, your eyes, your work, your future. To be sure, Rachel's consolation is to come through the return of her sons; yet they are mentioned with restraint. Yahweh first refers to the children only as "they" (v. 16) and in the parallel line (v. 17) where "they" becomes "sons" (this word providing another verbal link with the first strophe), God neither names these children nor attaches them to Rachel. In spite of translations,[25] Yahweh does not say "your sons." On the whole, the divine voice in this stanza emphasizes neither the deity nor the sons but rather the woman. She dominates.

But the third strophe changes emphasis (vv. 18–19). Concern for a mother leads to consideration of her children. The sons are named and they are quoted. Ephraim, at the center of the poem, is the center of attention. With verbal emphasis,[26] Yahweh introduces him: "Truly I have heard Ephraim rocking in grief." The verb *hear* (*šāmaʿ*) is a specific link between strophes one and three, but with differences. As the third word in strophe one, it is a passive voice, with no agent of hearing specified: the voice of Rachel can be heard on a height. As the first word(s) in strophe three, it is an active voice, with the *I* of Yahweh as subject and the son *Ephraim* as object. This object speaks remorse. Although Rachel's voice was so pervasive that it lacked a specific audience, the words of her children address God directly:

> You whipped me, and I took the whipping
>   like an untrained calf;
> bring me back that I may come back,
>   for you are Yahweh my God.
> For after I turned away, I repented;
>   and after I came to my senses, I slapped my thigh.[27]
> I was ashamed, and I was confounded,
>   because I bore the disgrace of my youth.

Ephraim implores and confesses. Three times he uses the verb *turn* (*šûb*) in the double sense of physical movement and religious change. The last of these usages recalls his exile and apostasy: "after I turned away." The other two ask God to restore him to the land and to his deity: "bring me back that I may come back." Theologically, the repentance of Ephraim is an act of God; geographically, the return of Ephraim is the work of God. These two occurrences of the verb echo Yahweh's promise to Rachel in strophe two: "they shall return from the land of the enemy . . . sons shall return to their own country." Now strophe three accounts for that promise: Ephraim implores God with a voice of repentance and confession.

Rachel cries; Yahweh consoles; Ephraim confesses. Thus the poem has moved to its center. Words of a mother and words to a mother converge upon her child. Then, with variations in order and in content, this pattern recurs in the next two strophes so that female semantics encircle the voice of the son.

Strophe four, which contains our metaphor, sounds Yahweh's voice (v. 20). The Revised Standard Version translates it:

Is Ephraim my dear son?
Is he my darling child?
For as often as I speak against him,
I do remember him still.
Therefore my heart yearns for him;
I will surely have mercy on him,
                    says the Lord.

As in the preceding strophe, God speaks in the first-person singular and names Ephraim, the name occurring in approximately parallel places (vv. 18a, 20a). Verbal links continue between adjoining stanzas. At the same time, however, strophe four matches strophe two in position and in speaker. Together they surround the center. On the one side, Yahweh consoles; on the other, Yahweh contemplates. But these similarities involve dissimilarities. For instance, the first-person singular of the deity, as well as the divine possessive pronouns, controls the language of strophe four. Neither appeared in strophe two, where Rachel dominated. Consequently, attention belongs here to Yahweh (not to Rachel). Moreover, Ephraim is the object of this attention. God names him, as the deity failed to do in strophe two, and God claims him—for the first time ever. A threefold utterance of question, motivation, and conclusion probes the divine relationship to this child. Particles introduce each of the three sections.

An interrogative particle poses a rhetorical question: "Is Ephraim my dear son? my darling child?" Having heard Ephraim rocking in grief (v. 18), Yahweh now considers him. But the question is a moment of hesitation that combines distance and intimacy. If Ephraim is the darling child of Yahweh, it is that Ephraim whom God has punished; it is also this Ephraim who is seeking restoration. In contemplating the child, Yahweh hesitates with a question that suggests but does not declare tenderness. Perhaps this deity shares a mother's suffering. After all, are not the children for whom Rachel weeps also the children of Yahweh?

The motivational clause, introduced by the particle *kî-middê* ("as often as"), moves toward a resolution; yet it elicits opposing interpretations.[28] Do its two cola contrast divine judgment with divine mercy?

> As often as I turn my back on him,
>   I still remember him.
>   (*NEB*; cf. *JB*)

Or are these cola a totally negative statement?[29]

> For since I spake against him,
>   I do earnestly remember him still.
>   (KJV; cf. RSV)

Or are the cola a full affirmation of love?

> That as oft as I mention his name
>   I so longingly think of him still?
>   (*AB*)

Context joins content to decide meaning. Preceding this line Yahweh has already promised Rachel that sons will return to their own land, and Ephraim has already repented. Following this line, Yahweh speaks of compassion for the children, and they are urged to return home. In other words, judgment has no power in the poem. This motivational clause proclaims love: "For the more I speak of him, the more I do remember him." To speak of the child is to remember him lovingly,[30] even as Rachel remembers him. Indeed, God's memory is the hope for Rachel's future (cf. v. 17).

Finally, with striking imagery, the climactic line of strophe four confirms God's love for Ephraim. Here all distance is overcome. To introduce this line, the particle *'al-kēn* ("therefore") points not to a logical progression of thought but rather to the energizing power of language.[31] Moving from anthropomorphic speech in the rhetorical question of the first line to anthropopathic utterances in the motivational clause of the second, Yahweh comes, in the conclusion of the third line, to the inner recesses of human existence where the physical and the psychic unite to convey the depths of divine love. Female imagery abounds. First, Yahweh speaks words that the woman in the Song of Songs uses to describe erotic play:

My lover put his hand to the latch,
and my inner-parts trembled [*mē'ay hāmû*] within me.
(SS 5:4)

Reversing the order of the two words,[32] Yahweh speaks here of the divine inner-parts trembling for Ephraim the child. In some other passages, the word *inner-parts* parallels *womb* (Gen. 25:23; Ps. 71:6; Isa. 49:1; cf. Ruth 1:11).[33] Hence, the first colon of this concluding line can be appropriately read "therefore, my womb trembles for him."[34] Support for this translation comes in the second colon, where the root *rḥm* appears in two verbal forms. Thus an exclusively female image extends its meaning to a divine mode of being: "I will truly show motherly-compassion upon him," says Yahweh. Furthermore, these two verb forms parallel the verb forms of the preceding line. Together they emphasize the tender memory and the earnest love of Yahweh for Ephraim: "I do remember him lovingly" (v. 20b); "I will truly show motherly-compassion upon him" (v. 20c).[35]

In summary, strophe four is the voice of Yahweh the mother. Parallels between Rachel and Yahweh occur in each of its three sections. The rhetorical question calling Ephraim a "darling child" suggests that God identifies with Rachel's caring for her children. The motivational clause recalls Rachel remembering her lost sons with tenderness. And the conclusion makes explicit the maternal metaphor for God. As Rachel mourns the loss of the fruit of her womb, so Yahweh, from the divine womb, mourns the same child. Yet there is a difference. The human mother refuses consolation; the divine mother changes grief into grace. As a result, the poem has moved from the desolate lamentation of Rachel to the redemptive compassion of God. Female imagery surrounds Ephraim; words of a mother embrace her son. My translation is the following:

Is Ephraim my dear son? my darling child?
For the more I speak of him,
    the more I do remember him.
Therefore, my womb trembles for him;
I will truly show motherly-compassion upon him.
                    Oracle of Yahweh.

Still there is more. Ephraim confesses; Yahweh contemplates; now Jeremiah commands. The message of God's maternal compassion must be delivered to her child, and that is the role of the prophet. Hence, strophe five is the voice of Jeremiah.[36] Speaking to the child, his voice lacks the tenderness of Yahweh's, although it carries the divine words of restoration. Mood, but not message, changes. This strophe absorbs form, content, and meaning from throughout the poem; at the same time it is full of surprises. The finale is both summary and innovation. In the overall structure it corresponds to strophe one; yet it is longer, a sign of end-stress.[37] It also has a verbal link to the opening strophe, but with a different meaning. The nouns *tamrûrîm* appear at the end of the first line of both strophes. In the former instance, the word means "bitterness"; in the latter, "guideposts." A poem beginning with a mother crying bitterly for her lost children concludes with a prophet commanding them to make guideposts for their return home. Despair has become hope. Moreover, along the way a new thing has happened to the children: they change sex. At first, male; at last, female. Ephraim the son becomes Israel the daughter. Jeremiah speaks to a woman. This change of imagery converges upon the center of the poem to surround male with female.

Jeremiah speaks with imperative and impatience. After all, since Israel has been granted restoration, the nation ought to return immediately. Five feminine-singular imperatives urge haste. Their form matches Yahweh's command to Rachel in strophe two, "Keep your voice from weeping" (v. 16, RSV). Similarly, feminine second-person pronouns also recall other language of this strophe (v. 21):

> Set up waymarks for yourself;
>   make yourself guideposts;
> consider well the highway,
>   the road by which you went.
> Return, O virgin Israel,
>   return to these your cities.
>   (RSV)

Of these five imperatives, two return to the verb *šûb*. Twice this verb appeared in strophe two as God's pledge to Rachel that her children would return. Twice this verb appeared in strophe three as Ephraim's request that he be returned. Now twice this verb appears in strophe five as Jeremiah's command that Israel return. What was promised and what was requested, God has made possible. To return to the land is to return to God. But the vocabulary of return had still another meaning in strophe three, the meaning of exile and apostasy. Ephraim said, "For after I had turned away . . ." (v. 19). In a rhetorical question[38] strophe five incorporates this meaning too (v. 22a):

> How long will you dillydally,
> O turnabout [*haššōbēbâ*] daughter?
>
> (*AB*)

Hence, between strophes three and five, three verbs correspond to three verbs in sequence and in meaning.

Jeremiah's question of urgency leads to the final, climactic line of the poem (v. 22b):

> For [*kî*] Yahweh has created a new thing in the land:
> female surrounds man.

Like the rest of strophe five, this line absorbs and provides meaning for the entire poem. Its words move between repetition and innovation. At the very beginning of the poem stands the prophetic formula "thus says the Lord," so that even the voice of Rachel comes under its rubric.[39] This formula comes again at the opening of strophe two, which is indeed Yahweh's speech. Further, the two phrases "oracle of Yahweh" (RSV: "says the Lord") emphasize the point. In strophe three, Ephraim confesses faith with the words "for you are Yahweh my God." Strophe four, the voice of Yahweh, concludes with the formula "oracle of Yahweh." Thus the appearance of the Tetragrammaton in strophe five belongs to a constant pattern. The difference is that here Yahweh neither speaks nor is addressed; rather, Yahweh is spoken about. The poet has taken over to announce God's new creation, and this new thing requires a new word, *bārā'*, a verb used throughout the Old Testament only for the creative work of God (cf. Gen. 1:27). Accordingly, verb and object match to proclaim the unique. Yet this new creation is "in the land," a word that echoes strophe two even as it reverses meaning. Yahweh who promised that "they will return from the land ['ereṣ] of the enemy" (v. 16) now creates a new thing in the land ('ereṣ) of their home. Altogether, then, the form and content of this declaration alternates between innovation and continuation.[40] Such activity mirrors the whole of strophe five.

The reversal of meaning for the term *land* recalls other reversals. For instance, the bitterness of Rachel has become guideposts for the return home. More importantly, the male Ephraim has become the female Israel. This switch in sexual identification anticipates the final colon, where language is again out of order. Subject and object turn sexual patterns upside down: "female surrounds man." The colon moves between mystery and meaning. All its words are new; none of them has appeared elsewhere. They are what they say: a new thing in the land. But this new thing belongs in the poem and in the poem finds its meaning. Innovation and continuity interact. Accordingly, the two nouns of this proclamation—one female, the other male—belong to a series of images developed throughout the poem. Specific female images are Rachel weeping for Ephraim, Yahweh showing him motherly compassion, and Israel replacing him. In the last line of the poem, the word *female* (*nᵉqēbâ*) resonates with all these images. As we have already seen, this word occurred in Genesis 1:27 as a generic term to include all females. Moreover, it was used there in poetic parallelism to the phrase "image of God," a parallelism approximated in Jeremiah 31:22b. In both these passages this noun is the object of the verb *create* (*bārā'*) with *God* (or *Yahweh*) as subject. Thus, the text of Genesis 1:27, which is the clue for our entire study, provides an external witness to the kind of internal function the noun *nᵉqēbâ* has here in Jeremiah. As an inclusive and concluding referent, *nᵉqēbâ* encompasses poetically all the specific female images of the poem.

But to encompass is to surpass. The verb *surround* contributes to its subject *female* a power that moves beyond comparable images in the poem. Although it is present in the connotations of the verb itself,[41] this power becomes apparent through a wordplay in the last two lines. After calling Israel a "turnabout [haśśôbēbâ, v. 22a] daughter," the poet juxtaposes immediately the description of female surrounding (tᵉśôbēb, v. 22b) man. Two very different portraits of the female are thus associated through assonance; yet this association yields a radical transformation with the positive image superseding the negative in Yahweh's new creation. Hence, the climactic affirmation that female surrounds man moves beyond other female images even as it includes them.[42]

The male images, on the other hand, are reinforced by the poem's last word, *man* (*geber*). In strophes one through four, the male vocabulary has terms designating youthfulness: *son* (*bēn*) in strophes one, two, and four; *young man* (*na'ar*) in strophe three; and *child* (*yeled*) in strophe four. All these words refer to Ephraim. Parenthetically, the female words for Israel in strophe five also stress youth: *virgin* (*b^etûlâ*) and *daughter* (*bat*). Thus the nation, male or female, is portrayed as young throughout. Yet at the same time Ephraim suggests in strophe three (the center strophe) that he is a grown man with the disgrace of his youth behind him (v. 19). The term *geber* can absorb all these male meanings.[43] Outside witnesses include Job 3:3, where *geber* describes a baby boy; Proverbs 30:19, where it portrays a young man; and Exodus 12:37, where it specifies adult males. In general, these meanings fit Ephraim so that the word *geber* develops further continuity in the male vocabulary of the poem. But it is also a new word that contributes new meaning: the nuance of virility. Perhaps the frequent application of *geber* to warriors or to heroes demonstrates best this persistent connotation.[44] The nuance itself, rather than its military applications, participates in our poetic context to enhance further the radical reversal that is the new thing of the poem. Thus it is the virile male, child to adult, who is surrounded by female. As both continuity and innovation, the term *man* (*geber*) completes the phrase "female surrounds." Altogether these new words interact with images throughout the poem.

Having no one specific referent, then, the three words of the final colon wander throughout a work of art to receive and give meanings. Accordingly, female surrounding man is Rachel the mother embracing her sons with tears and with speech; it is Yahweh consoling Rachel about Ephraim; it is Yahweh declaring motherly-compassion for Ephraim; it is the daughter Israel superseding the son Ephraim. And it is more than these images.

Female surrounding man has power to dry up the tears of
Rachel; to fulfill the compassion of Yahweh; and to overturn the
apostasy of Israel. And it is other than all these images, for it is
Yahweh's creation of a new thing in the land. In short, it is the
poem itself:

> Words of a *woman*: Rachel cries (v. 15)
> Words to a *woman*: Yahweh consoles (vv. 16–17)
> Words of a man: Ephraim confesses (vv. 18–19)
> Words of a *woman*: Yahweh contemplates (v. 20)
> Words to a *woman*: Jeremiah commands (vv. 21–22)

Within this new creation, our specific interest is strophe four.
There the uterine metaphor encompassed by the root *rḥm*
signifies the image of God female:

> Is Ephraim my dear son? my darling child?
> For the more I speak of him,
>   the more I do remember him.
> Therefore, my womb trembles for him;
>   I will truly show motherly-compassion [*raḥēm 'ăraḥămennû*]
>   upon him.
>
> > Oracle of Yahweh.

As we have demonstrated, this strophe belongs to an interlocking rhetoric that is replete with female semantics. More particularly, the very form and content of the poem embodies a womb:
woman encloses man. The female organ nourishes, sustains, and
redeems the male child Ephraim. Thus, our metaphor is surrounded by a cloud of witnesses.

Along with Hosea and Jeremiah, Second Isaiah also gives his
testimony.[45] Within the Servant Song of chapter 49, he depicts
the return from exile as a new Exodus in which Yahweh the
shepherd will lead the people (vv. 9c–11), thereby "showing
compassion upon them" (*mᵉraḥămām*).[46] The word *compassion* is
repeated in the exuberant hymn that follows. The heavens and
the earth are called to rejoice

> because [*kî*] Yahweh has comforted the people
>   and upon the afflicted will show compassion [*yᵉraḥēm*].
> > (Isa. 49:13)

A chiasm (verb-object-object-verb) encircles the suffering people with divine comfort and compassion. Yet the many assurances of mercy that have been given thus far, including two usages of the root *rḥm*, occasion the antithesis which introduces the second half of the poem (vv. 14–26). Zion is not convinced. Prophetic emphasis upon the restorative mercy of Yahweh does not persuade. As a result, the people speak, also in a chiastic structure, to surround God with human misery and despair:

> But Zion said:
> "Forsaken me has Yahweh
> and Adonai has forgotten me."
> (49:14)

Human reality confronts divine promise. Immediately the deity replies, and for the third time the root *rḥm* appears. Yet this usage differs significantly from the other two to reveal divine love in a way that surpasses human comparison. Yahweh poses a question:

> Can a woman forget her sucking baby
> that she should have no compassion [*mĕraḥēm*]
> on the child of her womb [*beṭen*]?[47]
> (v. 15, RSV*)

Physical and psychic meanings unite here in an illuminating manner. As the locus of birth, the womb is one of the most profound symbols of human love. Surely no woman can fail to show womb-love for the child of her own womb.[48] Nevertheless, if the inconceivable should happen, Yahweh will not forget Zion:

> Even these may forget,
> yet I will not forget you.
> (49:15cd, RSV)

In this divine speech our metaphor takes a new direction. Heretofore its journey has accented similarities between the womb of woman and the compassion of God. But now the metaphor suggests the limitations of this comparison in order to show the unfathomable depths and integrity of divine love:

Can a woman forget her sucking baby
    that she should have no compassion on the child of her womb?
Even these may forget,
    yet I will not forget you.

(49:15, RSV*)

By juxtaposing divine compassion to one supreme expression of human love, the poetry creates a new presence of Yahweh among the exiles.[49] Their protest ceases. The turn of the metaphor has left no room for doubt: Yahweh is the merciful God who will deliver the people.

Contributing further to the peregrinations of this metaphor, sections of a poem in Third Isaiah reflect tension between God the lover and God the enemy (Isa. 63:7—64:12).[50] In an intercessory prayer, the poet begins by praising Yahweh who has granted goodness to Israel "according to his mercy" ($k^e rah^a m\bar{a}yw$) and by recalling the rebellion of the people that evoked the enmity of the deity (63:7-10). Next Yahweh remembers the divine leadership in "the days of old" (63:11-14), a memory that returns the poem to the tragic situation of the exiled present. Thereupon, the prophet implores God, as the Revised Standard Version translates:

Look down from heaven and see,
    from thy holy and glorious habitation.
Where are thy zeal and thy might?
    The yearning of thy heart and thy compassion
    are withheld from me.
For thou art our Father,
    though Abraham does not know us
    and Israel does not acknowledge us;
thou, O Lord, art our Father,
    our Redeemer from of old is thy name.

(63:15-16)

Following this request, the poem continues with an appeal that Yahweh return the people to the sanctuary, for meanwhile they have become "like those who are not called by thy name" (63:17-19, RSV).

Of special interest to us in the request quoted above are the words "the yearning of thy heart and thy compassion." The phrase rendered "the yearning of thy heart" (*hᵃmôn mē 'eyka*) is a variation of the words in Jeremiah 31:20c that we have translated "my womb trembles." Moreover, this phrase joins a noun form of our metaphor, *rahᵃmeykā*, "thy compassion." Again comparable to Jeremiah 31:20c, the resulting parallelism of these words indicates maternal imagery for Yahweh. The entire phrase can be appropriately read "the trembling of thy womb and thy compassion." In other words, the two nouns interpret each other to establish the fullness of the metaphor: the God of the womb is compassionate. So the poet implores:[51]

> Where are thy zeal and thy might,
> the trembling of thy womb and thy compassion?

Immediately, however, he shifts from maternal to paternal language, with the word *father* forming an inclusion for v. 16:

> [Restrain not thyself,] for thou art our Father,
> though Abraham does not know us
> and Israel does not acknowledge us;
> thou, O Lord, art our Father,
> our Redeemer from of old is thy name.
>
> (RSV*)

This shift in parental language approaches a balance that recalls our basic metaphor, the image of God male and female. Accordingly, Third Isaiah beseeches the God of the womb to be a compassionate father.[52] Yet the interrogative form of this petition hints at the possibility that the deity may indeed not be compassionate. Other passages develop this tension.

BY WAY OF DENIAL

The metaphor of the God of the womb also journeys in scripture by way of denial. Though both harlots were mothers, only one merited the name. For her the maternal mode became selfless love as "her *rahᵃmim* yearned for her child." But for the other woman the maternal mode was selfish possession. While on a height Rachel wept for her children, in houses of harlotry Gomer betrayed her own. The daughter of her womb was named Not Loved. Further, in those dark days following the destruction of Jerusalem by the Babylonians,

the hands of compassionate [rah͛amāniyyôt] women
   have boiled their own children;
   they became their food
   in the destruction of the daughter of my people.
                        (Lam. 4:10, RSV; cf. 2:20)

If not all mothers are compassionate, not all compassionate mothers are always compassionate.

Thus, the inconceivable does happen. A mother can forget her child and have no compassion on the fruit of her womb. Although for Second Isaiah not even this reality could alter the persistence and stability of the love of God, others in Israel were not so certain. Indeed, they had already denied the compassion of God. In an oracle of unrelieved doom, Isaiah of Jerusalem castigated Judah in the eighth century for its rebellion against God as well as for its refusal to heed divine warnings (Isa. 9:8— 10:4; cf. 5:24–30).[53] Each strophe of his judgment concluded with the uncompromising refrain:

For all this his anger is not turned away
and his hand is stretched out still.
                        (RSV)

Among other effects, the awful extent of this punishment showed unmistakably in the withholding of mercy from the young, the weak, and the helpless:

Therefore, over their young men Yahweh does not rejoice,
   and on their fatherless and widows has no compassion [lō' y͛eraḥēm].
                        (Isa. 9:17[16], RSV*)

Divine anger has eliminated even the possibility of an appeal to love. More than a century later, on the eve of the Exile, Jeremiah's parable of wine jars (Jer. 13:12–14) concluded with equally harsh words upon Judah:

And I will smash them one against another, old and young alike.
No pity, no mercy, no compassion [lō' 'a͛raḥēm] will deter me from destroying them. (13:14, AB)

A yet more devastating indictment surfaced in post-exilic reflections. In spite of Second Isaiah's intervening assurance that the compassion of God superseded even the love of a mother for the child of her womb, another poet dared to say that Yahweh may indeed deny the meaning of creation as love. These words found a place in the scroll of Isaiah also. They begin with a motivational clause, indicated by the particle *kî* ("since"), that supplies the basis for the judgment to come. The judgment itself commences with the particle *'al-kēn* ("therefore"), which both continues the sentence and introduces a chiastic unit:

> Since [*kî*] this is not a people of understanding,
> Therefore ['*al-kēn*], [God]
>   will not be merciful to them [*lō' yᵉraḥᵃmennû*];
>   the one who made ['*śh*] them;
>   the one who formed [*yṣr*] them
>   will not be gracious to them [*lō' yᵉḥunnennû*].
> (Isa. 27:11)

At the center of this chiasm two verbs proclaim the creative activity of God. Elsewhere these words have been associated explicitly with the womb. The verb *make* was used by Job, for example, when he described the womb as a place of human equality created by God: "Did not he who made ['*śh*] me in the womb make ['*śh*] him?" (Job 31:15, RSV). And the verb *form* was used in Jeremiah when God described the prophet's origin: "Before I formed [*yṣr*] you in the womb, I knew you" (Jer. 1:5, RSV). Surrounding these two verbs of creation in the chiasm are two additional verbs whose adjectival forms have uniquely depicted Yahweh in many traditions of Israel: "God merciful [*raḥûm*] and gracious [*ḥannûn*]." As we have seen, this depiction of God the lover has been associated intimately with the motif of creation. Indeed, the root *rḥm* unites these themes: the place of birth is the vehicle of compassion. To create is to love. But now in this dreadful prophecy a poet wrenches apart the inseparable. Love and creation are set in antithesis. Moreover, love itself, symbolized by the pair of words *mercy* and *grace*, is both split apart and negated. God will not be merciful is the first line of the unit; God will not be gracious, the last line. Separating these denials of mercy and grace is divine creativity. In the structure of the poetry, then, the absence of love encircles creation. Indirectly, this passage witnesses to the freedom of God; directly, it testifies to a divine judgment that shatters life. Israel can appeal no more to the maternal love of the deity. If a mother shows no compassion on the child of her womb, how much more does God show no compassion on creation. The impact of these words is terrifying. And even though such sentiments are exceedingly rare in the memories of Israel, they do not let us forget that our metaphor has its negative side.

With persistence and power the root *rḥm* journeys throughout the traditions of Israel to establish a major metaphor for biblical faith: semantic movement from the wombs of women to the compassion of God. Though readers of the Old Testament have often been slow to perceive this speech, they have long been recipients of its manifold blessings. For us the language has unfolded new dimensions of the image of God male *and* female. This disclosure in turn has pointed beyond itself to the freedom of the Creator who is Lover. Thus, a partial metaphor has illuminated the basic metaphor that yielded the clue for our journey. Pursuing this clue further, let us explore other passages along the way.

NOTES

1. In its biblical setting this folktale demonstrates the great wisdom of the king, who is presumed to be Solomon, although the story itself does not name him. A concluding statement, extraneous to the story proper, makes explicit this function (1 Kings 3:28).

2. Translations do not always convey this subtle use of the word *mother*. E.g., the *NEB* introduces the word into v. 26, where it does not occur in Hebrew.

3. Cf. Georg Schmuttermayr, "RHM—Eine lexikalische Studie," *Biblica* 51 (1970): 499–532; Israel Eitan, "An Unknown Meaning of *Rahamīm*," *JBL* 53 (1934): 269–71.

4. To emphasize: I speak of semantic correspondences, not of etymologies. On root fallacies, see James Barr, *The Semantics of Biblical Language* (New York: Oxford University Press, 1961); cf. John F. A. Sawyer, "Root-Meanings in Hebrew," *Journal of Semitic Studies* 12 (1967): 37–50.

5. For a discussion of the root *rḥm* that emphasizes its affinities to the word *ḥesed*, see Alfred Jepsen, "Gnade und Barmherzigkeit im Alten Testament," *Kerygma und Dogma*, vol. 7 (Göttingen: Vandenhoeck and Ruprecht, 1961), pp. 261–71.

6. Though source analysis of this text is difficult, the issue does not affect our point; cf. Gerhard von Rad, *Genesis* (Philadelphia: Westminster Press, 1961), pp. 292–97.

7. On the phrase "God remembers," see Brevard S. Childs, *Memory and Tradition in Israel* (Naperville, Ill.: Alec R. Allenson, 1962), pp. 31–44, esp. p. 41.

8. On the verb *to form* (*yṣr*), cf. Gen. 2:7; Isa. 27:11; 45:9–10.

9. The word *beṭen*, which parallels *reḥem* in this poetry, is a general term designating the abdomen. Though frequently it means womb, it may also designate the male abdomen (Judg. 3:21–22). Only *reḥem*, the vehicle in our metaphor, is unique to the female. See Hans Walter Wolff, *Anthropology of the Old Testament* (Philadelphia: Fortress Press, 1974), pp. 63–64.

10. On the design of this poem, see William L. Holladay, *The Architecture of Jeremiah 1—20* (Lewisburg, Pa.: Bucknell University Press, 1976), p. 133; on the parsing of *mrḥm* in Jer. 20:17, cf. M. Dahood, "Denominative *rihham*, 'to conceive, enwomb,' " *Biblica* 44 (1963): 204–5.

11. For a discussion of this soliloquy, see Samuel Terrien, *Job: Poet of Existence* (New York: Bobbs-Merrill, 1957), pp. 40–50. For an alternate vocalization of the consonants *mrḥm* in Job 3:11, see Dahood, "Denominative *rihham*," p. 205.

12. Yet, God's meaning may also include death; see Hos. 9:11–14, 16 and the comments on this passage in Chapter 3.

13. Cf. the words of Aaron to Moses that the leprous Miriam "not be as one dead, of whom the flesh is half consumed when he comes out of his mother's womb [*mēreḥem*]" (RSV). After seven days of isolation, Miriam was restored by Yahweh (Num. 12:9–15).

14. On links between Jer. 1:5 and Ps. 22:9–10, see William L. Holladay, "The Background of Jeremiah's Self-Understanding," *JBL* 83 (1964): 153–64.

15. For further comments on this passage, see Chapter 3.

16. See Chapter 1.

17. The possible exception is Ps. 112:4; the Hebrew text lacks a specific reference to deity, though the Greek (A) supplies it. On this formula, see David Noel Freedman, "God Compassionate and Gracious," *Western Watch* 6 (1955): 10–11; also idem, "The Name of the God of Moses," *JBL* 79 (1960): 151–56.

18. Some scholars have proposed a maternal meaning for the term *hannûn* also; see, e.g., Johs. Pedersen, *Israel*, vols. 1–2 (London: Oxford University Press, 1926), pp. 309, 525; Samuel Terrien, "Toward a Biblical Theology of Womanhood," *Religion in Life* 42 (1973): 328; idem, *The Power to Bring Forth* (Philadelphia: Fortress Press, 1968), p. 115; David Noel Freedman and Jack Lundbom, " חנן ," *Theological Dictionary of the Old Testament*, ed. G. Johannes Botterweck and Helmer Ringgren (Grand Rapids, Mich.: Eerdmans, forthcoming).

19. My discussion is drawn from "The Gift of a Poem: A Rhetorical Study of Jeremiah 31:15–22," *Andover Newton Quarterly* 17 (March 1977): 271–80.

20. Not all scholars recognize Jer. 31:15–22 as a poetic unit. For instance, though allowing for a discernible pattern in vv. 15–20, Brevard S. Childs calls this section "a series of separate units loosely joined together"; vv. 21–22 are not included (*Memory and Tradition in Israel*, p. 40). See also Guy P. Couturier, "Jeremiah," *The Jerome Biblical Commen-*

tary, vol. 1 (Englewood Cliffs, N.J.: Prentice-Hall, 1968), p. 326. On the other hand, John Bright sees vv. 15–22 as a poetic unit (*Jeremiah, AB* [New York: Doubleday, 1965], pp. 275–76, 284–86); also James Muilenburg, "Jeremiah, the Prophet," *The Interpreter's Dictionary of the Bible* (Nashville: Abingdon Press, 1962), p. 834.

21. For this reading, rather than the traditional "in Ramah," see Matitiahu Tsevat, "Studies in the Book of Samuel," *Hebrew Union College Annual* 33 (1962): 107–9; also Herbert Brichto, "Kin, Cult, Land, and Afterlife—A Biblical Complex," *Hebrew Union College Annual* 44 (1973): 38–39.

22. At several places, including these two tricola, my translation of this poem is indebted to William L. Holladay. Following his suggestion, I understand the introductory word of this last colon as an emphatic *kî* preceding words of lamentation; cf. Jer. 4:8; 6:26. Cf. William L. Holladay, *A Concise Hebrew and Aramaic Lexicon of the Old Testament* (Grand Rapids, Mich.: Eerdmans, 1971), p. 155; see also James Muilenburg, "The Linguistic and Rhetorical Usages of the Particle כי in the Old Testament," *Hebrew Union College Annual* 32 (1961): 135–60.

23. The word order in Hebrew is chiastic, with the imperative at the center: "from weeping your voice keep and your eyes from tears."

24. The two occurrences of the phrase "oracle of Yahweh" have been a problem for translators and interpreters as far back as the LXX, which omits both phrases as well as the entire beginning of v. 17; it also has a different reading for the ending of v. 17 (LXX Jer. 38:16b–17). Cf. *JB, NEB*. My approach is to interpret the final form of the Hebrew text.

25. E.g., KJV, RSV, *AB, JB, NEB, NAB*.

26. The infinitive absolute *šāmôaʿ* precedes the finite form *šāmaʿtî*, "I have heard"; see Ronald J. Williams, *Hebrew Syntax* (Toronto: University of Toronto Press, 1976), pp. 37–38 (sec. 205).

27. For this translation, see Bernhard W. Anderson, "'The Lord Has Created Something New': A Stylistic Study of Jer. 31:15–22," *CBQ* 40 (1978): 463–78.

28. Differences in interpretation hinge on the meaning of the preposition *bᵉ* in the first colon and of the verb *zākar* ("remember") in the second. The preposition may have either a positive or a negative value. Similarly, memory may be for weal or for woe; cf. Ps. 25:6–7; 74:22; 79:8; Jer. 31:34.

29. When translators choose a negative meaning for the first colon, it is not always certain whether they intend a negative or a positive meaning for the second; e.g., KJV.

30. Like the verb *hear* in v. 18, the verb *remember* is an emphatic statement with the infinitive absolute preceding the finite form.

31. See Pedersen, *Israel*, vol. 1, pp. 116–23.

32. For the words *mēʿay hāmû*, cf. also Isa. 16:11.

33. In these parallels, the Hebrew word for womb is *beṭen*, not *reḥem*.

34. A translation arrived at in discussion with William L. Holladay; cf. KJV: "therefore my bowels are troubled for him."

35. Thus three of the four first-person speeches of Yahweh are syntactically the same (vv. 18a, 20b, 20c); see nn. 25 and 29, above.

36. Since strophe five does not identify its speaker, I cannot prove

that the voice belongs to Jeremiah. Actually, silence about the identity of the speaker focuses attention solely upon the speech—which is replete with female semantics.

37. On end-stress, see Axel Olrik, "Epic Laws of Folk Narrative," *The Study of Folklore*, ed. Alan Dundas (Englewood Cliffs, N.J.: Prentice-Hall, 1965), pp. 129–41.

38. Cf. the use of a rhetorical question in strophe four, v. 20a.

39. Although these rubrics may have been, in the words of Holladay, "added secondarily," they belong to the final form of the poem, and it is this form that I am interpreting rhetorically.

40. The Hebrew order of words shows this alternation clearly: "for creates [innovation] Yahweh [continuation] a new thing [innovation] in the land [continuation]."

41. Cf. Ps. 55:10; 59:6, 14; Jon. 2:3, 5.

42. For $t^e s \hat{o} b \bar{e} b$ ("surround") as a verb giving power to God, see Deut. 32:10; Ps. 32:7, 10.

43. My purpose is not to discuss all meanings of *geber* but to focus upon those congenial to the male images within this poem.

44. E.g., 1 Sam. 14:52; 17:51. For discussions of this verse that develop the meaning of *geber* as warrior or he-man, see William L. Holladay, "Jer. xxxi 22B Reconsidered: 'The Woman Encompasses the Man,'" *VT* 16 (1966): 236–39; idem, "Jeremiah and Women's Liberation," *Andover Newton Quarterly* 12 (March 1972): 213–23; idem, *Jeremiah: Spokesman Out of Time* (Philadelphia: Pilgrim Press, 1974), pp. 116–17.

45. On the structure of Second Isaiah, I follow the delineation of strophes set forth by James Muilenburg, "The Book of Isaiah, Chapters 40–66," *The Interpreter's Bible*, vol. 5 (Nashville: Abingdon Press, 1956), pp. 381–773. For a different rhetorical analysis, based on the study of genre rather than of strophe, see Roy F. Melugin, *The Formation of Isaiah 40–55* (Berlin: Walter de Gruyter, 1976).

46. See Muilenburg, "The Book of Isaiah," pp. 564–78.

47. For a similar use of these two Hebrew words, cf. Isa. 13:18. In 46:3, Second Isaiah parallels the nouns *rehem* and *beṭen*. For an alternate pointing of the consonants *mrhm* (49:15a), with the reading "one pregnant," see Dahood, "Denominative *riḥḥam*," p. 204.

48. But cf. the woman Babylon who failed to show womb-love (*raḥ°mim*) on the children of Yahweh (Isa. 47:5–6).

49. For a similar rhetoric indicting the people, cf. Jer. 2:32.

50. See Muilenburg, "The Book of Isaiah," pp. 728–44.

51. For this translation, cf. ibid., p. 736. On the words "the trembling of thy womb and thy compassion," cf. KJV: "the sounding of thy bowels and of thy mercies."

52. Cf. the balancing of female and male language in Isa. 45:10; 49:23; 51:2; also Ps. 123:2; Jer. 16:1–3, 7, 9. Jer. 31:8 pairs masculine singular forms ("the blind and the lame") with feminine singular forms ("pregnant and giving birth") (RSV).

53. On compositional questions, see Otto Kaiser, *Isaiah 1—12* (Philadelphia: Westminster Press, 1972), pp. 131–40.

CHAPTER 3

Passages Along

the Way

POINTS OF DEPARTURE

The word *womb* (*reḥem*) belongs to a lexicon of birth that further enriches creation in the image of God male and female. Among the passages we have already cited, Psalm 22:9–10[10–11] hints at this larger vocabulary:

> For [*kî*] you [*attâ*] brought me forth from the womb [*beṭen*],
>
> made me safe upon ['*al*] the breasts of my mother.
>
> Upon you [*āleykā*] was I cast from the womb [*reḥem*];
>
> from the womb [*beṭen*] of my mother, my God are you [*attâ*].

Earlier we observed Yahweh's involvement with the womb as it relinquishes life for the sake of life. Now a close reading of these verses underscores further connections between the deity and the female. Praying to God, the psalmist uses the divine pronoun *you* at the beginning, middle, and end of this two-line unit. Each occurrence links God with psychophysical aspects of birth. In the first line, the divine *you* receives the infant from the womb and places it safely upon the breasts of the mother. Deity and mother appear at the beginning and end of this sentence, respectively. Their syntactic distance signals a content difference between divine midwife and human mother.[1] But at the center of the poetry this distance lessens. The end of line one and the beginning of line two contain parallel prepositional phrases whose meanings converge. "Upon the breasts ['*al-šᵉdê*] of my mother" leads directly to "upon you" (*āleykā*). Subject has become object; divine midwife has become divine mother. To be kept safe upon the breasts of the mother is to be cast upon God from the womb.[2] This identification culminates in the final colon

60

where "my mother" adjoins "my God": "from the womb of my mother, my God are you." Distance and difference have yielded to proximity and approximation. Although the poetry never explicitly calls God midwife and mother, its form and content disclose these metaphors. In addition, the chiastic arrangement of the last line, as well as the inclusion of the entire unit, suggests the transcendence of the deity. The divine *you* encloses child and mother. Hence, the image of God female points to the Creator.

In Genesis 49:25 breasts and womb occur together again. The tribes of Joseph receive blessings

> by the God of your father who will help you,
> by God Almighty [*'ēl šadday*] who will bless you
> with blessings of heaven above,
> blessings of the deep that couches beneath,
> blessings of the breasts [*šādayim*] and of the womb [*rāḥam*].
> (RSV)

At first glance, this ancient poetry seems to associate God solely with a father who gives blessings (see also v. 26). Yet a wordplay between the epithet *šadday* ("mountains") and the noun *šādayim* ("breasts") connotes a maternal aspect in the divine.[3] Accordingly, though the verse combines two partial metaphors, the explicit father and the implicit mother, we accent here the female dimension of the God *šadday*, who gives the blessings of the breasts and the womb. Moreover, in contrast to Psalm 22:9–10, this passage extends these maternal benefits beyond an individual to a people.

Centuries later, however, the prophet Hosea reverses the meaning of these symbols. What was given as blessing becomes judgment. First, God declares:

> Ephraim's glory shall fly away like a bird—
> no birth, no pregnancy, no conception!
> Even if they bring up children,
> I will bereave them till none is left.
> (Hos. 9:11–12a, RSV; cf. v. 16)

To these divine words of destruction, the prophet adds his own:[4]

> Give them, O Yahweh—
> What wilt thou give?
> Give them a miscarrying womb [*reḥem*]
> and dry breasts [*šādayim*].
> (Hos. 9:14, RSV*)

For Hosea, signs of female infertility have become symbols of corporate sterility. In response to sin, the God of womb and breasts aborts fetuses and dries up milk. This link between the divine and the maternal speaks death, not life. Yet even in judgment these symbols are for us points of departure in a continuing journey to explore the image of God female.

ALONG THE WAY

Besides the words *womb* and *breasts*, other language discloses the contours of our journey. Let us examine first a passage within the Song of Moses (Deut. 32:1–43). Following the introduction (vv. 1–6), a major section of this poem is devoted to the history of Israel.[5] This history is reviewed from two perspectives: (1) the gracious acts of Yahweh for the people (vv. 7–14); (2) the apostasy of the people that leads to indictment (vv. 15–18). The Revised Standard Version translates the last verse of the history as follows:

> You were unmindful of the Rock that begot you [$y^e lād^e kā$],
> and you forgot the God who gave you birth [$m^e ḥōl^e lekā$].
> (v. 18)

In Hebrew this unit is a chiasm of object and subject. "The Rock that begot you" and "the God who gave you birth" surround the forgetfulness of the people. These phrases use two metaphors for God: rock and birthing. Occurring throughout much of the poem, the word *rock* signifies God's integrity and stability in contrast to Israel's corruption and mutability.[6] In verse 18 this noun is modified by a verbal form that introduces the second metaphor, that of procreating: $y^e lād^e kā$. The root *yld* can describe either the begetting of a father or the birthing of a mother. Proverbs 23:22, 25 shows both meanings within one pericope:[7]

> Hearken to your father who begot [$y^e lādekā$] you
> and do not despise your mother when she is old.
> ....
> Let your father and mother be glad,
> let her who bore you [$yôladtekā$] rejoice.
> (RSV; cf. Job 38:28–29)

In Deuteronomy 32:18, then, the divine image suggested by the word $y^e l\bar{a} d^e k\bar{a}$ may be either maternal or paternal: the Rock that bore you or the Rock that begot you. By contrast, the corresponding image at the end of this verse, "the God who gave you birth," is exclusively maternal.[8] The word $m^e \hbar\bar{o} l^e l e k\bar{a}$ only designates a woman in labor, and this activity the poetry ascribes to the deity.[9] With labor pains, God gave birth to Israel.

Thus the extremities of this chiasm present either complementary or identical parental metaphors. In the first instance, the Rock is the father who begot, and God is the mother who writhed at birth.[10] Isaiah 45:10 provides an external witness to this complementary interpretation of the two verbs:[11]

> Woe to him who says to a father, "What are you begetting [$t\hat{o}l\hat{i}d$]?"
> or to a woman, "With what are you in travail [$t^e \hbar\hat{i}l\hat{i}n$]?"
>
> (RSV)

In the second instance, both phrases yield maternal meanings.[12] The Rock is the mother who gave birth; indeed, God is the mother who experienced the pangs of childbirth. Isaiah 66:7a provides an external witness to this identical interpretation of the two verbs:[13]

> Before she was in labor [$t\bar{a}\hbar\hat{i}l$]
> she gave birth [$y\bar{a}l\bar{a}d\hat{a}$].
>
> (RSV)

Viewing this latter interpretation in light of the beginning of the Song of Moses, we discover a complementary balance between the conclusion of the introduction (Deut. 32:6) and the conclusion of the first major section (32:18). They both indict the people, one in interrogative form and the other in declarative. Moreover, they use language of creation, and they focus on God as the giver of life. The first conclusion calls God father:

> Is not he your father, who created you,
> who made you and established you?
>
> (v. 6, RSV)

The second describes God as mother:

> The Rock who gave you birth you forgot,
> and you lost remembrance of the God
> who writhed in labor pains with you.
>
> (v. 18)

These birth pangs of God appear again in Second Isaiah.[14] At a time when great empires have collapsed, when defeat and destruction rule the affairs of people, when in particular the nation Israel has lost its land, Yahweh cries out:[15]

> Like a travailing woman [kayyôlēdâ]
> I will groan; I will pant.
> I will gasp at the same time.
>
> (Isa. 42:14b)

Historical chaos has become divine labor pains. Out of God's travail a new creation will emerge (42:5–13). Nature will reverse; history will alter; prisoners will be set free; the blind will receive their sight; indeed, praise of Yahweh will fill the earth. Although she has restrained herself for a long while (v. 14a), now God will cry out, gasping and panting, as she gives birth to these new realities in the world.[16]

Third Isaiah pursues a similar theme in sections of a poem on the new birth of Zion and the fire of judgment (66:1–16).[17] Of the seven lines in its fourth strophe (vv. 7–9), the first five pertain to Zion giving birth suddenly and swiftly; and yet the specific identity of Zion comes only in the fifth line. Until that point the maternal subject hides in the feminine pronouns of the verb forms. Two verbs dominate: yld ("to give birth") and ḥwl ("to have labor pains"). As we have already seen, they appear side by side in the first line to announce an unusual birth:

> Before she was in labor [tāḥîl],
> she gave birth [yālādâ].
>
> (RSV)

With a different vocabulary, the second line reports again this surprise delivery:

> Before her pain came upon her
> she was delivered of a child.
>
> (v. 7b, RSV*)

Quick and painless birth elicits astonishment in the third line:

> Who has heard such a thing?
> Who has seen such things?
> (v. 8a, RSV)

The fourth line continues this interrogative wonder. Repeating the first two verbs of the announcement, it suggests the identity of female and nation:

> Shall a land be born [yûḥal][18] in one day?
> Shall a nation be brought forth [yiwwālēd] in one moment?
> (v. 8bc, RSV)

Astonishment leads at last to confirmation in the fifth line. Zion is named as mother and nation. And again the verbs are repeated:

> For as soon as Zion was in labor [ḥālâ],
>   she brought forth [yālᵉdâ] her children.
> (v. 8d, RSV)

Strikingly in Hebrew, both the subject (Zion) and the object (her children) of these final verbs have been delayed until the very end of the line. In its first colon, the two verbs appear; in its second, the two nouns. Separating the verbs is the adverb *gam* ("as soon as"); separating the nouns is the object sign *'et*. Although this order and structure cannot be retained in translation, it emphasizes the verbs that dominate the poetry (*yld* and *ḥwl*) and heightens suspense about the exact identity of their subject.

Three times within five lines, the same pair of natal verbs has occurred. With them God has proclaimed a new Zion bringing forth a new people in unprecedented wonder. Now in the finale of this strophe, Yahweh uses the first of these verbs again, but this time the deity shifts from speaking about Zion at birth to proclaiming identification with this birth:

> Shall I [ᵃnî] bring to the birth and not cause to bring forth [ʾôlîd]?
>   says Yahweh.
> shall I [ᵃnî], causing to bring forth [hammôlîd], shut [the womb]?
>   says your God.
> (v. 9, RSV*)

As questions, these closing lines complete a structural pattern in the strophe: the alternation between the declarative (vv. 7, 8d) and the interrogative (vv. 8abc, 9). Within these lines, two causative forms of the root *yld* ("to give birth") are enclosed by two related verbs. None of them signifies labor pains. Since Zion gave birth before pain came upon her, labor is not even mentioned by God. Instead, attention focuses solely upon the final act. Zion bearing children is Yahweh creating with swift surprise.

So liberating is this divine word of painless birth that immediately the poet bursts forth in an imperative of joy over Jerusalem the mother. This theme dominates strophe five of the poem (66:10–11). Those who heed the command to rejoice "may suck and be satisfied with her consoling breasts"; they may "drink deeply with delight from the abundance of her glory" (RSV; cf. Isa. 60:16). Thanks to God, the maternal city provides nourishment and comfort for the newborn child.

Similar images continue in strophe six, where Yahweh again speaks directly (66:12–14). The bounty of Jerusalem is derivative. Yahweh's generosity makes this city a prosperous mother, giving abundance of life to her children:

> For thus says Yahweh:
> "Behold, I will extend prosperity to her like a river,
>   and the wealth of the nations like an overflowing stream;
>   and you shall suck, you shall be carried upon her hip,
>   and dandled upon her knees.
>   (v. 12, RSV*)

Since Jerusalem is a loving mother by the grace of God, this act becomes in turn a clue for understanding the divine. The effect mirrors the cause. Thus, Yahweh declares:

> As one whom his mother comforts,
>   so I will comfort you;
>   you shall be comforted in Jerusalem.
>   (v. 13, RSV)

Throughout this verse emphasis falls upon the child Israel. He appears in the opening words, "as one whom"; in the pronoun object at the end of the first colon, "comfort *him*";[19] in the pronoun object at the end of the second colon, "comfort *you*"; and in the subject of the passive verb at the end of the verse, "*you* shall be comforted." In all three instances the single verb *comfort* (*nḥm*) directs its meaning to the child.

Clearly, the divine comforting of the inhabitants of Jerusalem is the tenor of a metaphor; its vehicle is maternal comfort. This correspondence flows freely from all the preceding language of the poem (vv. 7–12): "As one whom his mother comforts," says Yahweh, "so I ['*ānōkî*] will comfort you" (RSV). The use of the first-person pronoun, '*ānōkî*, stresses the divine agent. Although the comparison stops just short of calling God mother, it does not stop short of this meaning. Yahweh is a consoling mother to the children of Jerusalem. After these words of divine assurance, the poet bursts forth once again in joy:

> You shall see, and your heart shall rejoice;
>   your bones shall flourish like the grass;
> and it shall be known that the hand of Yahweh is with his servants,
>   and his indignation is against his enemies.
>
> (v. 14, RSV*)

Within this poem on the new birth of Zion, strophes four, five, and six have intertwined images of the divine and the female. A chart summarizes the overall pattern and central motifs of these units:

STROPHE FOUR (66:7–9)	STROPHE SIX (66:12–14)
Yahweh speaks about:	*Yahweh speaks about:*
Zion the mother (7–8)	Zion the mother (12)
Yahweh the mother (9)	Yahweh the mother (13)
STROPHE FIVE (66:10–11)	
The result of Yahweh's	The result of Yahweh's
speech: the poet rejoices	speech: the poet rejoices
over Jerusalem.	over Jerusalem (14).

The book of Job contributes another passage to the image of God male and female. Among the plethora of divine questions challenging Job is this couplet:

> Has the rain a father,
>   or who has begotten [*hôlîd*] the drops of dew?
> From whose womb [*beṭen*] did the ice come forth,
>   and who has given birth [*yᵉlādô*] to the hoarfrost of heaven?
>
> (Job 38:28–29, RSV)

The poetry balances parental images. As in Proverbs 23:22, 25, it uses the root *yld* for both the begetting of the father and the birthing of the mother. The questions are ironic; their purpose is to teach Job the transcendence of Yahweh. Thus, no human images, not even parental ones, can encompass divine creativity. No, the rain does not have a father; no male has sired the drops of dew. Rain and dew come only from God. No, the ice does not come forth from a woman's womb; no female has given birth to the hoarfrost of heaven. Ice and hoarfrost come only from God. Yet this irony has a double edge. Human images, especially parental ones, do suggest the activity of the divine. Yes, the rain does have a father; he has sired the drops of dew. God is this father. Yes, the ice does come forth from a woman's womb; a female has given birth to the hoarfrost of heaven (cf. Job 38:8). God is this mother. On the one hand, divine creation is not comparable to human procreation. On the other, it is through human comparisons that the transcendence of Yahweh is understood. Such perceptions continue as our journey concludes.

A RETURN TO THE BEGINNING

To the vocabulary of labor pains and birth belongs the initial stage of the process: conception. Our text comes from the traditions of the wanderings (Num. 11). Having been saved from bondage, Israel finds liberation a burden and so protests the gift of freedom. After all, slavery had its attractions, not the least of which was nourishing food (vv. 4–6). These complaints of a "liberated" people push Moses to anger and exasperation. Unable to meet their demands, he makes his own demands upon God. In a series of questions, he portrays himself as mistreated and burdened. The leader of the people is the victim of God:

> Why hast thou dealt ill with thy servant? And why have I not found favor in thy sight, that thou dost lay the burden of all this people upon me? (v. 11, RSV)

According to Moses, God is shirking responsibility. The people are as babes crying out for their mother. But who is this mother? With indirect language, Moses speaks boldly:

Did I conceive [*hārîtî*] all this people? Did I bring them forth [*yᵉlid-tihû*] that thou shouldst say to me, "Carry them in your bosom, as a nurse carries the sucking child, to the land which thou didst swear to give their ancestors?" (v. 12, RSV*)

In other passages, the verb *hrh* ("conceive") appears also in parallelism to *yld* ("give birth") to depict a woman who becomes pregnant and bears a child.[20] Implicitly, then, Moses says that Yahweh conceived and bore Israel. Next he carries the imagery further. Yahweh is to nurse the infant: "carry them in your bosom, as a nurse [*hā-'ōmēn*] carries the sucking child" (RSV). Although the word *hā-'ōmēn* is masculine in gender,[21] its context favors a female identity: a wet-nurse for the baby. Alternately, the word can be pointed *hā-'immōn*, a hypocoristicon for *'ēm*, mother.[22] The beloved mother herself caresses the sucking baby.[23] Either of these readings suggests, but does not assert, that God is a woman, whose bosom (*hēq*) gives care and nourishment to Israel, the newborn infant.

This last image, that of nursing the child, offers a return to our point of departure: the baby who is safe upon the breasts of its mother is cast from the womb upon God (Ps. 22:9–10). Along the way, the entire process of birthing has been attributed to the deity. In various passages, God conceives, is pregnant, writhes in labor pains, brings forth a child, and nurses it. With reticence characteristic of the poetic mode, such language expands, broadens, and deepens our understanding of the biblical God. Yet, like a finger pointing to the moon, our metaphor allows no resting place in the image of God female—nor in the image of God male (cf. Ps. 27:10). The One to whom it witnesses is the transcendent Creator going before us to make all things new.

Read with a rhetorical-critical methodology in light of a feminist critique of patriarchal theology, Genesis 1:27 has provided, first, the clue to a neglected dimension of biblical faith. Pursuing this clue, we have highlighted female metaphors for God and thus allowed scripture to interpret scripture for new occasions. This hermeneutical process continues as the text directs our attention next to traditions that embody male and female within the context of the goodness of creation. Genesis 2—3 is one such tradition.

NOTES

1. On midwife, cf. Gen. 35:17; 38:28; Exod. 1:15–21.

2. Cf. Ps. 131:2, which also suggests a comparison between God and a mother; contrary to RSV, however, the Hebrew does not mention the "breast" of the mother.

3. On the association of the words *šadday* and *šadayim*, cf. Frank Moore Cross, *Canaanite Myth and Hebrew Epic* (Cambridge: Harvard University Press, 1973), pp. 52–60, and the bibliography cited there; cf. also Maurice A. Canney, "Shaddai," *Expository Times* 34 (1922–23): 332. My stress is on the pun in Gen. 49:15, not on the etymologies of the two words.

4. Cf. James Luther Mays, *Hosea* (Philadelphia: Westminster Press, 1969), pp. 131–35.

5. On the Song of Moses, see G. Ernest Wright, "The Lawsuit of God: A Form-Critical Study of Deuteronomy 32," in *Israel's Prophetic Heritage,* ed. Bernhard W. Anderson and Walter Harrelson (New York: Harper & Brothers, 1962), pp. 26–67; C. J. Labuschagne, "The Song of Moses: Its Framework and Structure," in *De Fructu Oris Sui,* ed. I. H. Eybers, F. C. Fensham, et al. (Leiden: E. J. Brill, 1971), pp. 85–98; but cf. Patrick W. Skehan, "The Structure of the Song of Moses in Deuteronomy (Deut. 32:1–43)," *CBQ* 13 (1951): 153–63.

6. Deut. 32:4, 15, 18, 30, 31. Note also the chiastic arrangement of Rock and God in 32:4, 15, 18.

7. On the begetting of the father, see also, e.g., Gen. 4:18; 10:8, 15, 24, 26; 22:23; 25:3. On the birthing of the mother, see also, e.g., Gen. 4:1, 2, 17; 21:7; 29:32, 33, 34.

8. See, e.g., Isa. 13:8; 26:17; 51:2; 54:1. The verb is also used metaphorically of nature: Isa. 23:4; Hab. 3:10; Prov. 25:23; Job 15:7; 39:1.

9. The translation of *JB* is inadmissible: "You forget the Rock who begot you, unmindful now of the God who fathered [*sic*] you."

10. Salvador Carrillo Alday, *El Cantico de Moises* (Madrid: Pontificia Commissio de re Biblica, 1970), p. 85.

11. Cf. also Isa. 51:2; Prov. 1:8; 6:20; 30:11, 17. Although Jer. 2:27a is sometimes interpreted as complementary parallelism of father (tree) and mother (stone), the procreating verb in the second colon (*yelidtānû*) does not secure a maternal reading; rather, in light of Jer. 3:9, the verb may mean "you begot me" and refer to female adultery with male deities (tree and stone).

12. S. R. Driver, *A Critical and Exegetical Commentary on Deuteronomy, International Critical Commentary* (Edinburgh: T. & T. Clark, 1895), pp. 363–64.

13. Cf. also Isa. 66:8, 9; 23:4; Job 15:7; 39:1–3.

14. The poem in which this proclamation appears consists of an introduction and three strophes: Isa. 42:5, 6–9, 10–13, 14–17. The second strophe ends with Yahweh as a man of war (v. 13) and the third begins with Yahweh as a woman in labor (v. 14). On this shift, as well as on the entire poem, see James Muilenburg, "The Book of Isaiah, Chapters 40—66," *The Interpreter's Bible,* vol. 5 (Nashville: Abingdon Press,

1956), pp. 467–74. But cf. Roy F. Melugin, *The Formation of Isaiah 40—55* (Berlin: Walter de Gruyter, 1967), pp. 23, 64–69, 98–103.

15. Following Muilenburg, I read v. 14 as a contrast between then (14a) and now (14b); see "The Book of Isaiah," p. 473. Yahweh's restraint (14a) is the opposite of the deity's crying out like a woman in labor (14b). For a different view, see John McKenzie, *Second Isaiah*, AB (New York: Doubleday, 1968), p. 44.

16. "The figure of Yahweh's travailing has a profundity not easily discerned by modern minds" (Muilenburg, "The Book of Isaiah," p. 473).

17. See ibid., pp. 757–69.

18. On the form of this verb, see McKenzie, *Second Isaiah*, p. 205, n. 6.

19. This object does not appear in translation.

20. Judg. 13:3, 5; Isa. 26:17, 18; 33:11; Job 15:35.

21. Isa. 49:23; 2 Kings 10:1, 5; cf. KJV, *NAB*.

22. P. A. H. deBoer, *Fatherhood and Motherhood in Israelite and Judean Piety* (Leiden: E. J. Brill, 1974), p. 35; cf. G. B. Gray, *A Critical and Exegetical Commentary on Numbers* (Edinburgh: T. & T. Clark, 1912), p. 108.

23. Martin Noth, *Numbers* (Philadelphia: Westminster Press, 1968), pp. 86–87; also *NEB, JB*.

CHAPTER 4

A Love Story

Gone Awry

A love story gone awry—that is Genesis 2—3.

It is a simple story as stories go. Just three short scenes and four major characters; a single location and a single time; a circular design that contains the action; an easy movement of plot from entrance to exit with a definite turning point; straightforward narration, brief dialogue, and a small vocabulary that builds on repetition. Correspondingly, the narrative shows neither psychological development in the characters nor complicated interactions among them. Sparse in both description and explanation, it does not elaborate on the predicament of life nor fetter imagination with logic. Interpretive comments by the narrator are minimal. Details are few. And yet so simple a story has been made to bear the sins of the world, not excluding the complexities of scholarship.

If the story is simple, it is not, at the same time, neat and tidy. Abrupt, terse, elliptic, tentative, its language carries a plurality of meanings. From beginning to end the narrative is riddled with ambiguity. Embodying tension, connotations, hints and guesses, it compels multiple interpretations, as centuries of exegesis amply demonstrate. Accordingly, the task of the interpreter is not to eliminate this ambiguity but to illuminate it within the total unit. The task is not to circumscribe meaning but to enlarge it as the particularity of this tale engages the particularities of life.

This engagement is both intimate and explosive, since everybody knows the story and everybody has fixed ideas about it. Familiarity breeds stereotypes, mistakes, and, yes, contempt. According to traditional interpretations, the narrative in Genesis 2:7—3:24 (most interpretations bypass the preface in 2:4b–6) is about "Adam and Eve." It proclaims male superiority and female inferiority as the will of God. It portrays woman as "temptress" and troublemaker who is dependent upon and dominated by her husband. Over the centuries this misogynous reading has acquired a status of canonicity so that those who deplore and those who applaud the story both agree upon its meaning.[1] Impressive is even a partial list of specifics documenting this consensus:

- A male God creates first man (2:7) and last woman (2:22); first means superior and last means inferior or subordinate.
- Woman is created for the sake of man: a helpmate to cure his loneliness (2:18–23).
- Contrary to nature, woman comes out of man; she is denied even her natural function of birthing and that function is given to man (2:21–22).
- Woman is the rib of man, dependent upon him for life (2:21–22).
- Taken out of man (2:23), woman has a derivative, not an autonomous, existence.
- Man names woman (2:23) and thus has power over her.
- Man leaves his father's family in order to set up through his wife another patriarchal unit (2:24).
- Woman tempted man to disobey and thus she is responsible for sin in the world (3:6); she is untrustworthy, gullible, and simpleminded.
- Woman is cursed by pain in childbirth (3:16); pain in childbirth is a more severe punishment than man's struggles with the soil; it signifies that woman's sin is greater than man's.
- Woman's desire for man (3:16) is God's way of keeping her faithful and submissive to her husband.
- God gives man the right to rule over woman (3:16).

Although such specifics continue to be cited as support for traditional interpretations of male superiority and female inferiority, not one of them is altogether accurate and most of them are simply not present in the story itself. As ideas supposedly drawn out of the narrative, they fail to respect the integrity of this work as an interlocking structure of words and motifs with its own intrinsic value and meaning. In short, these ideas violate the rhetoric of the story. Keenly aware of the tenacity and power of such views, I propose not to defend the narrative against them—though I am tempted and may sometimes yield—but rather to contemplate it afresh as a work of art. A literary study of Genesis 2—3 may offer insights that traditional perspectives dream not of. At any rate, such a study fits the text.

Life and Death is the subject of the narrative in Genesis 2:4b—3:24. Life (Eros) means unity, fulfillment, harmony, and delight.[2] It is not, however, a paradise of perfection or purity untouched by loneliness, responsibility, or finitude. To the contrary, it is fulfillment within limits, a fulfillment that includes imperfections, makes distinctions, sets up hierarchies, and tempers joy with frailty. Death (Thanatos) is the loss of life. It means discord, strife, hostility, and danger. It is disintegration, the breaking of harmonious limits. As a result, imperfections become problems, distinctions become oppositions, hierarchies become oppressions, and joy dissipates into unrelieved tragedy. Life loses to Death.

This subject of Life and Death belongs to a particular structure of design and plot. Beginning with a lengthy introduction that moves from cosmos to earth (2:4b–7), the narrative proper falls into three scenes. Scene one is the development of Eros (2:7–24); scene two is the act of disobedience (2:25—3:7); and scene three is the disintegration of Eros (3:8–24). The overall design of the story is cyclic. By repetition of key words and phrases, the end (3:22–24) returns to the beginning (2:4b–9, 15). But in this return, meaning is reversed so that structural symmetry is semantic dissonance. Correspondingly, the plot unfolds by two opposite movements with an intermediate turning point. Entrance into a garden (scene one) opposes expulsion from a garden (scene three). Life opposes Death. Between these two opposite movements occurs disobedience, the turning point of the story (scene two). Thus the dynamics of plot coalesce with the statics of design to produce the structure of the story. This structure, which characterizes the entire narrative, appears with variations in both the whole and the parts of each scene.[3]

In addition to subject and structure, characters inhabit a narrative; yet for this particular tale, it is more appropriate to speak of four worlds: divine, human, plant, and animal. The plant world provides the setting; the other three, the characters. The divine world dominates in the two opposing movements of the narrative. First, Yahweh God decides life. The deity creates the plant, animal, and human worlds and brings each to fulfillment in differing ways. Conversely, Yahweh God decides death. The deity disrupts the plant, animal, and human worlds and brings each to loss of life in differing ways. Separating these two movements dominated by God is the participation of the plant, animal, and human worlds in disobedience. The plant world supplies the symbol of disobedience; the animal world provides the temptation; and the human world disobeys. In this middle scene the divine world is altogether silent. Taking over completely, the serpent, woman, and man turn God-the-subject into God-the-object. Their power to disobey leads, however, not to a change in the character of God (the divine continues to control the story) but rather to changes in their own portrayals: from creatures of delight (scene one) to creatures of death (scene three). Together these four worlds—divine, human, plant, and animal—both convey and reflect the artistry and meaning of the narrative.

EROS CREATED

INTRODUCTION: GENESIS 2:4b–7

This overview of subject, structure, and worlds prepares us to enter the story itself. And yet a compound-complex sentence, which prefaces the narrative, delays its beginning:

> When Yahweh God made earth and heavens—
> when no plant of the field was in the earth
> and no grain of the field had yet sprouted,
> because Yahweh God had not let it rain upon the earth,
> and [because] no earth creature was there to serve the earth—
> then a subterranean stream went up from the earth
> and watered the whole face of the earth;
> and then Yahweh God formed the earth creature,
> dust from the earth,
> and breathed into its nostrils the breath of life,
> and the earth creature became a living *nephesh*.
>
> (2:4b–7)

This tedious sentence struggles both to present and to limit a cosmic perspective, since it does not introduce a story about the universe but rather uses cosmic creation as a prelude to the advent and fulfillment of human life on earth. The tension between cosmic perspective and earthly focus threatens to explode grammar and syntax. Clause is heaped upon clause to move from one subject to the other. Accordingly, the introductory sentence begins with a circumstantial clause that utilizes a formulaic expression for cosmic creation: "When Yahweh God made earth and heavens . . ." (2:4b). Embracing everything, the phrase "earth and heavens" lacks the particularity by which stories unfold. At the same time it holds the key to this development. Inclusiveness moves toward specificity by a separation of its parts: earth and heavens split. The latter passes away; the former leads into the story. Earth ('*ereṣ*) becomes the key word of the prologue. Three times it appears before yielding completely to its synonym, *hā-'ᵃdāmâ,* the earth of the story.

Immediately following the making of earth and heavens, a clause interrupts to report the barrenness of the earth:

> when no plant of the field was in the earth ['*ereṣ*]
> and no grain of the field had yet sprouted.
>
> (2:5ab)

Since it interjects death in the presence of creation, a barren field requires explanation. Hence, this subordinate clause stretches beyond syntactical propriety to cite two reasons, one from the divine world and the other from the human:

> because [*kî*] Yahweh God had not let it rain upon the earth ['*ereṣ*]
> and [because] no earth creature ['*ādām*] was there
>   to serve the earth [*hā-'ᵃdāmâ*].
>
> (2:5cd)

By repeating the subject and one of the objects that occurred at the very beginning of the sentence, the first reason increases tension between Creator and creation: "When Yahweh God made earth . . . because Yahweh God had not let it rain upon the earth." The deity who has not let it rain upon the earth made the earth. Thus the negative of barrenness recalls the positive of creation, to return the form and content of this first reason to the beginning of the sentence with a countermeaning.

But the second reason moves the sentence forward. It enlarges the vocabulary of the earth (*hā-'ªdāmâ*) and it plays with this new language to introduce an earth creature (*'ādām*). Although God and an earth creature are the subjects of the verbs in the two parallel clauses, the parallelism itself is skewed. By a negative act of withholding rain, Yahweh God *causes* the barrenness of the earth. Strikingly, however, the passive absence of an earth creature *occasions* this barrenness. In other words, this second reason is attributed proleptically to the human world. But the account refrains from explaining that Yahweh God had not yet made a creature to serve the earth—even though such a statement would be an exact parallel to the first reason, would accord with the facts of the case, and would unequivocally assign cause to Yahweh God for the barrenness of the earth. Thus, the relationship between these two subjects, divine and human, awaits clarification.

Nevertheless, a play on words already establishes relationship between earth creature (*'ādām*) and the earth (*hā-'ªdāmâ*). This pun is accessible to sight and sound. While uniting creature and soil, it also separates them. *'Ādām* is not yet; *hā-'ªdāmâ* already is. Furthermore, this *'ādām* is described as potentially acting upon the *'ªdāmâ* (2:5d): "no earth creature [*'ādām*] was there to serve the earth [*hā-'ªdāmâ*]." An infinitive separates the subject from its cognate object, and this particular infinitive (*to till* or *to serve*) heightens the tension in the relationship because it connotes both lordship and servanthood. Hence, several formal and verbal structures in the introduction signal developments to come in the story itself.

Ironically, these two reasons that appear within a circumstantial clause to explain barrenness in the presence of creation have increased, rather than alleviated, tension.[4] Resolution comes in the remainder of the sentence, in the two independent clauses toward which the circumstantial clause has been moving. And this resolution compensates amply for the tension. Though each reason was stated negatively, each answer will be given positively. Though each reason was stated in a single line, the first answer will come in a double line and the second in a triple.

First, the barrenness of the earth happened "because Yahweh God had not let it rain upon the earth" (2:5c). Now the answer to this problem is an underground stream:

then a subterranean stream went up from the earth ['*ereṣ*]
and watered the whole face of the earth ['*ᵃdāmâ*].

(2:6)

If God has not caused rain from above, then water itself comes from below. Although this statement of two lines eliminates the first reason for barrenness, it corresponds in kind to the second reason, because it also lacks connection with the divine world. It refrains from claiming that the underground stream is the work of God. Further, this statement continues the parallelism between '*ereṣ* and '*ᵃdāmâ* that the preceding lines introduced. Yet with this report the use of the word '*ereṣ* ceases in the narrative. Separated originally from a traditional phrase ("earth and heavens") and repeated in every clause of the opening sentence so far, the word '*ereṣ* has moved the introduction from a cosmic perspective to an earthly focus. Its work is finished; now it yields completely, through parallelism, to '*ᵃdāmâ*, the word for earth that initiates the story proper. A subterranean stream from the '*ereṣ* waters the face of the '*ᵃdāmâ*.

Second, the barrenness of the earth ('*ereṣ*) was related to the absence of an earth creature ('*ādām*) to serve the earth (*hā-*'*ᵃdāmâ*) (2:5d). The answer to this problem is the forming of the earth creature:

then Yahweh God formed the earth creature [*hā-'ādām*]
dust from the earth [*hā-'ᵃdāmâ*]
and breathed into its nostrils the breath of life,
and the earth creature [*hā-'ādām*] became a living *nephesh*.[5]
(2:7)

In eliminating the second reason for barrenness in the earth, this triple verb statement also clarifies the relationship between Yahweh God and the earth creature. It declares unequivocally that the earth creature depends upon God for life. What the reason left unsaid, the response now specifies. Moreover, this response develops further the pun of earth and earth creature. Altogether this triple statement is the climactic ending of the tedious introduction and the grand beginning of the story. It is both end-stress and fore-stress. With it a convoluted sentence ends and a simple narrative begins. Cosmos yields to Eros.

SCENE ONE: THE DEVELOPMENT
OF EROS (GENESIS 2:7–24)

Scene one develops Eros in four episodes that are clearly delineated by stylistic devices and subject matter. At the same time, these episodes interlock and sometimes overlap so that the entire scene moves rhythmically from beginning to end. It progresses by repetitions, additions, and omissions. The repetitions provide continuity, while the additions and the omissions contribute differences in meaning.

Episode One: The Earth Creature (2:7–8)

Similar to the overall design of the story, the first episode is cyclic. It begins and ends with the repetition of key phrases. In addition, two full lines at the beginning match two full lines at the end in structure and content. These four lines surround one center line that differs from them. In the first line Yahweh God is the explicit subject of the verb; in the second line this deity is the implicit subject. The last two lines repeat this pattern. In the center line *hā-'ādām* is the subject of the verb, even as it is the object of verbs in the beginning and ending phrases. Altogether four actions by Yahweh God determine and encircle the earth creature:

A   <u>And Yahweh God formed *hā-'ādām*</u> [of] dust from *hā-'ᵃdāmâ*

    B   and breathed into its nostrils the breath of life

    C   and *hā-'ādām* became a living *nephesh*.

A'   And Yahweh God planted a garden in Eden in the east

    B'   and put there <u>*hā-'ādām* whom he had formed.</u>

Life begins with the creation of *hā-'ādām*. Creation is a process, not a *fait accompli*. Third-person narration depicts Yahweh God as potter, shaping the human creature of dust from the earth; as breather, animating the dust; as gardener, preparing a special plot of land; and as executive, determining the location of the creature. This divine work is pleasure, not toil. Forming *hā-'ādām* of dust from *hā-'ᵃdāmâ* (A), Yahweh creates a pun. Similarly, planting a garden in Eden (A'), Yahweh makes a place of delight, for the Hebrew word *'ēden* recalls the sound of another

Hebrew word meaning enjoyment.[6] Since these actions play with words, the deity is also portrayed as artist finding pleasure in the production of life. The creative process itself is erotic.

Hā-'ādām is the focus of God's pleasure. From beginning (A) to middle (C) to end (B'), it is the center of attention, both structurally and thematically. As presented in this first episode, with the definite article *hā-* preceding the common noun *'ādām*, this work of art is neither a particular person nor the typical person but rather the creature from the earth (*hā-'ᵃdāmâ*)—the earth creature.[7] The very words that differentiate creature from soil indicate similarity. Thus, through the pleasure of language Yahweh God makes distinctions that result not in oppositions but in harmony. A punned separation articulates unity. Other than this material image of dust, the description of the earth creature is sparse. Nostrils are mentioned. They indicate a sense of smell, though the text itself does not make this point. The suggestion becomes important as other senses emerge throughout the narrative. But apart from this reference to nostrils, no physical features are specified for the earth creature in this first episode. More important, this creature is not identified sexually. Grammatical gender (*'ādām* as a masculine word) is not sexual identification. Nor is sexuality assumed here, since it is created later in the fourth episode. In other words, the earth creature is not the male; it is not "the first man."[8] Although the word *hā-'ādām* acquires ambiguous usages and meanings—including an exclusively male reference—in the development of the story, those ambiguities are not present in the first episode. Instead, the earth creature here is precisely and only the human being, so far sexually undifferentiated. The complete story of creaturehood is a process, the tale that is being told. At the beginning some clues are given; further understanding awaits the end.

This sexually undifferentiated earth creature owes its existence to Yahweh God. It is not a "self-made man," a patriarchal figure, a superman, or *Übermensch*. Only two ingredients constitute its life, and both are tenuous: dusty earth and divine breath. One comes from below; the other from above. One is visible; the other invisible. Combined by Yahweh, these fragile ingredients unite to form the creature who is totally dependent upon God. Its life hangs on a breath that it does not control, indeed, that it does not breathe—for Yahweh is the breather. Moreover, God puts this creature in a garden of delight that the deity has already planted. Thus the earth creature does not create space; it is given a place. It does not make pleasure; it is assigned pleasure. The product and recipient of creation, it does not participate in creating. Human life, then, is God's gift; it is not possession. Playful creation is precarious existence.

The structure and key words of this first episode are paradigmatic of the entire first scene. From the beginning to the end, the earth creature is the center of attention. Yet, Yahweh God determines this center by introducing each of the four episodes. These two characters, divine and human, provide a continuity among all the episodes in the first movement. A third item from the first episode, *hā-'ªdāmâ* (the earth), also contributes continuity until the last episode where its absence tells of something new and different. Three other words, *life, garden,* and *Eden,* appear in the second episode, and the verb *form* is used again in the third. Hence, the first episode contains the main contours and key vocabulary for the entire scene.

Specifically, the last two lines of the first episode (2:8) provide the text for the second episode (2:9–17), and this continuity of theme matches a continuity of structure. These two episodes overlap in a pattern of alternated sequence that resembles the internal design of the first episode. In this pattern, four statements with Yahweh God as subject surround a center in which the deity does not appear. The word *garden* (*gan*) links all five statements. The four statements develop the garden and the relationship of the earth creature to it; the center statement describes the river that waters the garden. Although this description is often considered an insertion in the story,[9] design, context, and vocabulary argue for its final integrity. Water is as central to the life of the garden as it is to the literary structure that tells of this life:

A   And Yahweh God planted a garden in Eden from the east
     and there put *hā-'ādām* whom he had formed.

     B   And Yahweh God caused to grow from *hā-'ªdāmâ*
          every tree
          pleasant to see and good to eat—
          the tree of life in the midst of the garden
          and the tree of the knowledge of good and evil.

C   A river flowed out of Eden to water the garden
and there it divided and became four
rivers. . . .

A'   And Yahweh God took *hā-'ādām* and put it in the garden
of Eden
to till it and to keep it.

B'   And Yahweh God commanded *hā-'ādām* saying:
From every tree of the garden you may surely eat
but from the tree of the knowledge of good and
evil you may not eat,
for when you eat of it you will surely die.

(2:8–17)

Episode Two: Plants (2:9–17)

In the progression of the story, this concatenate arrangement,
provided by the word *garden,* leads from the first episode to an
examination of the internal design, content, and meaning of the
second. The word *tree* (*'ēṣ*) delineates its boundaries. Occurring
three times at the beginning (2:9), twice at the end (2:16, 17), and
nowhere else in the entire first scene, this word encloses the unit.
Associated with it is the verb *eat* (*'kl*) that likewise appears
nowhere else in scene one. This unit has a more complicated
structure and content than the first episode:

A   And Yahweh God caused to grow from *hā-'ᵃdāmâ* every tree
pleasant to see and good to eat—
the tree of life in the midst of the garden
and the tree of the knowledge of good and evil.

A river flowed out of Eden to water the garden
and there it divided and became four rivers. . . .

And Yahweh God took *hā-'ādām* and put it in the garden
of Eden
to till it and to keep it.

A'   And Yahweh God commanded *hā-'ādām* saying:
From every tree of the garden you may surely eat
but from the tree of the knowledge of good and evil
you may not eat
for when you eat of it you will surely die.

Life began with the oneness of the earth out of which Yahweh God formed the earth creature (2:7). Here that pattern of differentiation within earthly unity continues: out of the earth Yahweh God causes to grow every tree (2:9). The earth creature and the plants of the earth share common ground. Humanity and botany unite, though their unity is neither identity nor equality. Botany serves humanity. "Every tree pleasant to see and good to eat" provides aesthetic experience so that the senses of sight and taste now join that of smell (cf. 2:7). Thus far the relation of humanity and botany has been depicted in three ways: they have the same Creator; they are created from the same material; the human world absorbs the plant world through the delights of the senses. A fourth connection will follow later. Meanwhile, "every tree" narrows to two particular trees in the midst of the garden: the tree of life and the tree of the knowledge of good and evil. Although the tree of life may echo a motif from episode one (the breath of life and a living *nephesh*), the tree of the knowledge of good and evil has no antecedent.

A garden of trees requires attention—nourishment from nature and care from humanity (cf. 2:5cd). Accordingly, the next two sections of episode two speak to these needs. First is the requirement of water. "A river flowed out of Eden to water the garden" (2:10a). This statement reflects one tension present in the prelude to the story, the tension between the rain that Yahweh God did not send (2:5c) and the subterranean stream that watered the whole face of the earth (2:6). Now, with this report of a river, all three parts of the ancient universe have been examined for water: from above, no rain; from below, a stream; on the ground, a river. Moreover, this third reference deviates from the pattern prevalent throughout scene one, whereby Yahweh God controls the development of Eros, to return to the nondivine origin of water described in the prelude. If the stream from below the earth (*'ereṣ*) is not attributed to God, neither is the river on the earth (*'ᵃdāmâ*). Yet the river contributes life to the garden. So important is its presence that the narration strays temporarily from the story to follow its course: "A river flowed out of Eden to water the garden and there it divided and became four rivers" (2:10). Where the river divides, the episode divides to accommodate the names and descriptions of the four rivers (2:11-14).[10] Although more elaborate, these details correspond to the description of the two particular trees. In each instance the creation of life moves from a general classification (tree, river) to particular specimens. And what is true for plants and water will also be true for other parts of creation: the general moves to the specific. Harmony among the particularities of life begins to emerge. The need for water in a garden of trees has been answered by a river.

The second need of this garden is care from humanity. The end of episode one reported, first, that "Yahweh God planted a garden in Eden from the east" (2:8). A description of this garden, with its trees and water, then followed in the first half of episode two. Next, the second half of episode two continues to explicate the end of episode one by expanding upon the statement "and there [Yahweh God] put *hā-'ādām* whom he had formed." The expansion declares: "And Yahweh God took *hā-'ādām* and put it in the garden of Eden to till it and to keep it" (2:15). Care from humanity follows nourishment by the river. With this directive for human work, the earth creature appears in episode two, and the story returns to the established pattern of an action by God bringing fulfillment to creation. The first part of the sentence (2:15a) presents the creature exactly as it was at the conclusion of episode one—a passive object whom Yahweh God puts in a created place (2:8). Yet this presentation not only repeats; it also alters, and through this double process the story unfolds. Hence, while Yahweh God, the subject of these two corresponding passages, remains the same, the order of objects reverses. In the first text, the planting of the garden preceded the placing of the earth creature in it (2:8); in the second, the placing of the earth creature precedes the mention of the garden (2:15). This stylistic reversal coincides with the expansion of content that specifies the relationship of the two creations. Although at first Yahweh God simply made the garden and put the creature in it, now Yahweh God puts the creature there to till it and to keep it.

From being a totally passive object, the earth creature becomes an object who must work. Thus, its life develops further through the responsibility that Yahweh God has planned for it.

Earlier a clue to this responsibility appeared in the prelude of the story: "there was no earth creature to till the earth" (2:5). Here that statement of lack receives an answer, but with modifications. First, the earth creature is assigned the job of tilling a particular space, the garden of Eden, but not of tilling all the earth (cf. 3:23). Life expands within boundaries. Second, a new infinitive joins the tilling: *to keep it*.

These two infinitives, *to till* and *to keep*, give the earth creature power over the place in which Yahweh God put it. Hence, they signal a fourth connection between humanity and botany. We have already observed that the creature and the trees have the same Creator, that they are created from the same material, and that the human world absorbs the plant world through the delights of the senses. Now, in addition, the human world dominates the plant world. This last relationship is similar to the preceding one in establishing a hierarchy within creation. Humanity consumes the plant world through the senses and controls it through work. Both hierarchical postures signify harmony and fulfillment in creation, for if absorption of the trees through sight and taste is pleasant and good, so, too, is tilling and keeping the garden a pleasurable and loving activity— pleasurable and loving both for the doer and for the receiver. Since the garden of Eden is a place of delight, to till and to keep it is to foster pleasure. The Hebrew verb *'bd*, conventionally translated "to till," means to serve. It connotes respect, indeed, reverence and worship. To till the garden is to serve the garden; to exercise power over it is to reverence it. Similarly, to keep (*šmr*) the garden is an act of protection (cf. 3:24), not of possession. The two infinitives, *to till* and *to keep*, connote not plunder and rape but care and attention. They enhance the delight of the garden. By the same token, they give to the earth creature the joy of work. This work changes human life from passivity to participation. Indigenous to creation, work is not a role to be assumed. Moreover, it precedes sexuality to characterize total humanity. Work fulfills both creature and environment, providing dignity and integrity. It testifies to the oneness of humanity and soil at the same time that it establishes the responsibility of the earth creature for the earth. Distinction without opposition, dominion without domination, hierarchy without oppression: to serve and to keep the garden is to live life in harmony and pleasure. Work, then, is another way in which Eros unfolds.[11]

In episode one, God formed life through actions that produced human images of the divine: potter, breather, gardener, and executive. Each action was reported in third-person narration, a pattern that continues in the second episode, as do the images of gardener and executive. Yahweh causes trees to grow in the garden and assigns work to the earth creature. But the third appearance of the deity in episode two yields a new image in a new manner: God commands the earth creature in direct discourse. The deity speaks as legislator: "you may eat . . . you may not eat."

To understand this command, the earth creature must have the sense of hearing. From smell (2:7) to sight (2:9) to taste (2:9) to hearing (2:16)—in various ways these senses have emerged, and their gradual appearances correspond to other developments. In the beginning the creature was altogether a passive object, but as work and the senses of sight and taste come into play this passivity altered. Nevertheless, the duty to till and keep the garden was without choice or freedom on the part of the creature. It was prescribed. Consequently, the earth creature has remained the object controlled by Yahweh, even though it moved from total passivity to limited activity. Now another change occurs—the introduction of choice into life. This shift to moral responsibility comes precisely where the narrative changes style, where the deity acquires a new image, and where the earth creature receives the ability to hear. Although God first made the creature responsible by assigning it work, now God gives it the freedom to be responsible by commanding it to obey. These progressions in both the image of God and the power of the earth creature culminate in the conclusion of the second episode (2:16–17). While it returns to the beginning of this unit, specifically to the trees of the garden and to their desirability as food, this conclusion advances the story. At the start, all the trees are available for food. Yahweh ordains both freedom and authority over nature for the earth creature:

And Yahweh God commanded hā-'ādām saying:
"From every tree of the garden you may surely eat."

But, then, one tree is excepted:

> but from the tree of the knowledge of good and evil you may not eat.

The forbidden tree spells limits to human dominion. Nature itself also has God-given independence.

To eat and not to eat: permission and prohibition unite in a double command that is designed to preserve life. This command points up the opposites that can result from a single act. To eat is to live: "from every tree . . . you may surely eat," for the trees are "pleasant to see and good to eat." Yet to eat is to die: "for when you eat of it [the tree of the knowledge of good and evil] you will surely die." One act, eating, holds both life and death. The difference lies in obeying or disobeying the limits set by God.

With the divine words "You shall not eat" a negative command enters life. Earlier, negative statements appeared in the prelude of the story to describe chaos (2:5). Now a negative comes within the movement toward Eros; its purpose is not to revert to chaos but to assure the continuation of life: "you shall not eat . . . for when you eat of it you will die." Be these words of death a threat or a consequence, the result is the same. While all that the story may mean by death is not yet clear, certainly it signifies the loss of life—even as the conclusion of this episode (2:16–17) loses reference to the tree of life. Moreover, if this divine prohibition does not spell out the details of death, neither does it explicate the phrase "the knowledge of good and evil."[12] The meaning of this phrase lies not in its content but in its function. It symbolizes obedience and disobedience, so decreed by a God who does not explain why. If the tree of the knowledge of good and evil testifies to the freedom of God, it also witnesses to the integrity of nature apart from its use by the earth creature and to the moral responsibility of the earth creature.

Thus far in the progression of the story, which is the progression of life, the fragile and totally dependent creature of episode one has been given in episode two work and moral stature within a physical environment planned by God. Articulation of form and content has shown development in the activity of God, in the

portrayal of the earth creature, and in the composition of the
garden. The tenor of this development is harmony, joy, and
fulfillment. Specifically, botany and humanity are one in origin
and in substance: God made them both from the ground. Their
harmony is also hierarchy: botany serves humanity; humanity
preserves botany. The garden provides aesthetic pleasure, physical nourishment, significant work, and moral accountability. Yet
the earth creature has no license to plunder and exploit nature.
It must revere the soil and must not eat of the tree of the knowledge of good and evil. Its dominion is not domination. All in all,
the relationship between botany and humanity gives fulfillment,
for thus has Yahweh God created Eros. In episode three the
progression of life continues with the creation of the animal
world.

Episode Three: Animals (2:18-20)

Like the preceding sections, the third episode is set off from its
surroundings by an inclusive vocabulary. The phrase "a companion corresponding to it" occurs at its beginning and end and
nowhere else. In addition, a negative statement at the beginning
("it is not good") and at the end ("it did not find") distinguishes
this unit from the other episodes. Finally, the subject of animals
defines it, just as the subject of plants characterized episode two.

At the same time, vocabulary, form, and themes link episode
three to both of the preceding units. Three pervasive terms
continue in characteristic ways. First, Yahweh God initiates and
directs the action. Second, the word *hā-'ādām* occurs five times to
stress the centrality of the earth creature. And third, the word
hā-'ªdāmâ is the earth from which another creation comes.
Within this general pattern emerge particular nuances of discontinuity and continuity:

> And Yahweh God said,
>   "It is not good for *hā-'ādām* to be alone
>   I will make for it a companion corresponding to it."

> And Yahweh God formed from *hā-'ªdāmâ*
>   every beast of the field and every bird of the heavens
>   and brought [each] to *hā-'ādām* to see what it would call
>   each one.

And whatever *hā-'ādām* called each living *nephesh,*
that was the name.
And *hā-'ādām* called the names of all domestic animals
and the birds of the heavens and all the beasts of the field.

But as for *'ādām,* it did not find a companion corresponding to
itself.

Divine speech links the beginning of episode three with the
end of episode two—the only direct discourses of God in the
entire first scene. Overall, the narrative manners of these two
episodes relate chiastically. Episode two begins with third-person
narration and ends with direct discourse; episode three begins
with direct discourse and ends with third-person narration. The
content of the two narrations differs, with God present at the
beginning of episode two and absent at the end of episode three.
On the other hand, the content of the two direct discourses is
complementary. At the conclusion of episode two, Yahweh God
became a legislator, speaking directly to the earth creature with a
command to preserve life. That command had first a positive
and then a negative side: "You may freely eat of every tree; do
not eat of one tree." At the beginning of episode three, Yahweh
becomes an evaluator, speaking in a soliloquy about the life of
the earth creature. This speech has first a negative and then a
positive side—the reversal of order reflecting the overall chiastic
relationship of the two units. Without consulting the earth creature, Yahweh determines that its life is not yet fulfilled: "It is not
good for the earth creature to be alone." Although the divine
negative of episode two ("do not eat of one tree") functions to
preserve life, the divine negative of episode three discloses a lack
in life and, hence, leads to a declaration of positive intent: "I will
make a companion corresponding to it." God the evaluator is
God the rectifier.

The divine evaluation "it is not good for the earth creature to
be alone" contrasts wholeness with isolation. This contrast highlights distinctions that have appeared in the story from the first
moment that Yahweh God formed the earth creature out of the
earth. Although this original distinction indicated rapport between the creature and the soil, it also set the creature apart
from the earth. Moreover, in the second episode it set the crea-

ture over the earth with the assignment to till and keep the garden. Further, although the earth creature shares common ground with the plants that grow from the earth, the creature is set over the trees with the freedom to eat them and the restriction not to eat one of them. In episodes one and two, then, the creature's relationship to the rest of creation is ambiguous: a part of and yet apart from; of common ground but with power over; joined yet separated. Since the creature is not only of the earth but also other than the earth, it needs fulfillment from that which is other than in the earth. This need Yahweh God recognizes: "I will make a companion corresponding to it." The Hebrew word *'ēzer*, rendered here as "companion," has been traditionally translated "helper"—a translation that is totally misleading because the English word *helper* suggests an assistant, a subordinate, indeed, an inferior, while the Hebrew word *'ēzer* carries no such connotation. To the contrary, in the Hebrew scriptures this word often describes God as the superior who creates and saves Israel.[13] In our story the accompanying phrase, "corresponding to it" (*keneḡdô*), tempers this connotation of superiority to specify identity, mutuality, and equality. According to Yahweh God, what the earth creature needs is a companion, one who is neither subordinate nor superior; one who alleviates isolation through identity.

"I will make a companion corresponding to it." The word *make* (*'śh*) recalls the prelude of the story, where the same verb described God's creation of the earth and the heavens (2:4b). Since making is a familiar activity for God, this first-person pledge would seem to assure a happy ending to episode three. Furthermore, since life has unfolded thus far without delay, hesitation, or experimentation, we expect Yahweh to accomplish this goal immediately. After all, the endings of episodes one and two fulfilled the promise of their beginnings. Nevertheless, end-fulfillment does not come in episode three. The negative that flawed life at the beginning of this unit is still present at its end. Although God pledged to make a companion for the earth creature, the narrator reports, "but as for *'āḏām*, it did not find a companion corresponding to itself." This report is oblique, for it does not attribute the negative result directly to God. Indeed, for the first time, Yahweh does not appear in the conclusion of a pericope. The evaluation by God at the beginning of the episode and the observation by the narrator at the end surround the unit with negatives. And the animal world is the center of this nonfulfillment.

With the sole omission of the word *dust* (*ʿāpār*), the line that reports the creation of the animals (2:19) is identical to the line that reported the creation of the earth 'creature (2:7): "and Yahweh God formed . . . from the earth." The exact parallels of subject, verb, and material in the two accounts strongly suggest that the deity is making a creature corresponding to *hā-ʾādām*. And yet the repetition of this identical process produces a different object: "every beast of the field and every bird of the heavens." Although they are not fitting companions, the earth creature and the animals unite in the grammar and vocabulary of Yahweh's creative act. In fact, the verb *form* (*yṣr*) is used exclusively for these two creations, resulting in an identity unparalleled thus far in the story.

Humanity and zoology also unite with botany. The three share Creator and material, though not the same creative process. From the ground Yahweh God forms the earth creature (2:7), causes the plants to grow (2:9), and forms the animals (2:19). But then in contrast to humanity, both botany and zoology are immediately divided into particulars. Similar to the breakdown of the general category of trees into two particular specimens (and to the breakdown of a river into four rivers), the animal world appears from the beginning as two kinds: "every beast of the field and every bird of the heavens." These creatures of land and air recall the twofold division of the cosmos in the prelude of the narrative—the earth (2:4b) or the field (2:5), and the heavens (2:4b). But in keeping with the earthly focus of the story itself, God forms even the birds of the heavens from the earth. Absent altogether are the fish of the sea, an absence that meshes with the fact that nowhere in the narrative does God create water. Also missing in this third episode are sexual distinctions between the animals, an absence that corresponds to the sexual nondifferentiation of the earth creature.

Though the presentation of the animals began by stressing their similarities to the earth creature, it ends by focusing on their differences. By being divided into species, the animals are

comparable to the plants, not to the human creature. Furthermore, Yahweh God brings each animal to *hā-'ādām* "to see what it
would call each one. And whatever *hā-'ādām* called each living
nephesh, that was the name" (2:19b). Through the power of naming, the animals are subordinated to the earth creature. They
become inferiors, not equals. In this context the phrase "living
nephesh" is particularly striking, since it is the same phrase used
to describe the earth creature after it received the breath of life
(2:7). Thus the phrase is a reminder of the identity between
these creatures at the very point where the earth creature exercises power over the animals. Life continues to develop in ambiguity, but not in conflict. The identity of earth creature and
animals juxtaposed to the power of the earth creature over the
animals results in a hierarchy of harmony planned by God.

In two ways, then, the animals are subordinate to humanity.
First, they are categorized by species, like the plant world; second, they are named by the earth creature. These two elements
combine in the next sentence where the earth creature calls the
name of three categories of animals: "And *hā-'ādām* called the
names of all domestic animals and the birds of the heavens and
all the beasts of the field" (2:20). The distinction between domestic and wild animals, as well as the reference to naming each one,
prepares for the advent of a particular wild animal called the
serpent. Meanwhile, the repeated emphasis on naming underscores the subordination of the animal world to the earth creature and thus demonstrates the unsuitability of the animals for
humanity. "Helpers" they may be; companions they are not.
And Yahweh God caused this difference—the very God who
promised to make a creature corresponding to *hā-'ādām*.

The images of God expand in episode three. After forming
every animal, God the potter transports each one to the earth
creature, delegates power over each one to it, and then stands
aside to observe the outcome. The entire process depicts God as
flexible, not enslaved to an announced agenda but free to alter it.
Since Yahweh began this unit by promising to make a companion fit for the earth creature, we might expect the deity to bring
the animals to *hā-'ādām* as fit companions. Instead, God brings
each animal "to what it would call each one," and the narrative does not suggest failure, mistake, or fault on the part of

God. But it does indicate the deity's use of delay to build suspense. Yahweh is a skilled storymaker, faithful to the craft and hence not predictable.

Marking the beginning of human activity, the phrase "to see what it would call each one" also signals a cessation of divine activity, and, in fact, Yahweh God does recede from the episode at this point. What the story says, it does. This divine fading is unparalleled in the preceding episodes, where God determined the action from beginning to end. Accordingly, it shows this deity now not as the authoritarian controller of events but as the generous delegator of power who even forfeits the right to reverse human decisions: "whatever *hā-'ādām* called each living *nephesh,* that was the name" (2:19c). Without qualification God relinquishes dominion to the earth creature. As a result, episode three splits in the middle. Actions of the divine world shape the first half (2:18–19b); actions of the human world the last (2:19b–20). But this split is more decisive for God than for the earth creature. Although the creature appears throughout the episode, first as object and then as subject, God is not mentioned at all in the second half. *Deus absconditus;* the earth creature takes over.

This special status of the earth creature is not altogether new. The infinitive phrase "to see what it would call each one" parallels the infinitive phrase directed to the earth creature when Yahweh put it in the garden "to till it and to keep it." In each instance, Yahweh set the earth creature over the world of nature, though in this third episode the power of the creature expands even more with the fading of the deity. The human world has thereby received greater independence. This difference between the two instances of Yahweh's granting power and responsibility to the earth creature finds expression in both the form and content of the two reports. Whereas human action was implied in the duty to till and keep the garden, that action was not specifically performed. The earth creature never became the subject of the verbs *till* and *keep.* But now in episode three the earth creature becomes the active subject of an active verb: "and whatever the earth creature called each living *nephesh,* that was the name" (2:19c). Human action is now explicit, and it involves human speech.[14] Even though the earth creature does not yet speak directly, it exercises the power to name without being challenged or corrected by God. And what it decides comes to pass. From total passivity the earth creature has moved to active responsibility.[15] Yet through it all this creature has not found a fitting companion.

Indeed, episode three tantalizes. Yahweh announces one agenda only to precede immediately to another without explanation or apology. Then God disappears, and it is left to the narrator to conclude that the divine promise remains unfulfilled. Meanwhile, God's pursued agenda increases the stature of the earth creature, even to the point of replacing God in the action, and yet it leaves the earth creature unfulfilled. Power over creation has not alleviated human loneliness. As for the animals, their close identity with the earth creature has only heightened the differences between humanity and zoology. The animals disappoint rather than delight. Enclosed by negatives, their positive portrayal remains ambiguous—no doubt a foreshadowing of things to come. In fact, this entire episode is a foreshadowing. By contrast and juxtaposition, it prepares not only for the advent of disobedience in scene two, but also for the fulfillment of Eros in episode four of scene one.

Episode Four: Human Sexuality (2:21–24)

If no companion for the earth creature is found among the animals, there is another possibility: the creation of human sexuality. This divine act will alter radically the nature of *hā-'ādām* and bring about new creatures so that female and male together become the one flesh that is wholeness rather than isolation. With the creation of sexuality, episode four completes the development of Eros and concludes the first scene of the story. This unit has a circular design, similar to the three preceding episodes. The word *flesh* (*bāśār*) delineates the boundaries. It occurs once at the beginning, once at the end, twice in the middle, and nowhere else in the entire story. Encompassed by this circular design are four sections that correspond in form and content to episode three. In the first two sections, Yahweh God is the subject of active verbs. In the last two, the deity does not appear at all; rather, the earth creature speaks and the narrator comments.

And Yahweh God caused a deep sleep to fall upon *hā-'ādām*
and, while it slept, took one of its ribs
and closed up f̲l̲e̲s̲h̲ at that spot.

And Yahweh God built the rib
    which he took from *hā-'ādām* into woman ['*iššâ*]
    and brought her to *hā-'ādām*.

And *hā-'ādām* said:
    This, finally, bone of my bone
        and f̲l̲e̲s̲h̲ of my f̲l̲e̲s̲h̲.
    This shall be called woman ['*iššâ*]
        because from man ['*îš*] was taken this.

Therefore, a man ['*îš*] leaves his father and his mother
    and cleaves to his woman ['*iššâ*]
    and they become one f̲l̲e̲s̲h̲.
                                                    (2:21–24)

Like episode one but unlike episodes two and three, the deity
does not speak in this concluding unit. Similarly, the portrayal of
the earth creature as totally passive at the beginning of episode
four recalls its depiction in episode one. Yahweh God, who first
animated dust to form *hā-'ādām* and then put it in a garden and
delegated to it work, responsibility, power, and speech, now returns this creature to a state of inactivity, indeed, of uncon-
sciousness: "and Yahweh God caused a deep sleep to fall upon
the earth creature" (2:21a). This return to the beginning, however, is not regression but progress. Out of it comes the material
for a new creation: "and while [the earth creature] slept, Yahweh
God took one of its ribs and closed up flesh at that spot"
(2:21b).[16]

New images of deity emerge. God is anesthesiologist and sur-
geon. By administering an anesthetic sufficient for the operation
to come, Yahweh God causes a deep sleep in the creature. Immediately the deity removes a section of its body and then, concluding successfully this surgery, "closed up flesh at that spot."
The entire procedure is quickly and efficiently executed. In the
very next sentence the images of deity shift to architect, de-
signer, and builder: "and Yahweh God built the rib which he
took from the earth creature into woman" (2:22a). This work is

also accomplished swiftly so that in the next line Yahweh acquires still another image: the divine matchmaker brings the woman to the earth creature (2:22b).

Just as these opening verses of episode four expand the images of God in the story, so they develop the life of the earth creature in new ways. To be sure, the creature is totally passive here, as it was throughout episode one; yet this passivity, operated upon by God, results in new life through a unique creative act. All the other creations have originated from the earth, a material that is given, not created, in the story. In episode one Yahweh God formed *hā-'ādām* from *hā-'ªdāmâ* (2:7); in episode two Yahweh God caused every tree to grow from *hā-'ªdāmâ* (2:9); and in episode three Yahweh God formed the animals from *hā-'ªdāmâ* (2:19). The same material indicates physical, perhaps psychic, rapport between humanity, botany, and zoology. They share common ground, even though they are distinct and separate creations. Yet they are not equal creations. The earth creature is central, prior both in order and in responsibility and power; the plants and the animals are made for its sake so that the earth creature stands over them in a hierarchy of harmony. It tills the garden, with freedom to eat of every tree save one; and it names the animals, with power to determine their existence. Hence, the earth creature has dominion over the plants and the animals—over everything that comes from *hā-'ªdāmâ* and even over the earth of the garden.

Strikingly, the creation in episode four does not come from *hā-'ªdāmâ;* the word *earth* never appears. Instead, at the beginning of this unit the creative act comes out of the earth creature itself. Thus, the creature functions here precisely as the earth functioned in episode one. And the two episodes contain yet another parallel: the use of dust from the earth and rib from the earth creature. As specific parts of whole entities, these substances are fragile and require processing before creatures come into being. As Yahweh shaped dust and then breathed into it to produce the earth creature, so now Yahweh takes out the rib and then fashions it into woman.

Built of raw material from the earth creature, rather than from the earth, the woman is unique in creation. Her uniqueness is further indicated by the matchmaking activity of Yahweh God, who "brought her to *hā-'ādām*" (2:22b). Although the words "Yahweh brought . . . to the earth creature" are repeated from episode three (2:19), they carry a radically different meaning here. In the preceding episode, after God formed the animals from the earth, the deity brought them to *hā-'ādām* "to see what it would call each one and whatever it called each one, that was the name" (2:19bc). In other words, the earth creature was specifically given dominion over the animals through naming. Similar power was granted over the plant world by the infinitive phrase "to till and to keep" the garden (2:15). By contrast, in episode four no purpose at all is stated in Yahweh's bringing of the woman to the earth creature, whose very body has now been changed because of her. Specifically, God does not give *hā-'ādām* power over the woman. Hence, the omission of any infinitive clause of purpose in this episode further contrasts the relationship of the earth creature to the woman with that of the earth creature to the earth, to the animals, and to the plants. She does not fit the pattern of dominion that the preceding episodes have established. She belongs to a new order that will by itself transform the earth creature. Having made the proper introduction by bringing her to *hā-'ādām*, the divine matchmaker withdraws from the pericope and the earth creature takes over, a pattern that first appeared in episode three.

In becoming material for creation, the earth creature changes character. Whereas the making of the plants and the animals were divine acts extrinsic to the earth creature itself, the making of the sexes is intrinsic. Indeed, this act has altered the very flesh of the creature: from one come two. After this intrinsic division, *hā-'ādām* is no longer identical with its past, so that when next it speaks a different creature is speaking. To be sure, continuity exists in the oneness of humanity, but here stress falls upon the discontinuity that results from sexual differentiation. For the first time *hā-'ādām* employs direct discourse. Its language is the poetry of Eros; its subject, female and male:

> And *hā-'ādām* said,
>> This, finally, bone of my bones
>>> and flesh of my flesh.
>> This shall be called woman ['iššâ]
>>> because from man ['îš] was taken this.

Surrounding the poem and also occurring at its center, the feminine pronoun *this* (*zō't*) unmistakably emphasizes the woman whose creation has made the earth creature different. Only after surgery does this creature, for the very first time, identify itself as male. Utilizing a pun on the Hebrew word for woman, *'iššâ*, the earth creature refers to itself by the specific term for man as male, *'îš*. Sexuality originates in play, just as humanity did at the beginning of the story. The unit *'îš* and *'iššâ* functionally parallels *hā-'ādām* and *hā-'ᵃdāmâ*. Occurring at the beginning and the end of scene one, puns encircle Eros to give fulfillment and harmony through the delight of words.

With the advent of sexuality, the word *hā-'ādām* acquires a second usage in the story. In episodes one, two, and three it designated one creature who was sexually undifferentiated (neither male nor female nor a combination of both).[17] After God operates on this earth creature, to produce a companion, its identity becomes sexual. The surgery is radical, for it results in two creatures where before there was only one. The new creature, built from the material of *hā-'ādām*, is female, receiving her identity in a word that is altogether new to the story, the word *'iššâ*. The old creature transformed is male, similarly receiving identity in a word that is new to the story, *'îš*. At the same time, the basic word for humanity before sexual differentiation, *hā-'ādām*, now becomes a sexual reference so that it is used frequently, though not exclusively, for the male. With this altered meaning, the retention of the word *hā-'ādām* allows for both continuity and discontinuity between the first creature and the male creature, just as the rib allows for both continuity and discontinuity between the first creature and the female creature. The story itself builds ambiguity into the word *hā-'ādām*, an ambiguity that should prevent interpreters from limiting it to one specific and unequivocal meaning throughout. Furthermore, the ambiguity in the word matches the ambiguity in the creature itself—the ambiguity of one flesh becoming two creatures.

But no ambiguity clouds the words *'iššâ* and *'îš*. One is female, the other male. Their creation is simultaneous, not sequential. One does not precede the other, even though the time line of this story introduces the woman first (2:22). Moreover, one is not the opposite of the other. In the very act of distinguishing female from male, the earth creature describes her as "bone of my bones and flesh of my flesh" (2:23). These words speak unity, solidarity, mutuality, and equality.[18] Accordingly, in this poem the man does not depict himself as either prior to or superior to the woman. His sexual identity depends upon her even as hers depends upon him. For both of them sexuality originates in the one flesh of humanity.

In the last two cola of the poem to Eros appear its only two verbs: *call* and *take* (2:23). They have already appeared earlier in scene one. Indeed, the verb *call* (*qr'*) occurs three times in episode three with reference to the naming of the animals (2:19, 19, 20). Even as other parallels between episodes three and four have thus far highlighted the uniqueness of the creation of human sexuality, so likewise does a comparison of this verb in its two settings. *Call* appears first in episode three as part of that infinitive phrase which episode four omits, though it repeats verbatim the first part of the sentence to which the phrase belongs: "and Yahweh God brought . . . to the earth creature" (2:19, 22). With the bringing of the woman to the creature, episode four stops. By contrast, episode three, which reports the bringing of the animals to the creature, continues with the reason, "to see what it would call each one" (2:19). In the sentences that follow this infinitive phrase (2:19, 20), the verb *call* is joined to the noun *name* (*šēm*), and this complete activity of *calling the name* becomes the way in which the earth creature establishes power over the animals. The verb *call* by itself does not mean naming; only when joined to the noun *name* does it become part of a naming formula. The existence of such a formula is attested further in passages outside this particular story that belong, nevertheless, to the same literary tradition.[19] For instance, in Genesis 4 we read (RSV):

[Cain] built a city, and *called the name* of the city after the *name* of his son, Enoch (4:17).

And Adam knew his wife again, and she bore a son and *called his name* Seth (4:25).

To Seth also a son was born, and he *called his name* Enosh (4:26a).

At that time men began *to call* upon *the name* of the Lord (4:26b).

In these traditions, the act of naming, which can mean either power over an object or recognition of the object, requires the noun *name* joined to the verb *call*. Alone, the verb *call* does not signify naming. Although this naming formula appears in episode three of our story to signify the power of the earth creature over the animals, it does not occur in episode four. The earth creature exclaims, "This shall be called '*iššâ*." The noun *name* is strikingly absent from the poetry. Hence, in calling the woman, the man is not establishing power over her but rejoicing in their mutuality.

The word *woman* ('*iššâ*) demonstrates further that the issue is not the naming of the female but rather the recognition of sexuality. '*Iššâ* itself is not a name; it is a common noun, not a proper noun. It designates gender; it does not specify person. Moreover, this word appears in the story *before* the earth creature "calls" it: the narrator reports that "Yahweh God built the rib which he took from the earth creature into a woman ['*iššâ*]" (2:22). Thus, the creature's poem does not determine who the woman is, but rather delights in what God has already done in creating sexuality:[20]

> Bone of my bones and flesh of my flesh;
> This shall be called '*iššâ*
> because from '*îš* was taken this.

The phrase "taken from" requires investigation also. Does it indicate a derivative existence for woman? Some have claimed that it does, maintaining also that derivation means subordination: in being taken from man, woman is subordinate to man.[21] But that interpretation falters when the function of the phrase "take from" is examined throughout the story. Within episode four itself this phrase occurs three times, twice in prose and once in poetry (2:21, 22, 23). In prose the verb (*lqḥ*) is active; in poetry, passive. All three occurrences pertain to the woman, whose creation comes in stages. First, while the earth creature slept, Yahweh God "*took* one *from* its ribs" (2:21). Second, "Yahweh God built the rib which he *took from* the earth creature into woman" (2:22). As we have seen, the rib is raw material, comparable to dust from the earth. It requires processing before the woman is created. Clearly in the prose account, then, it is the raw material, not the woman herself, that is taken from the earth creature; furthermore, the earth creature is not the man. The difference in the third occurrence of the phrase "taken from" is poetic license: ". . . *'iššâ* because from *'iš* was taken this" (2:23). Here the phrase joins *'iš* and *'iššâ* to produce a pun, not to give information about the creative process (nor about philology). And the meaning of this pun is the similarity of woman and man, not the subordination of woman to man. Paradoxically, to be taken from man is to be differentiated from him while being bone of bone and flesh of flesh. Differentiation, then, implies neither derivation nor subordination. The poetic usage of the phrase "taken from" argues, in fact, for the mutuality of woman and man.

Investigation of this phrase outside of episode four confirms the contention that it does not indicate subordination. Twice in Genesis 3 the passive voice of the verb is used for the earth creature in relation to the earth. The first usage occurs in poetry: "till you return to the earth, for *from* it you were *taken*" (3:19). The second usage occurs in prose: "therefore, Yahweh God sent him forth from the garden of Eden to till the earth *from* which he was *taken*" (3:23, RSV*). As *'iššâ* is taken from *'iš*, so *hā-'ādām* is taken from *hā-'ªdāmâ* (cf. 2:7). Yet *hā-'ādām* is never portrayed as subordinate to the earth. On the contrary, the creature is given power over the earth so that what is taken from becomes superior to. By strict analogy, then, the line "this shall be called *'iššâ* because from *'iš* was taken this" would mean not the subordination of the woman to the man but rather her superiority to him.

Yet the practice of determining the nuances of a given word from its usages elsewhere in a text may mislead as well as enlighten. The meanings gleaned from such a procedure must fit the particular context in which the word being studied appears. Since the context for this statement concerning *'iššâ* and *'iš* is the preceding line, "bone of my bones and flesh of my flesh," the connotation of woman's superiority is inappropriate. The relationship of this couple is one of mutuality and equality, not one of female superiority and certainly not one of female subordination.[22] Nowhere in this entire story is subordination a connota-

tion of the phrase "taken from."[23] Finally, woman is not derived
from man, even as the earth creature is not derived from the
earth. For both of them life originates with God. Dust of the
earth and rib of the earth creature are but raw materials for
God's creative activity. Truly, neither woman nor man is an autonomous creature; both owe their origin to divine mystery. Differentiation from the earth, on the one hand, and from the man,
on the other, implies neither derivation from them nor subordination to them:

> This, finally, bone of my bones
> and flesh of my flesh.
> This shall be called *'iššâ*
> because from *'îš* was differentiated this.
>
> (2:23)

Although episode four expands images of God and develops
further the life of the earth creature, it focuses upon woman. In
her Eros finds fulfillment. Making her entrance in the last
episode of scene one, she is the culmination of the entire movement, in no way an afterthought. The process that creates her is
shrouded in mystery; Yahweh God makes certain that no one
shall witness it. Put into a deep sleep, the earth creature is
neither participant, spectator, nor consultant for this climactic
event. Indeed, the earth creature does not even know in advance
that she is coming. Her arrival is suspenseful, since God's promise of a companion did not materialize once before. This mystery
and suspense yield surprise and delight. Thus it is that the
transformed earth creature utters a poem upon meeting
woman. She is unique. Unlike all the rest of creation, she does
not come from the earth; rather, Yahweh God *builds* the rib into
woman. The Hebrew verb build (*bnh*) indicates considerable
labor to produce solid results.[24] Hence, woman is no weak,
dainty, ephemeral creature. No opposite sex, no second sex, no
derived sex—in short, no "Adam's rib." Instead, woman is the
culmination of creation, fulfilling humanity in sexuality. Equal
in creation with the man, she is, at this point, elevated in emphasis by the design of the story.[25] With her creation Eros reigns.
"Therefore a man leaves his father and his mother and cleaves to
his woman and they become one flesh" (2:24, RSV*).

This narrative report concludes episode four, even as a narrative report ended episode three. Indeed, the structure of these two units (2:18–20, 21–24) has been parallel throughout. Each is divided into two distinct parts, with Yahweh God controlling the action of the first part and then withdrawing altogether in the second. Moreover, in the first part of each pericope *hā-'ādām* is object: for it, Yahweh forms the animals in episode three; from it, Yahweh takes raw material to build the woman in episode four. And both units conclude with the deity bringing the newly made creatures to *hā-'ādām*. But, as we have seen, episode three contains an infinitive clause here that episode four omits, and this omission indicates a crucial difference in meaning. The latter parts of these two episodes begin with *hā-'ādām* speaking. In episode three the speech is indirect; in four, direct. In three it is prose; in four, poetry. In three, it asserts dominion through naming; in four, it exalts communion through punning. After the speech of *hā-'ādām*, each episode closes with a narrative comment. In three that comment is downbeat: no fit companion did the earth creature find among the animals. In four, it is upbeat: man and woman become one flesh. The conclusions of both episodes return to the themes of their beginnings. Actually, the parallels in design and vocabulary between these two episodes highlight their differences. What the creation of the animals cannot do for the earth creature, the creation of sexuality can. Loneliness, then, is overcome not by something other than humanity but by distinction within one flesh. Sexuality is the recognition not of division but of the oneness that is wholeness, bone of bone and flesh of flesh.[26] No fit companion among the animals gives way to the one flesh of female and male.

With the conclusion of episode four, the poetry of the earth creature yields to the silent communion of man and woman. This communion is protected from intruders through the distancing of third-person narration, which describes for us but does not allow us to witness. "Therefore a man leaves his father and his mother and cleaves to his woman and they become one flesh" (2:24, RSV*). The description employs the explicitly sexual terms *'îš* and *'iššâ* that have just been introduced into the story. To this vocabulary the narrator adds the terms for parental roles, achieving a juxtaposition of relationships: man and woman contrast with father and mother. Each couple is a unit of equality—one, the equality of creation; the other, the equality of roles. Interestingly, however, parents are not part of God's creative activity. They appear in the story as adjuncts to the creation of woman and man. In other words, sexuality makes father and mother possible; parental images are subordinate to and dependent upon sexual images. Roles, then, are secondary at best; they do not belong to creation.

In this description only the man is identified with father and mother; the woman continues to stand alone. Her uniqueness and independence as a human creature remain intact, and her prominence in the design of the story persists. To her the man comes. Though called "his woman," she is not his possession but rather the one in whom he finds fulfillment. She is gift—God's gift of life. The man does not control her; he moves toward her for union. Her advent has transformed the earth creature into a sexual being. Thus, in the design and content of the story she is elevated as the one to whom he must cleave.

The man's movement toward union with the woman involves its opposite: separation from the parents. Leaving and cleaving are interrelated: "Therefore a man leaves his father and his mother and cleaves to his woman" (RSV*). The result of this convergence of opposites is a consummation of union: "and they become one flesh." No procreative purpose characterizes this sexual union; children are not mentioned. Hence, the man does not leave one family to start another; rather, he abandons ('zb) familial identity for the one flesh of sexuality.[27] Beginning with the one flesh of the earth creature, episode four has described the creation of two sexual beings from it: woman and man. From one comes two; from wholeness comes differentiation. Now, at the conclusion of the episode, this differentiation returns to wholeness; from two come the one flesh of communion between female and male.[28] Thus is Eros consummated.

Not only does one flesh complete the cyclic composition of episode four, but it also completes the cyclic composition of the entire first scene. The creation of humanity, sexually undifferentiated in episode one, finds its fulfillment in the creation of sexuality in episode four. With it the development of Eros is completed, and the first movement of the narrative concludes.

Yet rest does not come;[29] over against Eros stands Thanatos.
And the movement from Life to Death is by way of disobedience.
At the very center of the story, scene two reverses the direction
to lead to Death. But this turning point is not totally surprising. A
forbidden tree; animals that do not fit; the withdrawal of God;
the increasing power and freedom of human creatures—all
these aspects of Eros now become the occasion for disobedience.

EROS CONTAMINATED

Scene Two: The Turning Point
of Disobedience (Genesis 2:25—3:7)

Located at the center of the narrative, scene two is shorter
than the surrounding scenes. This brevity juxtaposes the turning point of the story with the two opposing movements. Disobedience comes through a single decision and a single act,
whereas both the development (2:7–24) and the disintegration
of Eros (3:8–24) require a gradual process. Repeating the words
both and *naked*, the cyclic design of scene two opens (2:25) and
closes (3:7) in third-person narrations about the man and the
woman. With accompanying descriptions, these words constitute
an inclusion of contrast between the before and the after of
disobedience.[30] While parallel in subject matter, the two parts of
this inclusion differ in length, the end being twice that of the
beginning. Enclosed by these narrations of nakedness, the scene
of disobedience itself also begins (3:1) and ends (3:6) with
third-person narrations, though they are parallel neither in
length nor in subject matter. The beginning, the introduction of
the serpent, is brief; the end, the very act of disobedience, much
longer. Similarly, at the center of this scene a dialogue between
the serpent and the woman develops from one question to more
lengthy speeches. Initiating and concluding this conversation,
the serpent surrounds the woman. Her speech stands at the
heart of this center scene.

Overall, then, two designs interlock in scene two: three con-
centric circles of form, and sometimes of content, converge upon
the center, as their length progresses from short units that lead
to the center to longer units that proceed from it. The center

itself is expansive. This symmetry of form (and sometimes of content) pulls against the asymmetry of length. Still another tension emerges: though the three short units are generally the same length, the three longer units vary in length. Here, length itself connotes stress; variations in length, then, different stresses. Although relatively brief and absolutely decisive, the turning point of the story is by no means smooth. Disobedience upsets the orderly development of life, as design and content clearly indicate:

A   Now they <u>both</u> were <u>naked</u>, the man [*hā-'ādām*] and his woman,
and they were not ashamed.

B   But the serpent was the sliest of all the wild beasts that Yahweh God had made.

C   And he said to the woman:
"Did God really say, 'You shall not eat from every tree of the garden?' "

D   And the woman said to the serpent:
"From every fruit of the trees of the garden we may eat.
But from the fruit of the tree that is in the midst of the garden,
God said: 'You shall not eat from it,
and you shall not touch it,
lest you die.' "

C'   And the serpent said to the woman:
Indeed you will not die.
For God knows that when you eat of it,
then your eyes will be opened,
and you will be like God, knowing good and evil.

B'   And the woman saw that
good was the tree for food,
a delight it was to the eyes,
and the tree was desired to make one wise.

So she took from it
and she ate,
and she also gave to her man [who was] with her
and he ate.

A'   And the eyes of <u>both</u> were opened,
and they knew that <u>naked</u> were they;
and they sewed leaves together
and made for themselves clothes.

(2:25—3:7)

In the three short units that lead to the center of this scene, all four worlds of the narrative gradually merge. By concentrating upon the human couple, the first unit (A) maintains continuity with episode four of scene one.[31] By introducing the serpent, the second unit (B) returns to the animal world. By having the serpent speak to the woman about God and the trees of the garden, the third unit (C) brings together the animal, human, divine, and plant worlds. These units set the stage for the drama of disobedience.

"Now they were both naked, the man and his woman, and they were not ashamed" (2:25). In this opening sentence of scene two, the word *hā-'ādām* occurs for the first time since the narrative introduction to the poem on sexuality in episode four (2:23a). As we have seen, sexual differentiation has radically transformed the earth creature so that continuity in the presence of the word *hā-'ādām* has been broken by discontinuity in its function and meaning. After the creation of *'iššâ* and *'îš*, the sexually undifferentiated earth creature exists no longer. Accordingly, the word *hā-'ādām* has now acquired a second usage in the story: it designates the male character. A third usage is yet to come. Meanwhile, both the male creature, *hā-'ādām*, and the female creature, *'iššâ*, are depicted as naked and not ashamed. The one flesh of sexuality (2:24) is defenseless flesh.[32]

Even as the earth creature itself was formed of fragile dust and lived by the divine breath that it neither possessed nor controlled, so likewise the two sexes that happened through the differentiation of the earth creature live precariously in the world. Their lives are solely dependent upon God, who has, nevertheless, made them responsible creatures. This paradox of created helplessness and created responsibility encounters threats from both the plant and the animal worlds. One tree threatens death; the animals have threatened loneliness; and soon one animal will threaten the very integrity and truthfulness of God, the Creator. Against such threats, the only "security" of the man and the woman is obedience to Yahweh God. Obedience neither affirms nor denies defenselessness. Hence, the narrator reports that the man and woman are naked without ascribing knowledge of this condition to them. In holy insecurity they live without shame or fear (cf. 3:10). Thus Yahweh God has shaped Eros.

"But the serpent was the sliest of all the wild beasts that Yahweh God had made" (3:1). From the category of wild animals (2:20), the story narrows to one particular creature who differs in degree, but not in kind, from the rest. Like them, the serpent was made by Yahweh God. This double designation for deity occurs only this one time in scene two. Appropriately, its appearance with the verb *make* (*ʿśh*) is consistent with its use in episode three of scene one where Yahweh God promised to *make* (*ʿśh*) a companion for the earth creature (2:18). Although no fit helper was found among the animals, Yahweh God did establish the nature of the relationship between these two creations: the human world rules the animal world. To this hierarchy the serpent belongs, and yet the description of him as sly (*ʿārûm*)[33] preceded immediately by the description of the couple as naked (*ʿărummîm*) suggests that animal power may prevail over human power. Unlike the puns of scene one, this pun works for perversion, not for pleasure. Threatening the harmony of life, wordplay has become dis-ease. As scene two moves toward the act of disobedience, then, ambiguities mount in creation. A most cunning serpent, made by Yahweh God and named by the earth creature, now challenges its Creator and snares its ruler. Ambiguity about the nature of the serpent holds in tension its complicated dimensions.[34] Formed by divine activity, it is not the devil; directed by its own cunning, it becomes the tempter.

Although naming symbolizes the power of the human creature over the animal world (2:19–20), speech itself does not—at least, it does not for the serpent.[35] At the center of scene two is a dialogue between this animal and the woman. Initiating and concluding the conversation, the serpent surrounds her. Both form and content demonstrate that he has captured her. And to capture her is to capture the man, for the two are bone of bone and flesh of flesh. Hence, the serpent addresses the woman with plural verb forms, regarding her as the spokesperson for the human couple. As in episode four of scene one, the woman continues to be emphasized in the design of the story while being portrayed as equal with the man in creation.

The serpent and the woman discuss theology. They talk about God. Never referring to the deity by the sacred name Yahweh, but only using the general appellation God, they establish that distance which characterizes objectivity and invites disobedience. And, indeed, God-the-subject who acts and controls is altogether absent from scene two. Creation supplants Creator. The serpent poses a question to the woman: "And he said to the woman: 'Did God really say, you shall not eat from every tree of the garden?' " (3:1). It is a difficult question. Phrased in a cunning way, it cannot be answered by a simple yes or no, since God prohibited eating from one tree but not from every tree. The question, then, requires explanation and clarification.

In answering, the woman states the case even more strongly than did God. Like the divine word (2:16), her reply begins with the positive freedom that she and the man have been granted. In fact, the woman faithfully employs God's very sentence structure, which emphasized the availability of fruit by placing the object before the verb. Yahweh God had commanded, "From every tree of the garden you may freely eat" (2:16). The woman says, "From every fruit of the trees of the garden we may eat" (3:2). Although her report is not slavish repetition—something Hebrew rhetoric generally avoids—both her emphasis and her vocabulary parallel the original command. Continuing, she recounts God's prohibition, using a similar sentence order but changing the vocabulary. Yahweh God had specified, "From the tree of the knowledge of good and evil you may not eat." The woman cites this tree less specifically: "from the fruit of the tree that is in the midst of the garden." Even though this phrase "in the midst of the garden" originally identified the location of two trees, the tree of life as well as the tree of the knowledge of good and evil (2:9), no confusion exists in the story as to which of these trees the woman intends. She means the forbidden tree, as her next words will indicate. Furthermore, the serpent, in replying to her, employs the specific phrase "knowing good and evil" (3:5, RSV).

As the woman relates the actual words of prohibition, she invokes the deity in direct quotation: "From the fruit of the tree that is in the midst of the garden, God said, 'You shall not eat from it and you shall not touch it, lest you die' " (3:3). But this quotation embellishes the original with the phrase "you shall not touch it." The reference to *touch* completes the appearance of the five senses in the story,[36] and with these words the hermeneutical skills of the woman emerge. Not only can she relay the command of God; she can also interpret it faithfully. Her understanding guarantees obedience. If the tree is not touched, then its fruit cannot be eaten. Thus the woman builds "a fence around the Torah," a procedure that her rabbinical successors developed fully to protect the law of God and to insure obedience to it.[37]

The response of the woman to the serpent reveals her as intelligent, informed, and perceptive. Theologian, ethicist, hermeneut, rabbi, she speaks with clarity and authority. Although the divine words of prohibition were addressed to the earth creature, she assumes responsibility for obeying them. Clearly, this incident shows continuity between the earth creature and both human sexes. At the same time, the differentiation of sexuality indicates discontinuity with the earth creature and permits the woman and the man to appear as distinct and separate creatures within this unity. Since they are bone of bone and flesh of flesh, one can speak for two: "we may eat . . . you [plural] shall not eat." Yet their oneness does not level life to sameness; it allows for distinctions without opposition or hierarchy. The woman speaks; the man does not. Hence, the woman and the man can be compared and contrasted within their unity.

As spokesperson for the human couple, the woman has stated well what Yahweh God requires. Her words of uncompromising obedience are at the center of scene two (D). Yet the center cannot hold. The serpent challenges, indeed refutes, the logic of obedience, claiming for himself absolute knowledge of life and death:

> And the serpent said to the woman:
>   Indeed you will not die.
>   For God knows that when you eat of it,
>   then your eyes will be opened,
>   and you will be like God, knowing good and evil.
>   (3:4, RSV*)

The serpent's words are ambiguous. With whom is his quarrel? God? the human couple? or both? Taken at face value, his comments seem designed not to bring about the demise of the couple but to expose the deception of a God jealous of humanity. Thus, his quarrel is with his Creator, and the couple are but the means for pursuing it. On the other hand, the narrator has already warned that the serpent is the sliest of all the wild beasts and has suggested by a pun that his cunning may well snare the naked couple. In this light, the serpent's quarrel is with the human creatures who exercise power over him, and his impugning of God is but the means for destroying them. In either case the claims of the serpent are enormous: to have God's knowledge and to alter the meaning of the forbidden tree for the woman and the man.

Yet the motives of this animal are obscure. Certainly, he is the villain, but then the story itself is not about a villain. Nor is it about evil, cosmic or chthonic. Instead, it is about human obedience (life) and human disobedience (death) as defined by God. Hence, in scene two the serpent surrounds the woman to place the narrative focus directly upon the human couple. In this posture he is a literary tool used to pose the issue of life and death, and not a character of equal stress. A villain in portrayal, he is a device in plot. The ambiguity of his depiction highlights the complicated dimensions of his nature without explaining or resolving them.

These ambiguities in the serpent's portrayal epitomize the discrepancies suggested in the creation of the animals. What God promised at the beginning of episode three (2:18), a companion for the earth creature, did not come to pass in the making of the animals. Fitting neither the spoken intention of their Creator nor the observed need of humanity, they were, nevertheless, dominated by both the divine and human worlds. Even though they were formed of the same material in the same way as the earth creature, Yahweh God brought the animals to it to be named. Now, in the most cunning of the wild creatures, these discrepancies threaten to destroy Eros. The serpent becomes the "helper" that hurts. Ironically, the controlled one has become the controller. And while he works, the deity is silent, in fact, absent. Divine absence itself is not new to the animals since

Yahweh God withdrew when the narrator announced their unsuitability as companions. Although in scene one such discrepancies blended into the harmony of life, in scene two they
threaten to disrupt unity. Using the plant world, one animal
menaces both the divine and the human worlds.

After surrounding the woman with his words, the serpent
never talks again. His function in the story shrinks, though it
does not cease. With his last speech the dialogue ends; the act of
disobedience is yet to come. For this event the story returns to
third-person narration (3:6) that is unmatched in length and
content with any other unit in scene two. Disobedience stands
alone, a single act without parallel. Its uniqueness accounts for
the incongruity between this section (B') and its structural parallel (B).

Suspense characterizes this narration. First, the report concentrates exclusively upon the woman, withholding the fact that the
man is with her. This focus continues the emphasis placed upon
the woman in the dialogue. It also introduces tension by imply-
ing a splitting apart of the two human characters of one flesh, an
implication that is not corrected until the very end. Second, the
narration builds suspense by adding details that impede the action: an elaborate description of the tree, of the woman's delib-
erations about it, and of her conduct in eating it.

The woman contemplates the tree. It is good for food; it is a
delight to the eyes; and it is desired because it makes one wise
(3:6). All three insights have antecedents in the story. The first
two, in reverse order, originally described every tree Yahweh
God created (2:9). The third observation, though not explicitly
stated earlier, derives from the words of the serpent: "when you
eat of it . . . you will be like God, knowing good and evil" (3:5,
RSV). Yet, the woman, in quoting God to the serpent, had recounted something quite different: the tree brings death, not
wisdom. Hence, this last insight is the crucial one. Not only does
it distinguish the tree of the knowledge of good and evil from all
other trees to make it uniquely desirable, but it also offers, according to the serpent, knowledge not given by God, knowledge
that removes the limits of humanity and merges it with divinity.

The woman, then, finds the tree physically appealing, aes-
thetically pleasing, and, above all, sapientially transforming. She

is fully aware before she eats, her vision encompassing the gamut of life. Moreover, she does not discuss the matter with her man. She acts independently, seeking neither his permission nor his advice. At the same time, she is not secretive, deceptive, or withdrawn. In the presence of the man she thinks and decides for herself. Three actions immediately follow three insights: she took from the tree; she ate; and she gave some to her man who was with her.

Taking, eating, giving: these actions by the woman do not tell the whole tale of disobedience. The story is careful to specify that the man is with her (*'immāh*), just as it earlier included him by the use of plural verb forms in the dialogue.[38] Yet throughout this scene the man has remained silent; he does not speak for obedience. His presence is passive and bland. The contrast that he offers to the woman is not strength or resolve but weakness. No patriarchal figure making decisions for his family, he follows his woman without question or comment. She gives fruit to him, "and-he-ate." The story does not say that she tempted him; nor does its silence allow for this inference, even though many interpreters have made it. It does not present him as reluctant or hesitating. He does not theologize; he does not contemplate; and he does not envision the full possibilities of the occasion. Instead, his one act is belly-oriented, and it is an act of acquiescence, not of initiative. If the woman is intelligent, sensitive, and ingenious, the man is passive, brutish, and inept. This portrayal of his character in scene two contrasts with his ability in scene one to recognize sexuality, to speak sensitively of its delight, and then to decide the direction of his life by leaving father and mother and cleaving to his woman. Certainly his depiction in scene two does not reflect his position of equality with the woman in creation. Oppositions within one flesh have appeared at the turning point of disobedience.

These oppositions function in similar ways. Emphasis upon the woman throughout scene two leads directly to the man at its end. His transgression, reported in only one Hebrew word, *wayyō'kal*, concludes and climaxes the deed of the two who are one. Appearing at the end of the narration, he occupies a place of importance. Stress upon him comes through concealment and passivity; stress upon her through exposure and activity. Hence, the woman and the man are mutual foils. Two opposite narrative depictions converge to unite them in disobedience. Furthermore, these portrayals illustrate the wide range of human responses that participate in transgression. Both activity and passivity, initiative and acquiescence, are equal modes of lawlessness. Regardless of how differently they are characterized, the woman and the man are mutually responsible for their actions: "She ate and she gave some to the man who was with her and he ate" (3:6def). They do not talk to each other; their deeds speak for them. Thus, the narrator quickly reports their disobedience, omitting any theological judgment, psychological analysis, or moral evaluation. Simply put, the serpent has tempted both the woman and the man. Instead of consulting the God who gave them life, one flesh disobeys.

To this one flesh the narrator reverts explicitly in the closing comment of scene two (3:7), a verse that returns in semantic dissonance to the beginning of the scene. Before disobedience "they *both* were *naked,* the man and his woman, and they were not ashamed" (2:25). After disobedience, "the eyes of *both* were opened and they knew that *naked* were they" (3:7). Between these two kinds of defenselessness, one given in creation and the other acquired through knowledge, lies the single act of disobedience. It was fostered by the serpent's prediction: "your eyes will be opened, and you will be like God, knowing good and evil" (3:5, RSV). Now, in fact, "the eyes of both were opened," but ironically they know the opposite of what the serpent promised. They know their helplessness, insecurity, and defenselessness.[39] What characterized their life in creation now threatens it in disobedience.

The before and the after of disobedience contrast unselfconscious naked existence, on the one hand, with the knowledge of nakedness, on the other. The defenselessness that belongs to creation produces neither shame (2:25) nor fear (cf. 3:10). But the knowledge of defenselessness that is acquired through disobedience yields simultaneous affirmations and denials of itself: "and they sewed leaves together and made for themselves clothes" (3:7cd). What they conceal, they reveal. Having exceeded the limits set for Eros, this couple has destroyed its harmony. Instead of fulfillment, joy, and gift, they now experience life as problem that *they* must solve; as threat that *they* must eliminate; and as shame that *they* must cover up. God-given helplessness has become danger; existence has become burden.

In the early simplicity of creation two words sufficed to characterize the presence of nakedness: "and-they-were-ashamed not" (2:25b). Now in the growing complexity of disobedience, words triple to describe the plight of nakedness: "and-they-sewed leaves together and-made for-themselves clothes" (3:7c). Like the leaves, the words multiply to cover their transgression. With this cover-up, the movement of Eros has turned toward its opposite so that the conclusion of scene two portends a tragic ending to the entire story. Scene three is that ending.

EROS CONDEMNED

SCENE THREE: THE DISINTEGRATION
OF EROS (GENESIS 3:8-24)

As the countermovement to scene one (2:7-24), scene three details the disintegration of Eros. Here ambiguities thrive, ironies increase, clarity lessens, and design falters. All these difficulties have been foreshadowed in scene two, where disobedience upset the harmony of existence. Indeed, this act destroyed life at its source by turning God-the-subject into God-the-object; by exchanging God-the-authority for God-the-deceiver; and by asserting human autonomy over divine providence. Now, after disobedience, Yahweh God, the creator of life, returns to preside over its demise.

In full command, the deity controls the three parts of scene three. These parts do not parallel the four episodes of scene one because the two opposing movements of plot fundamentally clash.[40] Disintegration shatters Eros in unpredictable ways. With its particular content, then, the design of scene three evidences a decaying process at the same time that it sustains the integrity of the story. Third-person narration introduces the action by relating that the man and the woman hid themselves from Yahweh God among the trees of the garden (3:8). It concludes the scene by reporting that Yahweh God evicted *hā-'ādām* from the garden (3:23-24). Two occurrences of the word *garden* (*gan*) at the beginning parallel two occurrences of the phrase "garden of

Eden" at the end. In addition, the word *tree* (*'ēṣ*) appears once in each narration. This cyclic design encompasses the three parts of trial (3:8–13), judgment (3:14–19), and aftermath (3:20–24).

Part One: Trial (Genesis 3:8–13)

The opening verse that precedes the trial (3:8) has four functions: to recall aspects of scene one; to make the transition from scene two; to introduce the first section of scene three; and, in fact, to introduce all of scene three. Having already observed the last function, we turn to the other three, which intermingle. Scene two ended with the man and the woman clothing their nakedness. Scene three begins with the couple hiding from God:

> And they heard the voice of Yahweh God who was walking
> in the garden at the breezy time of day,
> and they hid—the man and his woman—from the presence
> of Yahweh God in the midst of the trees of the garden.
>
> (3:8)

Only once in scene two did the full designation *Yahweh God* appear (3:1), in contrast to its consistent use in scene one. In both scenes it occurred in narration, and likewise it appears at the beginning of scene three, where the voice of Yahweh God sounds again. This voice first commanded the earth creature to be obedient (2:16) and then declared that the earth creature needed a companion (2:18); yet it was ominously silent when the newly created couple chose disobedience. The silent God of scene two was also the absent and inactive one. But now in scene three this deity walks in the garden. The purpose of the walk is uncertain.[41] Is it a leisurely stroll? or a patrol? or a search for the couple? Whatever the reason, Yahweh God has returned to direct the story. Hearing the deity's voice, the man and his woman hide. The divine object causes the re-actions of the human subjects.

The words "the man and his woman" appeared first at the beginning of scene two to identify the newly created couple who "were both naked" and "not ashamed" (2:25). Now used a second time, at the beginning of scene three, they designate the clothed couple (cf. 3:7) who hide "from the presence of Yahweh

God in the midst of the trees of the garden." In scene one, the phrase "in the midst of" (*bᵉtôk*) described the tree of life and the tree of the knowledge of good and evil (2:9). In scene two this same term specifically identified the forbidden tree (3:2). Here in scene three it locates the couple. Occurring three times, the preposition *bᵉtôk* moves the story from creation to disobedience, to shame, and to fear. Their nakedness covered with leaves, the man and his woman hide precisely at the site of their disobedience. Ironically, both their dress and their position expose them.

Where they hide from the presence of Yahweh God, there the deity approaches them with questions. God becomes the prosecutor in a court of law. From passive object in scene two to active object in the introduction to scene three (3:8), the deity shifts to active subject for the remainder of scene three, the last a position Yahweh held throughout scene one. Thus the portrayal of the divine has come full circle. "And Yahweh God called to the man and said to him, 'Where are you?'" Although scene three opened with both the man and his woman hearing the divine voice, this voice first addresses only the man. Such individual treatment increases tension within the unity of the couple. The man, who ate last of the forbidden fruit, is the first to be questioned about it. One word suffices to inquire about the meaning of his behavior: "Where-are-you?" (*'ayyekâ*). The man answers only for himself. His reply (3:10) is a variation on the narrative description of the couple that introduced this scene (3:8):

And they heard the voice of Yahweh God who was walking in the garden at the breezy time of the day,

And he said, "Your voice I heard in the garden

and I was afraid, because I was naked,

and the man and his woman hid themselves from the presence of Yahweh God among the trees of the garden.
(3:8)

and I hid myself."
(3:10)

To a single word of God, "Where-are-you?" the man has given a seven-word answer: "Your-voice I-heard in-the-garden, and-I-was-afraid because-naked was-I and-I-hid-myself." This heaping of words upon words testifies to the damage of disobedience. Explanations, justifications, and rationalizations have entered life. Defenselessness has become defensiveness; selfcenteredness prevails. Four times the man speaks of himself: "I heard," "I was afraid," "I was naked," "I hid." Yet looming over all these expressions of the human ego is the divine voice. At the beginning of scene three (3:8), this voice as object determined the actions of the subjects. Here (3:10) its unusual syntactic position before the verb in the Hebrew sentence further emphasizes its power. Most assuredly, Yahweh God stands over this human assertion, as the man himself ironically acknowledges in his very word order: "Your voice I heard. . . ." Between the hearing and the hiding the man has interjected two declarations. The first is a confession of fear, totally new to the story. The second accounts for this fear by stating in the first-person singular what the narrator has twice reported of the couple: the fact of nakedness (2:25; 3:7). A Hebrew particle denoting motivation links fear and defenselessness: "I was afraid, because [kî] I was naked." Hence, knowledge of nakedness, not the presence of God, causes fear.

In the man's reply *naked* is the key word. The narrator has already shown its importance by encircling the act of disobedience with it (2:25; 3:7). Thus this word becomes the clue that Yahweh God pursues. Efforts to defend defenselessness lead not to resolution but rather to interrogation (3:11): "Who told you that you were naked?" (RSV). Although this divine question appears to seek the identity of a culprit, "Who told you . . . ," it actually focuses upon its object, "that you were naked?"

A second question immediately makes clear that the man alone must bear responsibility for his knowledge: "Have you eaten of the tree of which I commanded you not to eat?" (RSV). These words echo from scene one, where Yahweh God instructed the earth creature about the limits of freedom (2:16–17). The shared vocabulary of the two passages consists of the terms *command, not, eat,* and *tree.* The phrase "the knowledge of good and evil" in 2:17 is not repeated in 3:11, nor was it used by the woman in 3:3 to identify the forbidden tree. In all these instances the prohibition "do not eat" remains constant, while the description of the tree varies. The significance of the tree pertains, then, to obedience and disobedience rather than to the specific content of the phrase "the knowledge of good and evil." It is the tree of divine command.[42]

The deity's questions to the man seek to locate responsibility, which the man himself accepts reluctantly. First, he betrays the woman; second, he blames God; and only third does he confess: "And the man said, 'The-woman whom you-gave to-stand-with-me, she gave-me from-the-tree, and-I-ate' " (3:12). Before disobedience, distinctions within one flesh signified the fulfillment of Eros (2:22–24). With disobedience these distinctions become oppositions within one flesh (3:6–7). Now, after disobedience, these oppositions split one flesh, shattering its unity and harmony.[43] The man turns against the woman whom he earlier recognized as bone of bone and flesh of flesh.

Ironically, his opposition to her speaks of his solidarity with her in transgression. Though he betrays her, he does not say that she tempted him. He says, rather, that she gave him fruit of the tree, a report that accurately repeats the narrator's account of the incident (3:6). Moreover, this verb *give* (*ntn*) is the same verb that the man uses to describe the action of the deity toward him in the gift of the woman: "the woman whom you gave to stand with me." Neither God nor the woman has tempted the man, and yet he implicates them both in his guilt. He indicates that Eros, which he himself once celebrated in poetic language, is a mistake. If the serpent has suggested that God is jealous of the human couple (3:5), the man implies that the deity is culpable for making them female and male. Although the serpent spoke only indirectly, the man confronts God face to face. Only then, after seven words of accusation against creation and Creator, does he acknowledge, in one word, his own responsibility: "and-I-ate."

By turning immediately to the woman, God averts the attack by the man: "Then Yahweh God said to the woman, 'What is this you have done?' " (3:13). Unlike the two questions to the man, this one does not seek information to leave open the issue of guilt. Instead, it accuses (cf. Gen. 4:10). God has accepted the man's account of the woman's role in his disobedience, while ignoring his account of God's role. To the divine question the woman responds in a pattern similar to the man's reply. She accepts responsibility only after blaming another. "The-serpent beguiled-me, and-I-ate" (3:13). Yet her answer also differs from the man's in four remarkable ways. First, she does not blame God. She does not say, for example, "The serpent whom you made to dwell in the garden with me" (cf. 3:1). Second, she does not implicate her companion, for weal or for woe. She speaks only for and about herself. "The serpent beguiled me" (not "us"), she says, although in conversation with this animal she had used plural pronouns that included the man. Third, the woman's answer differs in its reference to the serpent as the tempter who deceived, beguiled, and seduced—all nuances of the Hebrew verb *nš'*, but not of the verb *ntn* ("give"), which the man used to characterize the actions of the woman and of God. Fourth, the woman confesses more quickly than did the man. After two words, which blame the serpent, she accepts responsibility: "and-I-ate."

By betraying the woman to God, the man opposed himself to her; by ignoring him in her reply to God, the woman separates herself from the man. Yet their mutual opposition unites them in the solidarity of separate confessions: "and I ate" . . . "and I ate." Split apart, one flesh awaits the outcome. The man and the woman speak no more in the story; God takes over to judge and then to punish.

The sequence and emphasis of these events in part one of scene three show inverse parallels to scene two. In other words, divine interrogation recapitulates in reverse order the main contours of disobedience. The chart on the following page demonstrates this process.

These inverse parallels bring artistic and thematic balance to the story. In both arrangements the woman is at the center, surrounded, on the one side, by the serpent who tempted her (3:1; 3:13–14) and, on the other, by the man who followed her (3:6ef) only to betray her (3:12). (She was also at the center of the dialogue with the serpent; see above.) Nevertheless, her depiction changes radically. In scene two she dominated the action (3:2–3, 6); in part one of scene three she speaks only three words (3:13cd). Correspondingly, emphasis upon the man reverses. In scene two he was the minor character who ate when she gave him

Scene Two (2:25—3:7)

e   After disobedience, the couple hide their nakedness by sewing leaves together (3:7).

d   The man appears last; the narrator reports, "and she gave some to her man, and he ate" (3:6ef).

c   The woman appears second; the narrator reports, "she took of its fruit and she ate" (3:6d).

b   The serpent, made by Yahweh God, appears first to make trouble (3:1).

a   Before disobedience there exists the unity of "the man and his woman" as defenseless creatures (2:25).

Scene Three, Part One (3:8–14a)

e'   "The man and his woman" hide from Yahweh God in the midst of the trees of the garden (3:8).

d'   Yahweh God addresses first the man, who says his woman gave him fruit and then acknowledges, "and I ate" (3:9–12).

c'   Yahweh God addresses, second, the woman, who finally acknowledges, "and I ate" (3:13).

b'   Yahweh God addresses last the serpent who beguiled (3:14a).

a'   (With the unity of the couple completely shattered in the preceding interrogation, there is no return to life before disobedience.)

the fruit (3:6ef); but in part one of scene three he dominates their response (3:10, 12). Thus, the portrayals of the man and the woman in disobedience and defense equalize them in narrative stress and moral responsibility. Once again, opposite depictions have converged to unite this couple, ironically, in the brokenness of life.

Parallels between the scene of disobedience and the trial by God underscore also the ambiguity of the serpent. In scene two he was villain in portrayal and device in plot. This tension persists in part one of scene three. The woman characterizes him as the tempter (villain in portrayal) precisely when she uses him (device in plot) as an excuse for her own disobedience. God's response confirms this ambiguity. The deity accepts the woman's portrayal of the serpent as villain and yet addresses no questions of responsibility to him, but does, in fact, curse him. The first to appear in scene two, the serpent sets the stage for human disobedience. The last to appear at the trial, he is blamed by the woman for that disobedience but is not asked by God to account for himself. Within the circle of the serpent, the human couple disobey, defend, and confess. Ironically, this animal surrounds those who were given power over him (cf. 2:19–20).

In reconstructing inversely the main contours of disobedience, Yahweh God has moved the story back to "the serpent who was the sliest of all the wild beasts that Yahweh God had made" (3:1, 14a). Inexplicably absent when this beast demonstrated his cunning, the deity is again in full control. Asking no question, God speaks to the serpent in judgment, and thereby this animal becomes the transitional figure between two sections.[44] From disobedience to trial to judgment, the story intertwines structurally and thematically. Though absent from the scene of disobedience, God-the-prosecutor now becomes God-the-judge. Moreover, the inverted order in which the animal and human characters appear in the three settings has moved the narrative cyclically to the judgment scene:[45]

Disobedience (2:25—3:7)	Trial (3:8–13)	Judgment (3:14–19)
serpent	man	serpent
woman	woman	woman
man	serpent	man

Part Two: Judgment (3:14–19)

In general outline as well as in specific parts, divine judgment recapitulates the sequence of human disobedience. Set over against the development of life in scene one, this judgmental process shows the disintegration that results when limits are exceeded. The divine speeches to the serpent, the woman, and the man are not commands for structuring life. To the contrary, they show how intolerable existence has become as it stands between creation and redemption. These judgments describe consequences; they do not prescribe punishment (that comes later in the scene).[46] They witness to living death, not to fulfilled life, and this witness is a protest, indeed a condemnation, against the contamination of creation. The brief poem to Eros that consummated creation in scene one (2:23) yields here to the extended poetry of Thanatos that forms the center of dissolution in scene three.

Similar to patterns throughout the story, this poetry is a cyclic composition with parallels in form and vocabulary between the first and last judgments that are absent in the second. At the same time, all three speeches are linked by the word *woman*; it alone occurs in every section (3:15, 16, 17). In length, the speeches differ. The words spoken to the man are the longest (3:17–19); to the woman, the shortest (3:16); to the serpent, the in-between (3:14–15). Interpretations of these general structural features will emerge in our study of the individual poems.

1. The Judgment upon the Serpent (3:14–15)

And Yahweh God said to the serpent:
"Because you have done this,
    cursed are you above all domestic animals
    and above all wild beasts."

(3:14a)

Although Yahweh God accused the woman through a question that permitted a reply, "What is this you have done?" (3:13), with this same vocabulary the deity accuses the serpent through a declaration that allows no defense: "Because [kî] you have done this." The serpent is guilty without a trial, and the result of his violation of life is a curse that differentiates him in degree, but not in kind, from the other animals. His superlative position here parallels his introduction in scene two. "The sliest [*ārûm*] of all the wild beasts that Yahweh God had made" (3:1) is now "cursed [*ārûr*] . . . above all domestic animals and above all wild beasts." A wordplay has transformed cunning into curse, and this change implicates the other animals. Only the birds of the air, specified in scene one (2:19, 20), are not explicitly mentioned here. As the superior member of the animal world, then, the serpent represents them while towering above them in disgrace.[47]

The severity of the curse upon him appears first in his peculiar posture and food (3:14b):

> upon your belly you shall go,
> and dust you shall eat
> all the days of your life.
> (3:14b, RSV)

The nouns *dust* ('*āpār*) and *life* (*hayyîm*), and the verb *eat* ('*kl*), are ironic references. From dust Yahweh God formed the fragile earth creature (2:7) and commanded it not to eat of one tree, lest it die (2:17). The very animal who tempted the human creatures of dust to eat the forbidden fruit and assured them that death would not result (3:1, 4) eats dust himself all the days of his life. When he was enticing the couple to disobey, the serpent spoke specifically to the woman but, through the use of plural pronouns, included the man also. Accordingly, the curse upon this animal continues with an explicit reference to the woman that also involves the man (3:15):

> Enmity I will put between you and the woman,
> between your seed and her seed;
> he will strike your head
> and you will strike his heel.

With these words, distinctions between the animal world and the human world become oppositions. The hierarchy of harmony that was established in scene one when the earth creature named the animals (2:18–20) and then was threatened in scene two when the sliest ('*ārûm*) of all the animals snared the naked ('*arûmmîm*) couple is now ruined in scene three when Yahweh

God curses (*'ārûr*) the serpent and declares perpetual enmity between the offspring of this animal and of the woman. God never discusses the enmity between deity and serpent that the latter's assertions in scene two might have occasioned (see above) and that the divine curse itself suggests. From Yahweh's perspective, the serpent's quarrel, indeed his hostility, is directed toward the human world that named him and yet was overpowered by him. The resulting enmity has shattered forever the unity of life, as reference to the woman's seed makes clear. This first mention of human progeny stresses the persistent consequences of disobedience. A power struggle prevails between the animal world and the human world, each striking to kill the other. Occasioned by the plant world (the tree), this hostility is one mark of the death of Eros, which the divine world had created but now judges as contaminated.

In summary, God's speech to the serpent recapitulates the order, vocabulary, and themes of the serpent's debut in the story (3:1–5). The first to appear in the narration of disobedience, this animal is the first to be addressed in the poetry of judgment. Having been called the most subtle (*'ārûm*) of all wild beasts, he is now cursed (*'ārûr*) above all wild beasts. Having introduced the idea of eating forbidden fruit without the consequence of death, he is now condemned to eat dust all the days of his life. Having spoken to the woman as the representative of the human couple, he now lives in hostility with the woman and her offspring. Repeatedly, Yahweh God denounces this animal by recalling his participation in transgression. The deity whom the serpent objectified in scene two judges the serpent in scene three.

Furthermore, this judgment contains allusions to each of the four episodes of scene one. The mention of dust returns to the forming of the earth creature in episode one (2:7). The single word *eat* recalls the exclusive use of this verb in reference to the trees of the garden in episode two. The description of animals domestic and wild alludes to episode three. And the reference to the woman reflects the creation of sexuality in episode four. Hints of the development of Eros suffice to report its disintegration. *Multum in parvo* is God's curse upon the serpent. After the curse, this wild beast disappears, bearing the unresolved ambiguity of villain in portrayal and device in plot. From this point on, God's attention focuses entirely, though not equally, upon the woman and the man.

2. *The Judgment upon the Woman (3:16).* "To the woman he said" (3:16a, RSV): Foreshadowed in the curse upon the serpent (3:15), this judgment upon the woman will, in turn, foreshadow the address to the man (3:16c). Yet it differs strikingly in form and content from the surrounding verses. First, it lacks an accusatory formula. On the one hand, the utterance to the serpent commenced, "because [kî] you have done this" (i.e., beguiled the woman, 3:13-14); on the other hand, the words to the man will begin, "because [kî] you have listened to the voice of your woman" (3:17). But in the middle of these judgments the woman herself is not accused, since the deity has already charged her in the interrogation at the trial. Unlike the two questions asked of the man there (3:11), the question to her assumed guilt, "What is this you have done?" Hence, all that remains is for Yahweh to describe the particular consequences of the woman's disobedience.

The lack of the word *curse* is a second difference between the judgments upon the woman and those upon the serpent and the man. Having accused the serpent, God cursed him directly (3:14): "*'ārûr 'attâ*" ("cursed are you"). After accusing the man (*'ādām*), God will curse him indirectly (3:17c): "*'ᵃrûrâ hā-'ᵃdāmâ ba'ᵃbûrekā*" ("cursed is the earth because of you"). Although surrounded by curses, the woman herself is never cursed, directly or indirectly, here or elsewhere in the story. Thus, any claim that Yahweh's judgment upon her is the most severe of the three falters at this very point (as well as at others). At the same time, the lack of a curse does not mean that she is less responsible than either the serpent or the man—or that she is less a human being than the man. As we have seen, the portrayal of the serpent wavers between tempter and technique, but the story itself is about neither villain nor device. Human obedience and disobedience is its subject, with the woman and the man equal characters, bone of bone and flesh of flesh (2:23). In the scene of disobedience, the woman was portrayed as intelligent, informed, and independent. The decision to eat of the fruit was hers alone, as was the man's decision his alone. At their trial, the questions of

God made clear their individual accountability; similarly, their confessions, although given separately, indicated mutual responsibility. Thus in judgment the woman is neither more nor less responsible than the man.

Speaking directly to the woman, Yahweh describes the particular consequences that disobedience has brought to her existence (3:16b):

> I will greatly multiply your pain and your childbearing [*or*, your pain in childbearing];
> in pain you will bring forth children.

The two objects of the verb *multiply* may be interpreted separately as two related ideas or together as one complex notion. According to the former view, the first object, *'iṣṣ^ebônēk* ("pain"), indicates suffering or toil in general for the woman, while the second object, *w^ehērōnēk* ("childbearing"), specifies suffering unique to her at particular times (cf. KJV).[48] The more she gives birth, the more her pain increases. Furthermore, by assigning the general meaning "toil" to the word *'iṣṣ^ebônēk*, this interpretation allows for a close parallel to the later usage of the same word to describe the work of the man: "in toil [*b^e'iṣṣābôn*] you shall eat of it all the days of your life" (3:17e, RSV). According to the latter view above, however, the two objects connote hendiadys, a rhetorical figure in which two words connected by a conjunction yield a single thought.[49] Hence, the phrase means "pain in childbirth." This interpretation draws support from the resultant parallelism in the succeeding line: "in pain [*b^e'eṣeb*] you will bring forth children." The seed that strikes the serpent's head (3:15) also hurts the woman.

The judgment upon the woman is pivotal. While the first part is linked primarily to motifs in the preceding poem, the second part connects with the unit to come by introducing the man (3:16c):

> For your man [*'îš*] is your desire,
> but he will rule over you.

The sexual vocabulary of *'iššâ* and *'îš* appeared first in the story at the fulfillment of Eros in episode four of scene one. The pun resulting there from the association of these words signified the unity of woman and man, even as it differentiated them (2:23). The equality of their union was immediately underscored again when the man ('îš) left his parents to cleave to his woman ('iššâ) and "they became one flesh" (2:24). Yahweh's words to the woman now allude to this event. As the man in creation joined her, so she continues, even at the place of judgment, to desire him. But between the then and the now, mutual disobedience has intervened. The woman ('iššâ) ate; she gave to her man ('îš) and he ate (3:6). At this turning point, distinctions within one flesh became oppositions (see above). Division followed, yielding "opposite sexes." To defend himself, the man (hā-'ādām) turned against the woman and betrayed her to God (3:12). Yet, according to God, she still yearns for the original unity of male and female: "for your man ['îš] is your desire [tešûqâ]." Alas, however, union is no more; one flesh is split. The man will not reciprocate the woman's desire; instead, he will rule over her. Thus she lives in unresolved tension. Where once there was mutuality, now there is a hierarchy of division. The man dominates the woman to pervert sexuality. Hence, the woman is corrupted in becoming a slave, and the man is corrupted in becoming a master. His supremacy is neither a divine right nor a male prerogative. Her subordination is neither a divine decree nor the female destiny. Both their positions result from shared disobedience. God describes this consequence but does not prescribe it as punishment.[50]

After only two lines the judgment upon the woman ends. Its brevity is a third contrast with the speeches to the serpent and the man. And the shortened form corresponds precisely to the closing words, subsuming the woman to the man: "he will rule over you." She shrinks in the story as hā-'ādām takes over. With this subordination of 'iššâ, the word 'îš disappears entirely. Eros has disintegrated. Thus, what the story describes it now becomes: oppression resulting from transgression is actualized by a design that emphasizes the man and minimizes the woman.

3. The Judgment upon the Man (3:17–19). The accusation against the man moves backward in the story:

> And to the man he said,
> "Because [kî] you have listened to the voice of your woman
>   and have eaten of the tree of which I commanded you,
>   [saying], 'You shall not eat of it.' "   (3:17, RSV*)

This reference to the woman completes the concatenate design of the three judgments: she is the common link (3:15, 16, 17). Her appearance here recalls, ironically, the man's joyful union with her in scene one (2:23–24). His listening to the voice of the woman is also a twist on two passages at the beginning of scene three. In that introduction, the narrator reported that the man and the woman heard (*šm‘*) the voice (*qôl*) of Yahweh God, and they hid (3:8). Later the man says to God, "Your voice [*qôl*] I heard [*šm‘*] . . . and I hid" (3:10). To hear the voice of God was to run away; not to heed it was to disobey. Yet this same vocabulary describes the opposite response. When the man listened (*šm‘*) to the voice (*qôl*) of his woman, to heed it was to disobey. The man is faulted for not being a responsible creature. Perhaps he is even charged with idolatry, since he set the voice of the woman over against the voice of God. But in no case is the man accused of failing to control the woman; after all, he has no right to do so. Instead, he is judged unfaithful to God. He has eaten of the forbidden tree, and his effort to blame the deity through betrayal of the woman counts for nothing.

Reference to the tree of divine command moves the accusation back to episode two of scene one. There the verb *command* was applied to God in the third person: "and Yahweh God commanded" (2:16). Here the deity speaks in the first person: "I commanded" (3:17). There the verb *eat* appeared twice in a negative context, once with the word *not* expressed and once with a negative meaning implied: "but of the tree of the knowledge of good and evil *you shall not eat*, for in the day that *you eat* of it you shall die" (2:17, RSV). Here parallel usages occur in reverse order. First, the negative meaning is implied, and, second, the word *not* is expressed: "Because . . . *you have eaten* of the tree of which I commanded you, '*You shall not eat of it . . .*' " (RSV). In both scene one and scene three, then, the content of the divine prohibition is identical: "you shall not eat of it." This formal and verbal return to episode two concludes the charge against the man. The specifics that follow extend back to episode one (2:7–8) and to the prologue (2:4b–7).

The judgment proper forms an inclusion with a postscript (3:17d–19). Like the address to the serpent, this one begins with the word *curse*. Yet, like the woman, the man himself is not

130   *GOD AND THE RHETORIC OF SEXUALITY*

cursed. Instead, the earth is cursed, as language plays again
upon the pun of *'ādām* and *hā-'ᵃdāmâ* (cf. 2:5d, 7). *Earth,* then, is
the word that delimits the inclusion. But the verb *eat,* with the
second-person pronoun as subject, dominates it: three occurrences continue the stress put upon eating in the accusation. Finally, the repetition of the verb *return* in the two lines of this
judgment binds the inclusion to a postscript, in which the noun
dust is the key term.

> Cursed is the earth because of you.
> In pain you shall eat of it all the days of your life.
> Thorns and thistles it will bring forth to you
>   as you eat the grain of the field.
> In the sweat of your face you shall eat bread,
> Until you return to the earth, for from it you were taken.
>
> For dust are you and to dust you shall return.
>   (3:17d–19)

The results of disobedience unite cause and effect. Caused by
'ādām, the curse upon *hā-'ᵃdāmâ* affects him. In toil he shall eat of
the earth all the days of his life. Originally assigned to serve and
keep the garden of Eden in harmony with the soil (2:15), the
man now must struggle to obtain food from it. Work, which was
an erotic activity of creation, has become alienated labor. As we
have seen, the word that denotes this labor (*'iṣṣābôn*) also
functioned in the judgment upon the woman (3:16). This verbal
parallelism indicates equal, though not identical, consequences
for the two sexes. However work is culturally conceived, be it
childbearing or farming, its execution comes in pain and toil
both for the woman and for the man. In addition, the curse
upon the earth that the man caused and now reaps links him to
the curse upon the serpent. The statement "dust you shall eat all
the days of your life" (3:14, RSV) reverberates in the words "in
toil you shall eat of it [earth] all the days of your life" (3:17,
RSV).

Joining in enmity *'ādām* and *hā-'ᵃdāmâ,* this third judgment
began with the man acting upon the earth:

> Cursed is the earth because of you.
> In pain you shall eat of it all the days of your life.

Conversely, the next line specifies the earth acting upon the man: "thorns and thistles it shall bring forth [ṣmḥ] to you" (3:18a). Moreover, similar to the preceding description of alienated labor, this declaration also returns ironically to episode two. There the verb *bring forth* (ṣmḥ) reported the activity of God:

> And Yahweh God *caused to grow* [ṣmḥ] from the earth every tree
> pleasant to see and good to eat—
> the tree of life in the midst of the garden
> and the tree of the knowledge of good and evil.
>
> (2:9)

In creating Eros, Yahweh caused joy and nourishment to come from the earth. But since disobedience has disrupted creation, the earth itself (not the deity) will now produce pain and famine: thorns and thistles contrast with every tree pleasant to see and good to eat. Connecting verbally these opposite descriptions, the verb ṣmḥ juxtaposes life and death. Furthermore, this present destructive context of the verb recalls the original barrenness of the earth in the prologue. And like the judgment in 3:18, that barrenness was not attributed to God:

> when no plant of the field was in the earth
> and no grain of the field had yet sprouted [ṣmḥ].
>
> (2:5ab)

Altogether these three occurrences of the verb ṣmḥ have suggested *in nuce* major aspects of the narrative plot. In the prologue this word reported chaos; in scene one, Eros; and now in scene three, Thanatos.

The return to the prologue continues in the phrase "the grain of the field." Yahweh God says to the man, "Thorns and thistles it [the earth] will bring forth to you as you eat the grain of the field." Before creation, "no grain of the field had yet sprouted" (2:5b); absence of food marked chaos. With creation came physical nourishment in abundance (2:9; cf. 3:6). After disobedience, "the grain of the field" is still available, although natural obstacles thwart it (3:18b). Only hard work will produce it:

> In the sweat of your face you shall eat bread,
> Until you return to the earth, for from it you were taken.

These closing lines of the inclusion parallel its opening (3:17ef). "In the sweat of your face you shall eat bread" corresponds to "in pain you shall eat of it." This repetition thus stresses alienated labor "all the days of your life," a living death that ends in physical demise: "until you return to the earth, for out of it you were taken."[51] Formed from the earth as the first act of creation (2:7), *'ādām* returns to *hā-'ᵃdāmâ* as the last act of disintegration. Although between beginning and end the word *'ādām* has altered in meaning from the earth creature to the man, it has nevertheless retained its punning usage. Originally, *hā-'ādām* separating from *hā-'ᵃdāmâ* signified life. Finally, *'ādām* reuniting with *hā-'ᵃdāmâ* means death. While differentiation was wholeness and harmony, union is disintegration and enmity:

> Cursed is the earth because of you.
> . . . .
> Until you return to the earth,
>   for out of it you were taken.

The postscript of this judgment continues to emphasize death: "For dust you are and to dust you shall return" (3:19c). Formed of dust, the earth creature lived precariously (2:7). Now in life's disintegration, the man is poignantly reminded of this fragility. And yet in judgment irony overtakes poignancy. "Dust you are and to dust you shall return" is the very dust that the serpent shall eat all the days of his life.

Part Three: The Aftermath (Genesis 3:20–24)

The trial established guilt: the man ate; the woman ate; and the serpent beguiled. Three separate judgments have described the outcome of their actions: the good earth is cursed; plants give way to thorns and thistles; fulfilling work has become alienated labor; power over the animals has deteriorated to enmity with the serpent; sexuality has splintered into strife; human oppression prevails. With such consequences, a happy ending to the story is impossible; only the aftermath of disaster remains. To relate it, the narrator takes major responsibility. The poetry of Thanatos leads, then, into the prose of a tragic conclusion.

The ending of scene three is uneven in composition. Whatever its history in the transmission of tradition,[52] its final disjointed form matches the content. After human disobedience and its effects, the narration, like existence itself, lacks harmony, manifests incongruities, and teems with perplexities. Nevertheless, within this composite section, two divisions can be discerned. The first (3:20, 21) is set apart by the presence of the words the man (hā-'ādām) and woman ('iššâ). In part three 'iššâ appears only at this point, and only here does hā-'ādām refer exclusively to the male. In quite different ways, the two verses of this division report on human sexuality in disarray. The second division (3:22–24), using the word hā-'ādām generically, relates the divine punishment that concludes the story.

1. Human Sexuality in Disarray (3:20, 21). The two verses on sexuality allude to the motifs that have foreshadowed them:

> Now hā-'ādām called the name of his woman Eve,
> because she was the mother of all living.
> And Yahweh God made for 'ādām and his woman garments of skin
> and clothed them.

In the judgment to the woman, the sexual term 'iš ("man") was used for the last time when Yahweh described the breakdown of equality between female and male (3:16). Although the erotic desire of 'iššâ for 'iš continued after disobedience, the man would not reciprocate. Instead, 'ādām would rule over the woman. What the deity told in judgment now comes to pass as "the man calls the name [šēm] of the woman Eve." While this language differs radically from the portrait of female and male in episode four of scene one, it chillingly echoes the vocabulary of dominion over the animals in episode three. There the earth creature called the name (šēm) of each animal (2:19). Now, in effect, the man reduces the woman to the status of an animal by calling her a name. The act itself faults the man for corrupting one flesh of equality, for asserting power over the woman, and for violating the companion corresponding to him. Ironically, he names her Eve, a Hebrew word that resembles in sound the word life, even as he robs her of life in its created fullness. The motivational clause that comments on this naming highlights the incongruity: "because she was the mother of all living."[53] The one who in creation stood alone, without parental identity (in particular, without a mother), is now assigned the role of mother (cf. 3:16). What alone might be a title of honor, "mother of all living," is in context intertwined with a position of inferiority and subordination.

Although the disaster to human sexuality that has resulted from disobedience is final, Yahweh God tempers it with kindness: the deity makes clothes for the man and the woman (3:21). This activity yields still another image of God—the tailor. It also recalls the inclusion of contrast that surrounded the scene of disobedience. In the beginning, "hā-'ādām and his 'iššâ were both naked ['ᵃrûmmîm], and were not ashamed" (2:25). In the end, "they knew that they were naked ['ᵃrûmmîm]; and they sewed fig leaves together and made themselves aprons" (3:7, RSV). Realizing their defenselessness, they could no longer live unprotected in creation. But how pathetic and insufficient was their solution. So now Yahweh intervenes to make garments of skin ('ôr). Neither erasing nor ignoring their transgression, the deity equips them to endure its shame and fear. Though certainly an improvement over leaves, garments of skin are, nevertheless, a sad commentary on the death of Eros (cf. 2:25).

For the last time the woman qua woman has appeared in the narrative. Here Yahweh God has treated her and her man as distinct and equal; yet, this divine touch of mercy is juxtaposed to the man's naming of the woman. Equality under God, after disobedience, does not translate, then, into equality between the sexes.

2. The Punishment (3:22-24). In the aftermath of judgment has come, first, a human act of corruption and, second, a divine act of help. But the latter does not overturn the former. God's gift of garments does not restore mutuality to male and female. Instead, the rule of the man over the woman is completed by a change in word usage. In episodes one, two, and three of scene one the term hā-'ādām described the sexually undifferentiated creature from the earth. But after the creation of 'iššâ and 'îš in episode four, the earth creature no longer existed, and hā-'ādām designated the male character. This usage persisted throughout scene two and has continued in scene three until the closing paragraph where hā-'ādām now becomes a generic term that

keeps the man visible and renders the woman invisible (3:22–24). Artistically, this accent upon the man at the end of scene three balances the stress upon the woman at the end of scene one. At the same time, this artistic symmetry yields a semantic dissonance. In scene one, the emphasis upon the woman in the design of the story demonstrated her equality with the man in creation. In scene three, however, the emphasis upon the man in the design of the story shows his rule over the woman in the aftermath of disobedience. What God described to the woman as a consequence of transgression, the story not only reports but actually embodies. Generic *hā-'ādām* has subsumed *'iššâ*.

If the sartorial mercy of Yahweh did not alter the oppression of female by male (3:20–21), neither does it prevent divine punishment of the couple. In fact, God's kindness leads immediately to expulsion. In an unfinished speech, the deity first comments on what has happened:

> Then Yahweh God said:
> "Lo, the man [*hā-'ādām*] has become like one of us,
>   knowing good and evil;
> now, lest he put forth his hand and take also
>   from the tree of life
>   and eat and live forever"—
>   (3:22, RSV*)

The speech is puzzling. To whom is Yahweh speaking? The phrase "like one of us" alludes to unspecified dimensions of the divine world that the story does not clarify. Even more baffling is the portrayal of *hā-'ādām*, "like one of us, knowing good and evil." This description has ambiguous antecedents. When God forbade the earth creature to eat of the tree of the knowledge of good and evil, the deity warned, or threatened, death as the consequence (2:17). Nothing was said about the earth creature partaking of the divine world. In her conversation with the serpent, the woman repeated this theme of death, but the serpent himself denied it (3:3–5). He claimed that divinity, not death, would result from eating the fruit and suggested further that God was jealous of humanity. Yet the narrator refuted the serpent's contention and declared that the couple, after eating the forbidden fruit, knew precisely the opposite of divinity: "they knew that they were naked" (3:7, RSV). All that ensued in the story, including God's act of mercy to clothe their nakedness (3:21), has spelled out this existential death, until the closing speech by Yahweh (3:22).

Taken at face value, this speech confirms the serpent in his claim that the couple would become divine and in his suggestion that God is jealous of humanity. After all, Yahweh moves quickly to prevent the man from acquiring immortality, a second quality of divinity that the tree of life symbolizes. But this apparent meaning clashes with the dynamics of the narrative itself. Nothing before or after Yahweh's closing speech indicates that the human couple are in any way like the divine world. They hide from God; they receive divine judgment; they exhibit no transforming wisdom (cf. 3:6); and they revert to total passivity when God inflicts punishment. Moreover, the fact that Yahweh God did not forbid the earth creature to eat of the tree of life at the beginning of the story suggests that God's jealous protection of divine prerogatives is not the issue.

Perhaps irony, a device that has appeared often in scene three, best interprets this closing speech by God. Helpless creatures, their lives shattered by strife, discord, and enmity, are hardly candidates for divinity. Hence, the observation by Yahweh that "the man has become like one of us, knowing good and evil" (RSV) mocks the serpent and convicts the couple through the incongruity of the promised and the actual. They expected divinity but disaster came. Eating the forbidden tree has brought death to "the mother of all living" (RSV) and to the husband who now rules over her. As God punishes them, existential death merges with mortality. The tree of life, available in Eros, is denied in Thanatos. The man shall not live forever. And furthermore, unlike the human prerogative in creation, the man in the aftermath of disaster has no freedom to obey or to disobey the divine restriction placed on the tree of life. He will not have access to it. How ungodlike his existence has become; "now, lest he put forth his hand and take also of the tree of life, and eat, and live forever—" (RSV). Abruptly, the speech stops. Its completion is the act of expulsion from the garden.

Linking the divine speech with the divine deed is the verb *šlḥ*, "put forth" or "send forth." In order that the man not put forth (*yišlaḥ*) his hand to take of the tree of life, Yahweh God sent him forth (*wayᵉšallᵉḥēhû*) from the garden. A second verb underscores the severity of the punishment: "he drove out." Appearing at the center of the divine action, this word confirms that expulsion is not a mere exit but a permanent exile. Finally, a third verb, also with Yahweh God as subject, results in protecting the tree of life itself from the human world: "he put . . . the cherubim and a flaming sword to guard the way" to this tree.

A circular design contains these divine deeds that conclude the story. The phrase "garden of Eden" appears at the beginning (3:23) and end (3:24). Parallel infinitive phrases also occur. The first specifies labor in exile for the man; the second describes work in the garden by its protectors:

> And Yahweh God sent him forth from the garden of Eden
> to serve the earth [*hā-'ᵃdāmâ*] from which he was taken.
>
> And he drove out the man (*hā-'ādām*).
>
> And he put at the east of the garden of Eden the cherubim and a
> flaming sword
> to guard the way to the tree of life.
>
> (3:23–24, RSV*)

In highly compressed form all the closing verses of the story (3:22–24) return to its beginnings (2:4b–9, 15–17). Symmetry is asymmetrical, since with punishment existence has shrunk, indeed, shriveled. Moreover, repetitions of key words, phrases, and motifs reverse meanings; the disintegration of life replaces creation. As a central word in this dissonant ring composition, *hā-'ādām* is used exclusively for humanity at the beginning and the end of the story, yet with two very different meanings: at first, the sexually undifferentiated earth creature (2:7); at last, the generic man who renders the woman invisible (3:24).[54]

The closing speech by Yahweh God, beginning in 3:22, reaches back to the divine command to the earth creature in 2:16–17. The tree of the knowledge of good and evil echoes in the phrase "knowing good and evil." The command against eating of this tree is recalled in the new prohibition not to eat of the tree of life. The statement about death in the day that the forbidden fruit is eaten is juxtaposed to the reference to life forever if the fruit of the second tree be consumed. The first divine speech emphasized freedom and accountability for *hā-'ādām:* "You may freely eat of every tree" save one. Since that one was available, *hā-'ādām* was responsible to obey. By contrast, the last divine speech stresses that human freedom is gone and that responsibility has been forfeited. Yahweh makes it impossible to eat of the tree of life. Finally, this closing speech also reaches back to the creation of the trees in 2:9. Only in these two places does the tree of life appear in the story—first, in pleasure; last, in punishment.

The report of divine punishment (3:23–24) returns to still other parts of the narrative beginnings. Sending the man forth "from the garden of Eden to serve the earth from which he was taken" (3:23) reverses the action in two earlier verses, while repeating some of their vocabulary. In 2:15 "Yahweh God took *hā-'ādām* and put him in the garden of Eden to serve it and guard it." In 2:8 "Yahweh God planted a garden in Eden, in the east; and there he put *hā-'ādām* whom he had formed." In addition, this report of banishment from the garden moves yet further back into the beginnings of the story. Reference to the earth (*hā-'ᵃdāmâ*) from which the earth creature was taken recalls Yahweh God forming *hā-'ādām* of dust from *hā-'ᵃdāmâ* (2:7). And the phrase "to serve the earth" is repeated verbatim from the prologue: "no earth creature was there to serve the earth" (2:5d).

Allusions to the beginnings of the story continue in the final verse (3:24). "He drove out the man" is another reversal on the entry of the earth creature into the garden (2:8, 15). The phrase "at the east of the garden of Eden" matches "a garden in Eden, in the east" (2:8). The duty of the cherubim and a flaming sword "to guard [*šmr*] the way to the tree of life" employs another of the infinitives that describe the responsibility of the earth creature for the garden: to keep (*šmr*) it (2:15). Whereas in 2:15 the two infinitives *to serve* (*'bd*) and *to keep* [*šmr*] appeared together to designate work in the garden, in 3:23–24 they are separated in order and in meaning. "To till [*'bd*] the ground" is the labor of the man outside the garden (3:23); "to guard [šmr] the way to the tree of life" is the duty of the cherubim and a flaming sword within the garden (3:24). These very last words of the story, "tree of life," echo again the words of 2:9.

All in all, the end of scene three recapitulates in a highly compressed form the opening sections of the story. Beginning with one reference in the prologue (2:5), and continuing through episodes one (2:7–8) and two (2:9, 15–17) of scene one, the conclusion reiterates with semantic dissonance key words, phrases, and motifs. Omitted only are the references to water (2:6, 10–14). Thus, the expansion of life at the beginning of the story disintegrates at its end. God-the-creator becomes God-the-punisher. Joy in the garden dissipates in the sorrow of exile, with disobedience as the turning point.

Life has lost to Death, harmony to hostility, unity and fulfillment to fragmentation and dispersion. The divine, human, animal, and plant worlds are all adversely affected. Indeed, the image of God male and female has participated in a tragedy of disobedience. Estranged from each other, the man and the woman are banished from the garden and barred forever from the tree of life. Truly, a love story has gone awry.

Yet Genesis 2—3 is not the only word in scripture on human sexuality. What it forfeits in tragedy, the Song of Songs redeems in joy.

NOTES

1. Documentation of this statement by theologians and biblical scholars is hardly necessary. For recent expositions of misogynous readings, see Merlin Stone, *When God Was a Woman* (New York: Dial Press, 1976), pp. 5–8, 198–233; June Singer, *Androgyny: Toward a New Theory of Sexuality* (New York: Anchor Press/Doubleday, 1976), pp. 85–100.

2. My understanding of Eros draws upon, though it is not identical with, Sigmund Freud, *Beyond the Pleasure Principle* (New York: W. W. Norton & Co., 1961), pp. 44–55; Herbert Marcuse, *Eros and Civilization* (Boston: Beacon Press, 1955); and Norman O. Brown, *Life Against Death* (Middletown, Conn.: Wesleyan University Press, 1959), esp. pp. 40–54. I am particularly influenced by Marcuse's "notion that Eros and Agape may after all be one and the same—not that Eros is Agape but that Agape is Eros . . ." (p. 210); cf. Paul Tillich, *Dynamics of Faith* (New York: Harper & Row, 1957), pp. 114–15. Thus, my use of the word

140   GOD AND THE RHETORIC OF SEXUALITY

Eros contrasts sharply with Anders Nygren, *Agape and Eros* (Philadelphia: Westminster Press, 1953), and with Ernest Becker, *The Denial of Death* (New York: Free Press, 1973), pp. 150–75.

3. For a different structural analysis, with corresponding differences in meaning, see Jerome T. Walsh, "Genesis 2:4b—3:24: A Synchronic Approach," *JBL* 96 (1977): 161–77.

4. Ironies persist throughout Gen. 2—3. Cf., e.g., Edwin M. Good, *Irony in the Old Testament* (Philadelphia: Westminster Press, 1965), pp. 81–84. One recent literary-critical study of the phenomenon of irony is Wayne C. Booth, *A Rhetoric of Irony* (Chicago: University of Chicago Press, 1974). Since it is limited to "stable irony," however, Booth's discussion is not as helpful as it might be.

5. I choose not to translate the word *nephesh*, which connotes the totality of the "self." Cf. Hans Walter Wolff, *Anthropology of the Old Testament* (Philadelphia: Fortress Press, 1974), pp. 10–25.

6. Cf. Terence E. Fretheim, *Creation, Fall, and Flood* (Minneapolis: Augsburg, 1969), pp. 70–71.

7. For the translation of *hā-'ādām* as "the earth creature," I am indebted to Professor Prescott Williams of Austin Presbyterian Theological Seminary, Austin, Tex. Cf. "the earthling" in Adrien Janis Bledstein, "The Genesis of Humans: The Garden of Eden Revisited," *Judaism* 26 (1977): 190; also in E. A. Speiser, *Genesis, AB* (New York: Doubleday, 1964), p. 16. On the four occurrences of the word *'ādām* without the definite article (Gen. 2:5, 20; 3:17, 21), see Ernest Lussier, "Adham in Genesis 1, 1–4, 24," *CBQ* 18 (1956): 137–39; also Speiser, *Genesis*, p. 18.

8. To avoid any suggestion of sexual differentiation in the earth creature before episode four (Gen. 2:21–24), I use the neuter pronoun "it."

9. Gerhard von Rad, *Genesis* (Philadelphia: Westminster Press, 1961), pp. 79–80.

10. On Gen. 2:10–14, see U. Cassuto, *A Commentary on the Book of Genesis*, Pt. I (Jerusalem: Magnes Press, 1961), pp. 114–21.

11. Cf. Marcuse's distinction between labor and work, *Eros and Civilization*, pp. 212–21; also Hannah Arendt, *The Human Condition* (Chicago: University of Chicago Press, 1970), pp. 79–174.

12. Scholarly attempts to explicate the phrase "the knowledge of good and evil" are legion. See W. Malcolm Clark "A Legal Background to the Yahwist's Use of 'Good and Evil' in Genesis 2—3," *JBL* 88 (1969): 266–78 and the bibliography cited there.

13. Exod. 18:4; Deut. 33:7, 26, 29; Ps. 33:20; 115:9–11; 121:2; 124:8; 146:5. Cf. Clarence J. Vos, *Women in Old Testament Worship* (Amsterdam: N.V. Verenigde Drukkerijen Judels and Brinkman-Delft, n.d.), p. 16.

14. Cf. Susanne K. Langer, *Philosophy in a New Key* (Cambridge: Harvard University Press, 1973), pp. 103–43.

15. Cf. David Tobin Asselin, "The Notion of Dominion in Genesis 1—3," *CBQ* 16 (1954): 277–94.

16. Though I retain the traditional translation "rib" for the Hebrew word *ṣēlā'*, I do not regard that meaning as sacrosanct. The word may indicate "side" rather than "rib"; see Koehler-Baumgartner, *Lexicon in Veteris Testamenti Libros* (Leiden: E. J. Brill, 1958), p. 805.

17. Elsewhere I have proposed an interpretation of *hā-'ādām* as androgynous until the differentiation of female and male in Gen. 2:21–24 ("Depatriarchalizing in Biblical Interpretation," *JAAR* 41 [1973]: 35, 37–38). I now consider that description incorrect because the word *androgyny* assumes sexuality, whereas the earth creature is sexually undifferentiated. To understand the earth creature as either humanity or proto-humanity is, I think, legitimate.

18. See Walter Brueggemann, "Of the Same Flesh and Bone (Gen. 2, 23a)," *CBQ* 32 (1970): 532–42.

19. Trible, "Depatriarchalizing," p. 38.

20. Although I have retained the traditional reading "she shall be called" (so RSV), this Hebrew verb may also be rendered in the present tense: "she is called." The latter translation is indeed preferable in this context, since it connotes simple recognition without an act of determination (cf. Isa. 54:5; Prov. 16:21).

21. See Fretheim, *Creation, Fall, and Flood*, pp. 78–79; Eugene C. Bianchi and Rosemary R. Ruether, *From Machismo to Mutuality* (New York: Paulist Press, 1976), pp. 12–13.

22. *Contra* Walsh, "Genesis 2:4b—3:24: A Synchronic Approach," p. 174, n. 32.

23. Cf. Vos, *Women in Old Testament Worship*, p. 17.

24. The verb *bnh* is used of towns, towers, altars, and fortifications as well as of the primeval woman (Koehler-Baumgartner, *Lexicon*, p. 134). In Gen. 2:22 it may mean the fashioning of clay around the rib (Ruth Amiran, "Myths of the Creation of Man and the Jericho Statues," *Bulletin of the American Schools of Oriental Research* 167 [1962]: 24–25).

25. See John L. McKenzie, "The Literary Characteristics of Gen. 2—3," *Theological Studies* 15 (1954): 559–60; cf. John A. Bailey, "Initiation and the Primal Woman in Gilgamesh and Genesis 2—3," *JBL* 89 (1970): 143; Claus Westermann, *Genesis, Biblischer Kommentar* 1/4 (Neukirchen-Vluyn: Neukirchener Verlag, 1970), p. 312.

26. *Contra* Norman O. Brown, *Love's Body* (New York: Vintage Books, 1966), p. 84.

27. *Contra* Cassuto, *Commentary on the Book of Genesis*, p. 137; but cf. Wolff, *Anthropology of the Old Testament*, p. 172.

28. Westermann, *Genesis*, pp. 316–17. For different views, cf. von Rad, who claims that "one flesh" signifies progeny (*Genesis*, p. 82), and Hermann Gunkel, who holds that the phrase means sexual intercourse (*Genesis, Handbuch zum Alten Testament* [Göttingen: Vandenhoeck and Ruprecht, 1902], p. 10).

29. Cf. Freud, *Beyond the Pleasure Principle*, p. 56.

30. On inclusion, see Chapter 1, n. 61.

31. Gen. 2:25, then, serves a double function: (1) the epilogue to episode four of scene one and (2) the prologue to scene two.

32. On the connotation of defenseless in the word *naked* (*'ārôm*), see Good, *Irony in the Old Testament*, p. 83, n. 3.

33. For some scholars the word *'ārûm*, along with other words and themes, indicates a sapiential milieu for Gen. 2—3; see Luis Alonso-Schökel, "Sapiential and Covenant Themes in Genesis 2—3," in *Studies*

142   *GOD AND THE RHETORIC OF SEXUALITY*

in Ancient Israelite Wisdom, ed. James L. Crenshaw (New York: KTAV, 1976), pp. 468–80; George E. Mendenhall, "The Shady Side of Wisdom: The Date and Purpose of Genesis 3," in *A Light Unto My Path: Old Testament Studies in Honor of Jacob M. Myers*, ed. Howard N. Bream, et al. (Philadelphia: Temple University Press, 1974), pp. 319–34.

34. On this type of ambiguity, cf. William Empson, *Seven Types of Ambiguity* (New York: New Directions, 1966), pp. 133–54. On the background of the serpent in Gen. 3, see Brevard S. Childs, *Myth and Reality in the Old Testament* (Naperville, Ill.: Alec R. Allenson, 1960), pp. 42–48; Karen Randolph Joines, *Serpent Symbolism in the Old Testament* (Haddonfield, N.J.: Haddonfield House, 1974), pp. 16–41. For an interpretation of the serpent, see Paul Ricoeur, *The Symbolism of Evil* (Boston: Beacon Press, 1967), pp. 252–60; and cf. Thomas Hora, *Existential Metapsychiatry* (New York: Seabury Press, 1977), pp. 216–20.

35. Cf. Langer, *Philosophy in a New Key*, pp. 104, 200.

36. See above on Gen. 2:16, pp. 86–87: smell (2:7); sight (2:9); taste (2:9); hearing (2:16).

37. See George Foot Moore, *Judaism*, vol. 1 (Cambridge: Harvard University Press, 1950), pp. 258–59; Phyllis Trible, "Biblical Theology as Women's Work," *Religion in Life* 44 (Spring 1975): 8.

38. On the presence of the man, see Katharine D. Sakenfeld, "The Bible and Women: Bane or Blessing?" *Theology Today* 32 (1975): 225, Jean M. Higgins, "The Myth of Eve: The Temptress," *JAAR* 44 (1976): 646–47.

39. Good, *Irony in the Old Testament*, p. 84.

40. To accord with the disparities between scenes one and three, then, I have chosen intentionally a different terminology for their respective divisions. Thus scene one was divided into four *episodes;* scene three is divided into three *parts.*

41. Cf. Cassuto, *A Commentary on the Book of Genesis*, pp. 150–55.

42. Clark, "A Legal Background," pp. 277–78.

43. Cf. Good, *Irony in the Old Testament*, p. 84: "As soon as man's created oneness is a solidarity in sin, it splits apart."

44. Throughout the narrative, then, several verses function as transitions between sections: 2:7 (see p. 78); 2:25 (see p. 107); 3:8 (see p. 116); and here 3:14a.

45. Similarly, Fretheim, *Creation, Fall, and Flood*, p. 82.

46. The punishment is not these judgments but rather expulsion from the garden; see below on Gen. 3:22–24. Cf. George W. Coats, "The God of Death," *Int.* 29 (1975): 231–32.

47. *Contra* Speiser, *Genesis*, p. 24.

48. Cassuto, *A Commentary on the Book of Genesis*, p. 165.

49. Speiser, *Genesis*, p. 24.

50. For a different view, see Susan T. Foh, "What Is the Woman's Desire?" *Westminster Journal of Theology* 37 (1974–75): 376–83; also Vos, *Women in Old Testament Worship*, p. 24.

51. Cf. Marcuse, *Eros and Civilization*, pp. 212–21.

52. See von Rad, *Genesis*, pp. 96–98.

53. Cf. Isaac M. Kikawada, "Two Notes on Eve," *JBL* 91 (1972): 33–37.

A LOVE STORY GONE AWRY

54. If the word *hā-'ādām* in these closing verses (3:22–24) is read not as a generic term but as an exclusively male reference, then the story never says that the woman was driven out of the garden (cf. Higgins, "The Myth of Eve," p. 645). Though this interpretation may be tempting, the interlocking structures and motifs of the story do not validate it.

CHAPTER 5

Love's Lyrics Redeemed

Love is bone of bone and flesh of flesh. Thus I hear the Song of Songs.[1] It speaks from lover to lover with whispers of intimacy, shouts of ecstasy, and silences of consummation. At the same time, its unnamed voices reach out to include the world in their symphony of eroticism. This movement between the private and the public invites all companions to enter a garden of delight.

Genesis 2—3 is the hermeneutical key with which I unlock this garden. That narrative began with the development of Eros in four episodes: the forming of the earth creature, the planting of a garden, the making of animals, and the creation of sexuality. Alas, however, the fulfillment proclaimed when 'îš and 'iššâ became one flesh disintegrated through disobedience. As a result, Yahweh God drove out generic man and invisible woman from the garden, and "at the east of the garden of Eden he placed the cherubim, and a flaming sword which turned every way, to guard the way to the tree of life" (Gen. 3:24, RSV). Clearly, Genesis 2—3 offers no return to the garden of creation. And yet, as scripture interpreting scripture, it provides my clue for entering another garden of Eros, the Song of Songs. Through expansions, omissions, and reversals, this poetry recovers the love that is bone of bone and flesh of flesh. In other words, the Song of Songs redeems a love story gone awry. Taking clues from Genesis 2, then, let us acquire first an overview of the form and content of the Song.

READING THE MUSICAL SCORE

Expanding upon the lyrics of eroticism in Genesis 2, three human voices compose this new song. They belong to a woman, a man, and a group of women, the daughters of Jerusalem. Independent of logical progression or plot development, these voices flow freely and spontaneously to yield a series of metaphors in which many meanings intertwine simultaneously. At times, the standard, the figurative, and the euphemistic converge so compellingly that one cannot discern where vehicle ends and tenor begins. Often the language is elusive,[2] holding its treasures in secret for the lovers themselves. Occasionally the identity of the speaker is uncertain,[3] creating a problem for observers but not for participants who know that in Eros all voices mingle. Hence, the poetry of the Song resists calculations and invites imagination. The visual must be heard; the auditory, seen. Love itself blends sight, sound, sense, and non-sense. In these ways, the voices of the Song of Songs extol and enhance the creation of sexuality in Genesis 2.

Of the three speakers, the woman is the most prominent. She opens and closes the entire Song, her voice dominant throughout. By this structural emphasis her equality and mutuality with the man is illuminated. The arrangement recalls the stress placed upon the woman at the conclusion of Genesis 2: although equal with the man in creation, she was, nonetheless, elevated in emphasis by the design of the story. In the Song of Songs, accent upon the female is further increased by the presence of the daughters of Jerusalem. As a foil and complement to the lovers, this group aids the flow of the action.[4] Women, then, are the principal creators of the poetry of eroticism.

Strikingly, God does not speak in the Song; nor is the deity even mentioned. This divine absence parallels the withdrawal of Yahweh God in Genesis 2 precisely where the poem of eroticism emerged. After making the woman and bringing her to the transformed earth creature, the deity disappeared from scene one. Then the earth creature spoke for the first time:

> This, finally, bone of my bones
> and flesh of my flesh.
> This shall be called 'iššâ
> because from 'îš was differentiated this.
> (Gen. 2:23)

Just as the tenor of this poem continues in the Song of Songs, so appropriately does its setting. Yahweh God, who created male and female, withdraws when lovers discover themselves, speak the revelation, and become one flesh.[5]

The cyclic design of Genesis 2 is also reflected and developed in the Song. Originally, the creation of humanity found its fulfillment in the creation of sexuality: the earth creature became two, male and female, and those two became one flesh. With such an erotic completion, the Song of Songs begins, continues, and concludes. As a symphony of love, it unfolds in five major movements of varying lengths.[6] At the conclusions of the first four sections, the woman utters a refrain that both separates and joins these movements. It begins, "I adjure you, O daughters of Jerusalem" (RSV). Clusters of verbal motifs that precede this refrain further interrelate the five movements, yielding an ebb and a flow among the images of the Song. An examination of the beginnings and endings of these movements shows the cyclic pattern of the overall composition.

The introductory movement extends from 1:2 to 2:7. By speaking first *about* her lover, rather than directly *to* him, the woman invites us to enter their circle of intimacy:

> O that he would kiss me with the kisses of his mouth!
>
> (1:2)

With the words of her mouth she reaches many; for the kisses of her mouth she desires only one. And by the end of the movement her yearnings are realized:

> His left hand is under my head,
>   and his right hand embraces me!
>
> (2:6)

This verse appears again at the conclusion of the fourth movement, thus providing one of the many verbal links between sections. Since, with these words, the woman's desire has been fulfilled, she completes the introductory movement by imploring the daughters of Jerusalem to let love happen according to its own rhythm:

> I adjure you, O daughters of Jerusalem,
>   by the gazelles or the hinds of the field,
> that you stir not up nor awaken love
>   until it please.
>
> (2:7, RSV)

Having begun the first movement by seeking the touch of her lover's mouth, the woman commences the second (2:8—3:5) by invoking the speech of his lips:[7]

> The voice of my lover!
> Behold, he comes,
> leaping upon the mountains,
> bounding over the hills.
> (2:8, RSV*)

She concludes this section by seeking and finding her man:

> Upon my bed by night
> I sought him whom my *nephesh* loves;
> I sought him, but found him not;
> I called him, but he gave no answer.
> "I will rise now and go about the city,
> in the streets and in the squares;
> I will seek him whom my *nephesh* loves."
> I sought him but found him not.
> The watchmen found me,
> as they went about in the city.
> Him whom my *nephesh* loves, have you seen?
> Scarcely had I passed them,
> when I found him whom my *nephesh* loves.
> I held him, and would not let him go
> until I had brought him into my mother's house,
> and into the chamber of her that conceived me.
> (3:1–4, RSV*)

The motifs of the search, the watchmen, and the mother's house surface again in various combinations in the conclusions of the third and fourth movements. Coming together here in the encounter of love, they allow the woman to close this second movement exactly as she did the first. Thus, she implores the daughters of Jerusalem to let love happen according to its own rhythm (3:5).

She opens the third movement (3:6—5:8) with a question about her lover:

> What is that coming up from the wilderness,
> like a column of smoke,
> perfumed with myrrh and frankincense,
> with all the fragrant powders of the merchant?
> (3:6, RSV)

To end this section, she returns, with variations, to two of the themes at the conclusion of the second movement: the seeking, but not the finding, of the lover and her discovery by the watchmen, who this time not only fail to help but actually assault her:

> My *nephesh* failed because of him.
> I sought him, but found him not;
>   I called him, but he gave no answer.
> The watchmen found me,
>   as they went about in the city;
> they beat me, they wounded me,
> they took away my mantle,
>   those watchmen of the walls.
>   (5:6c–7, RSV*)

Exact verbal correspondences between the endings of movements two and three establish parallelism in their structure and content. The differences between them, on the other hand, sustain the tempo and flow of the poetry. Point and counterpoint shape the rhythm of love:

3:1–3a (Second Movement)	*5:6b–7 (Third Movement)*
Upon my bed by night	My *nephesh* failed because of
I sought him whom my	him.
nephesh loves;	
I sought him but found him not;	I sought him, but found him not;
I called him but he gave no	I called him, but he gave no
answer.	answer.
"I will rise now and go about the city,	
in the streets and in the squares;	
I will seek him whom my *nephesh* loves."	
I sought him but found him not.	
The watchmen found me,	The watchmen found me,
as they went about in the city.	as they went about in the city;
(RSV*)	they beat me, they wounded me,
	they took away my mantle,
	those watchmen of the walls.
	(RSV*)

At the very end of the third movement, the woman alters the refrain of adjuration to fit the situation that now exists. Since,

contrary to the ending of the second movement (3:4), she does
not find her lover, she enlists the daughters of Jerusalem in her
search:

I adjure you, O daughters of Jerusalem,
 if you find my lover,
that you tell him
 I am sick with love.

(5:8, RSV*)

The words "I am sick with love" repeat a line from the closing
sentiments of the first section (2:5), thereby showing another
interplay among the motifs of the poem.[8] Although these words
led to fulfillment in the first movement, here they but long for
consummation.

Linked closely to the third movement, the fourth (5:9—8:4)
commences with questions by the daughters, who are responding to the woman's plea in the preceding refrain of adjuration:

What is your lover more than another lover,
 O fairest among women?
What is your lover more than another lover
 that you thus adjure us?

(5:9, RSV*)

This interrogative style parallels the woman's question at the
beginning of the third section. And the closing speech (8:1-3) of
the fourth movement belongs again to the woman. She caresses
the man with her voice:

O that you were like a brother to me,
 that nursed at my mother's breast!
If I met you outside, I would kiss you,
 and none would despise me.
I would lead you and bring you
 into the house of my mother,
 and into the chamber of her that conceived me.
I would give you spiced wine to drink,
 the juice of my pomegranates.
His left hand is under my head,
 and his right hand embraces me!

(8:1-3, RSV*)

Like the end of the third section, this conclusion also returns, with variations, to motifs first appearing at the end of the second movement: finding the lover and bringing him to the house of the mother who conceived her. In the second movement, the woman sought the help of the watchmen and then spoke about her actions toward her lover (3:1–3). Now in the fourth, she addresses her intentions to him directly. Though her reference to "none would despise me" may allude to the watchmen who have since assaulted her, that group is not involved in this ending. Once again, however, exact verbal correspondences between the conclusions of two movements confirm the parallelism in their structure and content, while, on the other hand, differences between them enhance the rhythm of the poetry:

3:3b–4 (Second Movement)	8:1–2a (Fourth Movement)
Him whom my *nephesh* loves, have you seen?	O that you were like a brother to me, that nursed at my mother's breast!
Scarcely had I passed them when I found him whom my *nephesh* loves.	If I found you outside, I would kiss you, and none would despise me.
I held him and would not let him go until I had brought him into my mother's house, and into the chamber of her that conceived me.	I would lead you and bring you into my mother's house and into the chamber of her that conceived me.
(RSV*)	(RSV*)

The word *kiss* in the speech of the woman to the man (8:1c) recalls the opening line of the first movement, "O that he would kiss me with the kisses of his mouth" (1:2). The touch she desired, she now gives: "If I found you outside, I would kiss you." Moreover, in the beginning of the first section, she declared that his "love is better than wine" (1:2b, RSV), and at its end she reported that "he brought me to the *house* of wine" (2:4). Now, immediately after leading her lover to the *house* of her mother, she says:

I would give you spiced wine to drink,
the juice of my pomegranates.
(8:2, RSV)

These allusions to the introductory movement are confirmed by the ensuing words of the woman. They repeat verbatim her last statement in the opening section:

> His left hand is under my head
>   and his right hand embraces me!
> (8:3)

With this description the woman ceases to address the man directly and returns to the pattern of third-person narration that she has consistently used at the end of all the preceding movements. Thus she wavers between distance and intimacy.

Finally, the refrain of the fourth movement echoes, with variation, the adjurations of the first and second. Though the gazelles and the hinds of the fields are missing, the rhythm of love is again affirmed:

> I adjure you, O daughters of Jerusalem,
>   that you stir not up nor awaken love
> until it please.
> (8:4, RSV)

Like the third and fourth movements, the fifth (8:5–14) begins with a question. Perhaps the daughters ask it, since they similarly introduced the fourth movement.

> Who is that coming up from the wilderness,
>   leaning upon her lover?
> (8:5, RSV*)

To conclude this unit, the woman speaks, as indeed she has done at the close of each section. In all these instances, she has referred to the man in the third person, though in the fourth movement she also addressed him directly. In this final movement, however, distance and ambivalence vanish altogether. Intimacy triumphs. The woman summons her man to love:

> Make haste, my lover,
>   and be like a gazelle
> or a young stag
>   upon the mountains of spices.
> (8:14, RSV*)

No refrain of adjuration follows these closing words: with the consummation of Eros it is unnecessary. Thus, the daughters of Jerusalem disappear, and we, the readers, must also withdraw. Just as the first words of the woman at the very beginning of the Song invited us to enter the circle of intimacy (1:2a), so her last words deny us further participation. In the end she speaks directly and only to her lover, the bone of her bone and the flesh of her flesh. The man of Genesis 2 once left his father and mother to cleave to his woman (v. 24); now the woman of the Song bids her man make haste, and in this bidding all others are left behind. The circle of intimacy closes in exclusion when two become one.

As a symphony of love, the Song of Songs unfolds in five major movements: 1:2—2:7; 2:8—3:5; 3:6—5:8; 5:9—8:4; 8:5-14. The beginnings and endings of these sections demonstrate the interweaving of cyclic patterns in the overall structure.[9] Through the convergence of form and content, these patterns recall cyclic designs throughout Genesis 2.[10] Moreover, several themes in Genesis 2:21-24 have also enhanced our reading of this musical score: the creation and consummation of sexuality; an erotic poem; emphasis upon the female in the design of the literature; and the absence of God when female and male unite. Building upon this interpretation, let us explore leitmotifs within the Song of Songs that further reflect and elucidate Genesis 2—3.

EXPLORING VARIATIONS ON A THEME

A garden (*gan*) in Eden locates the tragedy of disobedience in Genesis 2—3. But the garden itself signals delight, not disaster, and that perspective reverberates in the Song of Songs. The woman is the garden (*gan*), and to the garden her lover comes. This vocabulary appears first in the third movement when the man describes love withheld:[11]

A garden locked is my sister, my bride,
a garden locked, a fountain sealed.
(4:12, RSV; cf. 4:15)

Immediately the woman responds, offering her garden to him:

> Awake, O north wind,
>   and come, O south wind!
> Blow upon *my* garden,
>   let its fragrance be wafted abroad.
> Let my lover come to *his* garden,
>   and eat its choicest fruits.
>   (4:16, RSV*; cf. 4:13)

The man accepts the invitation, claiming her garden as his own:

> I come to *my* garden, my sister, my bride (5:1a, RSV).

This imagery of intercourse continues in the fourth movement. Answering questions from the daughters of Jerusalem, the woman says:

> My lover has gone down to his garden,
>   to the beds of spices,
> to pasture in the gardens,
>   and to gather lilies.
>   (6:2, RSV*; cf. 6:11)

And in the fifth movement, the last words of the man address the woman with the same motif:

> O you who dwell in the gardens,
>   my companions are listening for your voice;
>   let me hear it.
>   (8:13, RSV)

Male and female first became one flesh in the garden of Eden. There a narrator reported briefly their sexual union (Gen. 2:24). Now in another garden, the lovers themselves praise at length the joys of intercourse. Possessive adjectives do not separate their lives. "My garden" and "his garden" blend in mutual habitation and harmony. Even person and place unite: the garden of eroticism is the woman.

In this garden the sensuality of Eden expands and deepens. Emerging gradually in Genesis 2—3, all five senses capitulated to disobedience through the tasting of the forbidden fruit. Fully present in the Song of Songs from the beginning, these senses saturate the poetry to serve only love. Such love is sweet to the taste, like the fruit of the apple tree (2:3; cf. 4:16; 5:1, 13). Fragrant are the smells of the vineyards (2:13), the perfumes of myrrh and frankincense (3:6), the scent of Lebanon (4:11), and the beds of spices (5:13; 6:2). The embraces of lovers confirm the delights of touch (1:2; 2:3–6; 4:10, 11; cf. 5:1; 7:6–9; 8:1, 3). A glance of the eyes ravishes the heart (4:9; 6:13), as the sound of the lover thrills it (5:2). Taste, smell, touch, sight, and hearing permeate the garden of the Song.

Plants also adorn this place of pleasure—"every tree that is pleasant to the sight and good for food" (Gen. 2:9, RSV). Again, what the storyteller in Genesis reported succinctly, the voices in the Song praise extensively. They name not only the trees, but also the fruits and the flowers. For instance, in the first movement the woman describes herself to the man:

> I am a lotus of the plain,
>   a lily of the valleys.
>   (2:1)

The word *lily* suggests to the man an extravagant comparison, to which even the thorns and thistles of the earth (cf. Gen. 3:18) contribute:

> As a lily among brambles,
>   so is my love among women.
>   (2:2, RSV*)

The woman replies in kind:

> As an apple among the trees of the wood,
>   so is my lover among men.
>   (2:3a, RSV*)

Yet her comparison does not stop there. She expands upon images from the plant world to portray the joy her lover embodies:

> In his shadow I delight to rest
>   and his fruit is sweet to my taste.
> He brought me to the house of wine
>   and his emblem over me was love.

Strengthen me with raisin cakes,
   refresh me with apples,
for faint with love am I.
   (2:3b–5; cf. *NAB*)

Throughout the Song of Songs other members of the plant world further specify "every tree pleasant to the sight and good for food": the mandrake (7:13), the fig tree (2:13), the pomegranate (4:3, 13; 6:7), the cedar (5:15), the palm (7:8), and "all trees of frankincense" (4:14, RSV). And among these many plants, no tree of disobedience grows (cf. Gen. 2:16–17). Instead, the lovers offer an open invitation to eat freely of every tree of the garden, as well as to drink from its fountain of delight.[13] In their world of harmony, prohibition does not exist:

Eat, O friends, and drink:
   drink deeply, O lovers!
   (5:1e, RSV)

The invitation to drink follows a description of the abundance of water that fills the garden:

a garden fountain, a well of living water,
   and flowing streams from Lebanon.
   (4:15, RSV; cf. 4:12)

This imagery recalls the subterranean stream that watered the earth before creation (Gen. 2:6) and clearly invites comparison with the river flowing out of Eden to nourish that garden (Gen. 2:10–14). In both settings, food and water enhance life.

Animals as well inhabit these two gardens. In Genesis 2:18–20 their creation was marked with ambivalence. Closely identified with the earth creature, they were, nevertheless, a disappointment, for among them "was not found a companion fit for it." Indeed, the power which the earth creature exercised in naming the animals underscored their inadequacy for humankind. Yet, conversely, the animals provided a context for the joy of human sexuality. In Genesis 3, however, the ambivalence of their creation yielded completely to the villainous portrayal of the serpent. The most clever of all wild animals beguiled the naked couple to become their perpetual enemy (3:14). In the garden of Eden, then, the animals lived in tension with the human creatures.

But in the garden of the Song of Songs this tension disappears. No serpent bruises the heel of female or male; no animals are indicted as unfit companions for humankind. To the contrary, the beasts of the field and the birds of the air (cf. Gen. 2:19) now become synonyms for human joy. Their names are metaphors for love. Scattered throughout the movements of the poetry, these creatures are often used for physical descriptions of the lovers. In the opening poem of the second movement, for example, the woman limns her mate:

> leaping upon the mountains,
>   bounding over the hills,
> My lover is like a gazelle,
>   or a young stag.
>   (2:8, 9a, RSV*; cf. 2:17b)

To these images she returns in the closing lines of the Song (8:14). In other places she compares her lover's black hair to a raven and his eyes to "doves beside springs of water" (5:11–12, RSV). Similarly, the man depicts the beauty of the woman in animal metaphors:[13]

> Behold, you are beautiful, my love,
>   behold, you are beautiful!
> Your eyes are doves
>   behind your veil.
> Your hair is like a flock of goats,
>   moving down the slopes of Gilead.
> Your teeth are like a flock of shorn ewes
>   that have come up from the washing,
> Each having its twin,
>   and not one of them is bereaved.
>   (4:1–2, RSV*)
> . . . .
> Your two breasts are like two fawns,
>   twins of a gazelle,
>   that feed among the lilies.
>   (4:5, RSV; cf. 7:3)

The mare (1:9), the turtledove (2:12), and the lions and the leopards (4:8) also dwell in this garden where all nature extols the love of female and male. Clearly, the Song of Songs banishes the ambivalence toward animals that Genesis 2 introduced, just as it knows nothing of the villainous serpent in Genesis 3. Even the little foxes that spoil the vineyards can be captured by love (2:15). Thus, all animals serve Eros.

Work and play belong together in both the garden of creation and the garden of eroticism. To till and keep the garden of Eden was delight until the primeval couple disobeyed, causing the ground to bring forth thorns and thistles and work to become pain and sweat (Gen. 2:15; 3:16, 18–19). In the first movement of the Song of Songs, the woman transforms the pain of work into pleasure. At the command of her mother's sons, she keeps vineyards under the scorching sun; yet, undaunted by this experience of forced labor, she associates it with play:

> The sons of my mother were angry at me;
> they made me keeper of the vineyards.
> My own vineyard I have not kept![14]
> (1:6, RSV*)

Identifying herself with a vineyard, the woman hints that her lover is *its* keeper. Such playfulness directs her to the man, with another allusion to work:

> Tell me, you whom my *nephesh* loves,
> where do you pasture?
> (1:7a)

The man may well be a shepherd, but for the woman his occupation is the play of intercourse. After all, he pastures among the lilies (2:16; 6:3), and she herself is a lily (2:1, 2).[15] By analogy, the man is also a king (1:4, 12; 8:11, 12), but he neither rules nor dispenses wisdom. Instead, he provides luxury for the sake of love.[16] Hence, throughout the garden of the Song, sexual play intertwines with work, redeeming it beyond the judgments of Genesis 3:16–19.

Familial references offer still another study in contrasts. Although in Genesis 2 the creation of male and female was totally independent of parents, in the Song of Songs the births of the lovers are linked to their mothers, though the fathers are never mentioned. Seven times, at least once in every movement, the word *mother* appears in the poetry. The man calls his love the special child of the mother who bore (*yld*) her (6:9), even as the woman cites the travail of the mother who bore (*yld*) him (8:5). Appropriately, both these references allude to the beauty of birth; they know nothing at all of the multiplication of pain in childbearing (cf. Gen. 3:16). Moreover, in yearning for closeness with her lover, the woman wishes that he were a brother nursing at the breast of her mother (8:1). Again, she parallels the desire for sexual union with her own conception; thus, she wants to lead the man

> into the house of my mother,
> and into the chamber of her
> that conceived me.
> (3:4; 8:2, RSV*)

This entry into the mother's house for intercourse suggests its opposite in Genesis 2:24. There the man broke up a family for the sake of sexual union. He left his father and mother to cleave to his woman. Standing alone, without parents, the woman was highlighted as the one to whom he must come. In the Song, the woman is emphasized, by contrast, as the one who brings the man into her mother's house. From different perspectives, two other passages in the Song also mention the mother. The woman identifies her brothers as "sons of my mother" (1:6), and later she beholds King Solomon

> with the crown with which his mother crowned him
> on the day of his wedding,
> on the day of the gladness of his heart.
> (3:11, RSV)

Unquestionably, these seven references to mother, without a single mention of father, underscore anew the prominence of the female in the lyrics of love. Once again, then, the Song of Songs expands and varies a theme present in Genesis 2—3.

Belonging to a historical rather than a primeval setting, the Song also extends the witnesses to love beyond the human inhabitants of Eden.[17] Certain groups are hostile, for not all the world loves a lover. Specifically, the woman encounters anger from her brothers (1:6) and physical assault from the watchmen of the city (5:7; cf. 2:3). But other witnesses celebrate the happiness and beauty of the lovers: kings (1:9; 3:7; 4:4); queens and concubines (6:8, 9); warriors (3:7; 6:4), indeed, an army with banners (6:4, 10); merchants with their fragrant powders (3:6); shepherds (1:7–8); and the daughters of Jerusalem. Moreover, the woman herself exults that other women, as well as men, adore her mate. In their attraction for him, she finds joy, not jealousy:

> your name is oil poured out;
> therefore, *the maidens* love you.
> Draw me after you, let us make haste.
> The king has brought me into his chambers.
> We will exult and rejoice in you;
> we will extol your love more than wine;
> rightly do *they* [masculine] love you.
> (1:3b–4, RSV)

Similarly, the man rejoices that other men, as well as women, delight in his partner:

> O you who dwell in the gardens,
> *my companions* [masculine] are listening for your voice;
> let me hear it.
> (8:13, RSV)

> The maidens saw her and called her happy;
> *the queens and concubines* also, and they praised her.
> (6:9b, RSV)

Throughout the Song, Eros is inclusive; the love between two welcomes the love and companionship of many. Only at the end does exclusion close this circle of intimacy.

On two occasions (2:16; 6:3) the woman expresses intimacy by the formula "My lover is mine, and I am his." This interchange of pronouns parallels the union of "my garden" with "his garden" (4:16). Love is harmony. Neither male nor female asserts power or possession over the other. In light of Genesis 3:16, a third expression of this idea is particularly striking. The woman says, "I am my lover's and for me is his desire" (7:10). Her use of the word *desire* (*tᵉšûqâ*) echoes, in contrast, the divine judgment upon the first woman: "Your desire [*tᵉšûqâ*] shall be for your man, but he shall rule over you."[18] In Eden, the yearning of the woman for harmony with her man continued after disobedience. Yet the man did not reciprocate; instead, he ruled over her to destroy unity and pervert sexuality. Her desire became his dominion. But in the Song, male power vanishes. His desire becomes her delight. Another consequence of disobedience is thus redeemed through the recovery of mutuality in the garden of eroticism. Appropriately, the woman sings the lyrics of this grace: "I am my lover's and for me is his desire."

A further hint of redemption comes in the way the word *name* is used in the two gardens. When the transformed earth creature called the woman '*iššâ* (and himself '*îš*), he did not name her but rather rejoiced in the creation of sexuality (Gen. 2:23). But when the disobedient man called his woman's *name* (*šēm*) Eve, he ruled over her to destroy their one flesh of equality (Gen. 3:20). On the other hand, the opening lines of the Song of Songs convert the motif of the name to the service of sexual fulfillment. The woman herself utters this word in a pun of adoration for the man:

> For better is your love than wine;
>   your anointing oils are fragrant;
> oil [*šemen*] poured out is your *name* [*šᵉmekā*].
>   (1:2b–3, RSV*)

Rather than following her man out of the garden (cf. Gen. 3:23–24), this woman bids him bring her to his palace of pleasure: "Draw me after you, let us make haste" (1:4, RSV). For her, naming is ecstasy, not dominion. A new context marks a new creation.

Love redeemed meets even death unflinchingly.[19] Although the threat of death belonged to the creation of Eros (Gen. 2:17), it was through human disobedience that death became the disintegration of life. Harmony gave way to hostility; unity and fulfillment to fragmentation and dispersion. In the closing movement of the Song of Songs, this tragedy is reversed. Once again, eroticism can embrace the threat of death. The woman says:[20]

Let me be a seal upon your heart,
Like the seal upon your hand.
For love is fierce as death,
Passion is mighty as Sheol;
Its darts are darts of fire,
A blazing flame.

(8:6)

But she does more than affirm love as the equal of death. She asserts triumphantly that not even the primeval waters of chaos can destroy Eros:

Many waters cannot quench love,
neither can floods drown it.

(8:7, RSV)

As a "garden fountain, a well of living water [*mayîm ḥayyîm*]" (4:15, RSV), a woman in love prevails over the many waters (*mayîm rabbîm*) of chaos. With such assurances, the poetry moves inexorably to its consummation.

COMPLETING THE SONG

Using Genesis 2—3 as a key for understanding the Song of Songs, we have participated in a symphony of love. Born to mutuality and harmony, a man and a woman live in a garden where nature and history unite to celebrate the one flesh of sexuality. Naked without shame or fear (cf. Gen. 2:25; 3:10), this couple treat each other with tenderness and respect. Neither escaping nor exploiting sex, they embrace and enjoy it. Their love is truly bone of bone and flesh of flesh, and this image of God male and female is indeed very good (cf. Gen. 1:27, 31). Testifying to the goodness of creation, then, eroticism becomes worship in the context of grace.[21]

In this setting, there is no male dominance, no female subordination, and no stereotyping of either sex.[22] Specifically, the portrayal of the woman defies the connotations of "second sex." She works, keeping vineyards and pasturing flocks. Throughout the Song she is independent, fully the equal of the man. Although at times he approaches her, more often she initiates their meetings. Her movements are bold and open: at night in the streets and squares of the city she seeks the one whom her *neph-esh* loves (3:1–4). No secrecy hides her yearnings. Moreover, she dares to describe love with revealing metaphors:

> My lover put his hand to the latch,
> and my womb trembled within me.
>   (5:4)

Never is this woman called a wife, nor is she required to bear children. In fact, to the issues of marriage and procreation the Song does not speak.[23] Love for the sake of love is its message,[24] and the portrayal of the female delineates this message best.

Though love is fulfilled when the woman and the man close the circle of intimacy to all but themselves (8:13–14), my imagination posits a postlude to the poetry. In this fantasy "the cherubim and a flaming sword" appear to guard the entrance to the garden of the Song (cf. Gen. 3:24). They keep out those who lust, moralize, legislate, or exploit. They also turn away literalists. But at all times they welcome lovers to romp and roam in the joys of eroticism:

> Arise, my love, my fair one,
>   and come away;
> for lo, the winter is past,
>   the rain is over and gone.
> The flowers appear on the earth,
>   the time of pruning has come,
> and the voice of the turtledove
>   is heard in our land.
> The fig tree puts forth its figs,
>   and the vines are in blossom;
>   they give forth fragrance.
> Arise, my love, my fair one,
>   and come away.
>   (2:10–13, RSV*)

Thus far we have studied two portrayals of male and female in the Old Testament. Genesis 2—3 depicted a tragedy of disobedience; the Song of Songs, a symphony of eroticism. Yet somewhere between tragedy and ecstasy lie the struggles of daily life. For an understanding of male and female in this setting, we turn to the book of Ruth.

LOVE'S LYRICS REDEEMED   163

NOTES

1. On the history of interpretation, see H. H. Rowley, "The Interpretation of the Song of Songs," in *The Servant of the Lord and Other Essays* (London: Lutterworth Press, 1952), pp. 189–234; Christian D. Ginsburg, *The Song of Songs and Coheleth* (New York: KTAV, 1970), pp. 20–126. Cf. Roland E. Murphy, "Towards a Commentary on the Song of Songs," *CBQ* 39 (1977): 482–96. The commentary by Marvin H. Pope arrived too late to inform my essay (*Song of Songs, AB* [New York: Doubleday, 1977]).

2. This elusiveness is of two kinds: (1) passages where the meaning of the Hebrew itself is uncertain (see the notes in 'H. L. Ginsberg, *The Five Megilloth and Jonah* [Philadelphia: Jewish Publication Society, 1969], pp. 5–17); (2) passages difficult to understand in their present context (e.g., 2:15 and 8:8).

3. E.g., the invitation in 5:1ef to eat and drink deeply has been variously attributed to the poet (Gillis Gerleman, *Ruth—Das Hohelied, Biblischer Kommentar· Altes Testament* [Neukirchen-Vluyn: Neukirchener Verlag, 1965], p. 162); to some of the daughters of Jerusalem (Ginsburg, *The Song of Songs and Coheleth*, p. 163); to a chorus (Hugh J. Schonfield, *The Song of Songs* [New York: New American Library, 1959], p. 111); to the man (L. Krinetzki, *Das Hohe Lied* [Düsseldorf, 1964], p. 177); and to the woman (Robert Gordis, *The Song of Songs* [New York: Jewish Theological Seminary of America, 1954], p. 61). Similarly, 8:5a is assigned to the daughters of Jerusalem in the *NAB*, but to the man by Roland E. Murphy, "The Structure of the Canticle of Canticles," *CBQ* 11 (1949): 391. Other passages in which the identity of the speaker is uncertain include 3:6ff.; 7:1–2; and 8:11–12.

4. Cf. Roland E. Murphy, "Form-Critical Studies in the Song of Songs," *Int.* 27 (1973): 417.

5. Central in the erotic revelation of Gen. 2:23 are the sexual designations *'iššâ* and *'iš*. In the Song, the word *'iššâ* appears as a plural in a refrain that extols the beauty of the female lover above other women (1:8; 5:9; 6:1); the two occurrences of the word *'iš* (3:8; 8:7) do not refer to the male lover. Superseding this vocabulary, then, are terms of endearment, such as *sister* and *bride* (4:9–12), *brother* (8:1) and *king* (1:4, 12). The dominant expressions are *dôdî*, used by the woman for the man, and *ra'yāh*, used by the man for the woman. I translate the former as "lover" (so *NAB*) and the latter as "love" (so RSV). I avoid the word *beloved* altogether, but especially for the woman, since it connotes a passivity that is incongruous with her portrayal throughout the Song.

6. Stylistic and rhetorical analyses of the Song of Songs differ widely in their results; with the suggestions offered here, cf., e.g., Franz Landsberger, "Poetic Units Within the Song of Songs," *JBL* 73 (1954): 203–16; Krinetzki, *Das Hohe Lied;* J. Angénieux, "Structure du Cantique des Cantiques," *Ephemerides theologicae lovanienses* 41 (1965): 96–142; Gerleman, *Ruth—Das Hohelied*, pp. 52–62; J. Cheryl Exum, "A Literary and Structural Analysis of the Song of Songs," *Zeitschrift für die alttestamentliche Wissenschaft* 85 (1973): 47–79. Cf. the English verse translation by Marcia Falk, *The Song of Songs* (New York: Harcourt Brace Jovanovich, 1977).

7. Chapter 2:8–17 constitutes the first of the two major units within the second movement; 3:1 ʼ4, the second unit. Near the beginning of this first unit (2:9a) the woman describes her lover "like a gazelle, or a young stag" (RSV); at the end (2:17b), she urges her lover to be "like a gazelle, or a young stag . . ." (RSV). Within this inclusion is another ring composition enclosed by the words "Arise, my love . . ." (vv. 10, 13). Throughout the entire unit the motif of the voice (*qôl*) is prominent (vv. 8, 12, 14). The second unit also forms an inclusion. Seeking "him whom my *nephesh* loves" (3:1) concludes in "finding him whom my *nephesh* loves" (3:4). Observe also two additional occurrences of this phrase within the unit (3:2, 3). Cf. Exum, "A Literary and Structural Analysis," pp. 54–55.

8. Cf. also the sentiment "your love is sweeter than wine." In the first movement, the woman addresses these words to the man (1:2); in the third, the man to the woman (4:10).

9. I have not examined all correspondences among these five movements but rather have concentrated upon the repetitions that delineate each section. The overall cyclic design is further evidenced by words and themes within the fifth movement that return to the first. For example, 8:11–13 returns to 1:5–7 (cf. keepers, vineyards, Solomon, and companions). Cf. also the repetitions, with variations, of the motifs of love (1:3–4 and 8:6–7); mother (1:6 and 8:5); cedar (1:17 and 8:9); fruit (2:3 and 8:11–12); and apple tree (2:3 and 8:5).

10. Cf. the discussion of the structure of Gen. 2 in Chapter 4.

11. On the metaphors in 4:12—5:1, see Edwin M. Good, "Ezekiel's Ship: Some Extended Metaphors in the Old Testament," *Semitics* 1 (1970): 94–97.

12. On eating, see also SS 2:3; 4:16; 5:1c; on drinking, 5:1d.

13. These descriptions of the physical beauty of a lover are known by the Arabic term *wasf*. For a discussion of this genre in 4:1–7, see Murphy, "Form-Critical Studies," pp. 418–20. Cf. Richard N. Soulen, "The *Wasfs* of the Song of Songs and Hermeneutic," *JBL* 86 (1967): 183–90.

14. Note the chiasm of keeper/vineyard/vineyard/kept.

15. Used in 1:7, 2:16, and 6:3, the verb *pasture* (*rʻh*) has no direct object in the Hebrew text. Frequently, translators supply the object *sheep* (or *flock*) to make the man a shepherd (so RSV, *NEB, JB, NAB*). More likely, the verb is a *double entendre* for erotic play.

16. See Albert Cook, *The Root of the Thing* (Bloomington: Indiana University Press, 1968), pp. 106, 125.

17. The setting of the Song of Songs is neither primeval nor eschatological. The lovers do not live before the advent of disobedience. Nor do they belong to a future yet unrealized; *contra* Karl Barth, *Church Dogmatics*, vol. 3, pt. 2 (Edinburgh: T. & T. Clark, 1960), pp. 291–300. Instead, they depict a present reality.

18. Thus, two of the three occurrences of this word *desire* in the Old Testament belong to sexual contexts; the third (Gen. 4:7) is altogether different.

19. Cf. Cook, *The Root of the Thing*, pp. 146–51.

20. For this translation, see Ginsberg, *The Five Megilloth and Jonah*, p. 16.

21. Cf. Kornelis H. Miskotte, *When the Gods Are Silent* (London: Collins, 1967), pp. 265ff.

22. *Contra,* e.g., Franz Rosenzweig, *The Star of Redemption* (Boston: Beacon Press, 1972), pp. 156, 199–204; and Miskotte, *When the Gods are Silent,* pp. 268–71.

23. Note the absence of any reference to procreation for the couple in Gen. 2; see above, Chapter 4. Cf. also the references to the female bearing (*yld*) children in Gen. 3:16 and SS 8:5.

24. Cf. Brevard S. Childs, *Biblical Theology in Crisis* (Philadelphia: Westminster Press, 1970), pp. 192ff. Gerleman, *Ruth—Das Hohelied,* pp. 72–75, 83–85.

CHAPTER 6

A Human Comedy

A man's world tells a woman's story [1] With consummate artistry, the book of Ruth presents the aged Naomi and the youthful Ruth as they struggle for survival in a patriarchal environment. These women bear their own burdens. They know hardship, danger, insecurity, and death. No God promises them blessing; no man rushes to their rescue. They themselves risk bold decisions and shocking acts to work out their own salvation in the midst of the alien, the hostile, and the unknown.

Four scenes mark the contours of this story.[2] These scenes form a circular pattern whereby the third and fourth return to the concerns of the second and first. Variations of this design appear within each scene so that the parts shape the whole and the whole molds the parts. This total symmetry lends integrity to the story; it sets it apart as an aesthetic object; and it embraces meaning as inseparable from form and content.

Underlying this surface design are the deep structures of relations that generate it.[3] On the human level, females and males move between life and death. On the divine level, God works between blessing and curse. The human movements are open and deliberate, while the divine activity is hidden and fortuitous. In many forms, these basic opposites produce tension in the narrative even as they converge to effect transformation and resolution.

DEATH ABOUNDING

SCENE ONE: CHAPTER 1

A. Introduction: vv. 1–7. (1) The story begins in the tension of grammar (vv. 1–5). Third-person narration names the charac-

166

ters, specifies their relationships, and describes their plight, but
it does not allow them to emerge as human beings. Subjects of
verbs, they are objects of discourse; spoken about, they do not
speak. Accordingly, they hover between person and nonperson.
This grammatical tension is their existential tension. Confronted
with famine, four characters hover between life (person) and
death (nonperson). Thus the form of the introduction mirrors
content, and its content mirrors form.

A famine in the land of Judah motivates a sojourn in the
country of Moab. While native soil offers death, foreign soil
offers life. Hence, a healthy family departs a sick land. True
to patriarchal custom, Elimelech the father leads this journey. Accompanying him are Naomi, his devoted and traditional
wife, and *his*—thus the text reads—his two sons, Mahlon and
Chilion. The fullness of this family corresponds to fertility in the
land of Moab. Yet recovered harmony between land and family
shatters soon, this time not from the natural but from the human
side. Elimelech dies. Naomi becomes a widow, though not without hope, since the narrator transfers the parental claim from
the dead father to the living mother. Naomi is "left with *her* two
children" (v. 3).[4] Furthermore, the storyteller moves swiftly to
overcome the incompleteness of the family by reporting that the
sons take Moabite wives, Orpah and Ruth. These marriages contrast with that of Elimelech and Naomi. Exogamy opposes en-
dogamy.[5] But the opposition is complementary. The foreign
land of Moab, which has already given to a Judahite family food
(life) in the face of famine (death), now restores that depleted
family to a transformed whole and provides it with a possible
future (life) through the continuation of the family line.

The comfort of this news is short-lived. In four Hebrew words,
ten years pass without the arrival of a third generation. Mahlon
and Chilion die. With death again canceling life, a whole family
shrinks to a solitary figure. Naomi stands alone. The narration
focuses entirely upon her, but it avoids her name. "The woman,"
it says, "was bereft of her two children and her husband" (v. 5).
From wife to widow, from mother to no-mother, this female is
stripped of all identity. The security of husband and children,
which a male-dominated culture affords its women, is hers no
longer. The definition of worth, by which it values the female,

applies to her no more. The blessings of old age, which it gives through progeny, are there no longer. Stranger in a foreign land, this woman is a victim of death—and of life.

(2) The extremities of Naomi's predicament signal change, which both grammar and content confirm (vv. 6–7). For the first time, she becomes the subject of active verbs. A nonperson inches toward personhood. Still the storyteller is cautious. She or he continues to withhold the name of this woman while speaking about her. Thus it is the pronoun *she* who "started with her daughters-in-law to return from the country of Moab" (RSV). It is *she* who heard "that the Lord had visited his people and given them food" (RSV). It is *she* who then "set out from the place where *she* was" (RSV).

These words of change belong to a transitional passage that carries a double function: to complete the introduction and to prepare for the dialogue. It accomplishes the first function through inclusion. The introduction begins with an exodus from Judah (v. 1); now it ends with the announcement of a return to that land (v. 7). It begins with the problem of famine; now it answers with the promise of food. It begins with a man choosing a future for his family; now it ends with a woman—the sole survivor of that family—choosing her own future. Within this ring structure, the themes of land, food, and family have contrasted, crisscrossed, and coalesced as they alternate between life and death. In these ways the conclusion of the introduction completes the beginning, yet with differences.

The differences aid the second function of the passage: to prepare for dialogue. First, by making Naomi the subject of verbs, the third-person narration anticipates her active role. Second, by twice using the verb *return*, it heralds a central emphasis. Third, by reporting twice that the two daughters-in-law accompany the aged widow, it points to major tension. Thus by the structure of grammar, by the use of key words, and by the release of information, verses 6–7 lead the hearers from introduction to dialogue. This double function of completion and continuation resolves the grammatical-existential tension between person and nonperson, between life and death. Resolution comes along sexual lines. The males die; they are nonpersons; their presence in the story ceases (though their absence continues). The females live; they are persons; their presence in the story continues. Indeed, their life is the life of the story. One set of opposites has worked its way to a resolution that in turn generates other sets of opposites.

B. Body: vv. 8–21. (1) Precisely at the point where third-person narration yields to dialogue, where introduction leads to action, women take over the story (vv. 8–14). In this entire first episode, no men are present; women alone speak and act. And furthermore, that solitary widow, who has been stripped of all identity, is now, at the place of poetic speech, given back her name.[6] *Naomi* speaks to her daughters-in-law:

A   Go, return each of you to her mother's house.

B   May the Lord deal kindly with you,

C   as you have dealt with the dead and with me.

B'   The Lord grant that you may find a home,

A'   each of you in the house of her husband.

(1:8, RSV)

Age commands youth; a Judahite advises Moabites; one counters two. Yet as childless widows, these three are one.

Unexpected in a patriarchal culture is the phrase "mother's house."[7] Yet the words are singularly appropriate here. Mother-in-law opposes mother. In addition, this phrase emphasizes the radical separation of these females from all males. It juxtaposes present reality with past and future. Once these women were wives of husbands, and that status would be desirable again. Meanwhile, however, they are women without men. Hence, "to her mother's house" each young woman is urged to return (RSV).[8]

In this speech, Naomi invokes the *ḥesed* ("kindness") of Yahweh.[9] Now the basis for her invocation is not a past action by Yahweh to which Naomi can point as insurance for future goodness, because the past has meant only famine, dislocation, and death. It offers no intimations of divine blessing. Strikingly, the basis upon which Naomi invokes Yahweh's *ḥesed* is the gracious hospitality of her daughters-in-law: "May the Lord deal kindly with you, *as you have [already] dealt with the dead and with me*" (RSV). At the heart of Naomi's poem, both in structure and in meaning, these female foreigners become models for Yahweh. They show the deity a more excellent way. Once again, levels of opposites meet and crisscross: the past loyalty of human beings (foreign women, at that) is a paradigm for the future kindness of the divine being.

After her first speech, Naomi kisses her two daughters-in-law in an act of farewell. They lift up their voices and weep. But the scene is not over. Naomi has ordered, "Return each of you to her mother's house" (v. 8, RSV). The young widows reply by returning these words to their mother-in-law: "No, we will return with you to your people" (v. 10, RSV). The vocabulary of return, by which Naomi herself emerged as a person in the narrative, now functions similarly for Orpah and Ruth.[10] In using it, they seize the initiative and potential for a new direction that breaks with custom and with common sense.

Naomi does not understand. Her way cannot be their way. "Turn back, my daughters, why will you go with me? . . . Have I more sons in my womb [*mēʿay*][11] who could become husbands for you? . . . If I were to bear sons, would you wait until they were grown?" (vv. 11–13a). Rhetorical questions bring Naomi full circle. She returns to Yahweh, whose *ḥesed* she has invoked earlier for her daughters-in-law. That invocation was the irony of implied judgment. Now implication becomes explication. Yahweh is indeed found wanting: "No, my daughters, for it is exceedingly more bitter for me than for you that the hand of Yahweh has gone forth against me" (v. 13c). From seeking the kindness of Yahweh for the future, Naomi returns to citing the cruelty of Yahweh in the past and the present. These two disparate references to deity frame her consistent advice to Orpah and Ruth. Nowhere in the scene does God intervene in a direct way. Human speech alone interprets divine activity, and that speech is ambivalent: "May God deal kindly with you—that God who has dealt harshly with me."

Three times Naomi commands that the women turn back, and each time she cites the necessity for them to find husbands (vv. 9, 11, 12–13). If their lives are to be fulfilled, then they must remarry, because their male-structured society offers no other possibility. Moreover, their chances for remarriage are far greater in the native land of Moab than in the foreign land of Judah. Naomi herself is powerless to help. Throughout the exchange, her counsel is customary, her motive altruistic, and her theology tinged with irony.

As on the first occasion, a narrative report follows Naomi's second speech. The relationship between these two reports (v. 9b and v. 14) is chiastic in part and in whole:

	a b c		
A	Then she kissed them,	B'	Then they lifted up their voices and wept again.
			c' b'
B	and they lifted up their,	A'	And Orpah kissed her
			a'
	voices and wept.		mother-in-law, but
	(RSV)		c' b' a'
			Ruth clung to her.
			(RSV)

Besides being a mnemonic device, the similarities in both structure and content suggest consistency in the characters of all three women. But the differences give the crucial meaning, that meaning which enables the story to move forward. It comes with the reversal of subjects and objects in A and A'. Though intended as a farewell (A), Naomi's kiss lacks that power, for these young women are not objects at the control of their mother-in-law. They themselves choose their individual responses (A'). Perhaps this point needs elaboration with particular reference to Orpah. Although following the advice of Naomi, Orpah is nevertheless in charge. She does not submit; she decides. *Her* kiss of farewell—not Naomi's—signals her future. Thus the reversal of subject and object in A and A' allows Orpah to appear in the story, if only for one brief moment, as a whole human being, one who chooses her destiny. This structural change performs a similar function for Ruth, and there the break is even sharper. Not only does Ruth decide; she decides contrary to Naomi's orders.

In taking the initiative as subjects of verbs, these young women differentiate themselves from their mother-in-law. In choosing different responses to her, they differentiate themselves from each other. Once they spoke (v. 10); now they act (v. 14). Orpah does the expected, Ruth the unexpected. As a result, both emerge as persons. Use of their names, for the first time since the introduction (v. 4), clinches this point.

Two women of common age, country, and experience have faced together a crisis in life. At first responding identically, they have at last chosen differently. If there must be reasons for this divergence, the storyteller considers them superfluous. Evaluation is likewise unnecessary so that the decisions are recounted without praise or blame. Similarly, the young women neither explain nor evaluate. By contrast, Naomi herself speaks both reason and judgment. Having already cited the need to find husbands as the reason that these widows should return home, Naomi praises next the decision of Orpah and urges Ruth to emulate it: "See, your sister-in-law has returned to her people and to her god; return after your sister-in-law" (v. 15). Orpah is a paradigm of the sane and reasonable; she acts according to the structures and customs of society. Her decision is sound, sensible, and secure. Nevertheless, Orpah dies to the story. However commendable her way, it is not the dynamic of the tale.[12] Ironically, her alliance with Naomi means separation from that mother-in-law.

(2) The movement of life is with Ruth and Naomi (vv. 15–18). At the same time, however, Naomi has isolated Ruth by making Orpah the acceptable model. If Naomi stands alone by the force of circumstances, Ruth stands alone by the force of decision. Her choice makes no sense. It forsakes the security of a mother's house for insecurity abroad. It forfeits possible fullness in Moab for certain emptiness in Judah. It relinquishes the familiar for the strange. Naomi rejects this radical decision. Hence, the two women begin their lives together in separation. Ironically, Ruth's opposition to Naomi means unity with that mother-in-law:

> Entreat me not to abandon you,
>   to return from following you;
>
> For where you go, I will go;
>   where you lodge I will lodge.

Your people are my people
and your god my god.

Where you die, I will die
and there I shall be buried.

Thus may Yahweh do to me
and thus may he add,

If even death separates
me from you.
(1:16–17)

From a cultural perspective, Ruth has chosen death over life. She has disavowed the solidarity of family; she has abandoned national identity; and she has renounced religious affiliation.[13] In the entire epic of Israel, only Abraham matches this radicality, but then he had a call from God (Gen. 12:1–5). Divine promise motivated and sustained his leap of faith. Besides, Abraham was a man, with a wife and other possessions to accompany him. Ruth stands alone; she possesses nothing. No God has called her; no deity has promised her blessing; no human being has come to her aid. She lives and chooses without a support group, and she knows that the fruit of her decision may well be the emptiness of rejection, indeed of death. Consequently, not even Abraham's leap of faith surpasses this decision of Ruth's. And there is more. Not only has Ruth broken with family, country, and faith, but she has also reversed sexual allegiance. A young woman has committed herself to the life of an old woman rather than to the search for a husband, and she has made this commitment not "until death us do part" but beyond death. One female has chosen another female in a world where life depends upon men. There is no more radical decision in all the memories of Israel. Naomi is silenced by it (v. 18). She does not speak again to Ruth in this scene, nor does she speak about her. Ruth's commitment to Naomi is Naomi's withdrawal from Ruth.

(3) "So the two of them went on until they came to Bethlehem" (vv. 19–21, RSV). Of their journey from the plateau of Moab across the Jordan River to the hills of Bethlehem, we know nothing. Instead, the narrator rushes the story to Bethlehem, where "a whole town was excited because of these women." In-

terestingly, the town speaks through its women, another sign of the exclusively female character of the first scene. "Is this Naomi!" the women exclaim. Then that emptiness which has continued to triumph overwhelms in Naomi's response: "Do not call me Naomi" (sweet one), she says; "call me Mara" (bitter one).[14] The opposites of life and death are present within one person. Furthermore, Naomi, woman of reason and of judgment, pursues her suffering. True to her earlier portrayal, she speaks a chiastic language to explain the power of death in her life as divine curse:

> A   for Shadday has dealt very bitterly with me.
>
>   B   I went away full but Yahweh has brought me back empty.
>
>   B'   Why call me Naomi when Yahweh has afflicted me
>
> A'   and Shadday has brought calamity upon me?
>
>   (1:20c–21, RSV*)

Her words begin and end with Shadday who has wronged her. The two middle lines reiterate this calamity as they contrast fullness and sweetness with emptiness and affliction. These contrasts are variations of the underlying opposite, life/death. For Naomi, the divine is the author of death who has destroyed life on the human side. Overpowered by it all, this aged widow fails to acknowledge that Ruth is with her. Life is utter, total, complete emptiness—from famine on a physical level to famine on a familial level to famine at the very core of her being. "I went away full, but Yahweh has brought me back empty."[15] Yet Naomi does not have the final word; that word belongs to the storyteller.

C. Conclusion: v. 22. Having given the story to women after the introduction, the narrator takes it back for the conclusion. This ending mitigates the emptiness of Naomi. She is not alone. "Ruth the Moabite her daughter-in-law is with her." Every word counts in this corrective. Ruth is the name of radical decision and total commitment to Naomi. Ruth the Moabite has chosen Naomi the Judahite. Ruth the daughter-in-law has chosen Naomi the mother-in-law. Moreover, these two people have come to Bethlehem at the beginning of the barley harvest. The possibility of fullness in the harvest tempers the threat of famine. Accordingly, scene one closes not in the deep anguish that Naomi has sounded but in a cautious movement toward well-being. Ruth and the barley harvest are two signs of life opposing the death statements of Naomi.

THIS DAY OUR DAILY BREAD

SCENE TWO: CHAPTER 2

A. Introduction: v. 1. In scene two the narrator continues to affirm fullness over emptiness. Boaz is the third sign, though his name is given only at the close of the introduction (cf. v. 19c). Three brief phrases identify him, and all three contest the power of death in Naomi's life. First, Naomi has "a kinsman." To be sure, this person is "a kinsman of her husband's," but in the extended families of Israel that identity relates him to Naomi, so that in Bethlehem she is not completely bereft of family. Second, this kinsman is "a man of substance" (*'îš gibbôr ḥayil*).[16] The phrase opposes Naomi's emptiness, poverty, and powerlessness. Third, this man is "of the clan of Elimelech." Although the description may appear redundant, it carries a nuance. At the beginning of scene one, the family of Elimelech is equated with death. Elimelech and his two sons speak not at all, and they die quickly. Scene two begins by contrast. There is in the clan of Elimelech a male identified with life. He will speak and he will endure. His name is Boaz, and his appearance begins to restore a balance between female and male as creatures of life. By introducing him prematurely, while withholding his name until the end, the narrator arouses interest, creates suspense, and suggests importance.

B. Body: vv. 2–22. (1) After the introduction, the storyteller steps back and the women speak (v. 2). This structural pattern corresponds to scene one, but at the same time it reverses the order of speakers. Here Ruth leads. She informs Naomi of her decision to "glean among the ears of grain after him in whose sight I shall find favor" (RSV).[17] If these women live in social and familial famine, they need not yield to physical hunger. The young foreigner sees an opportunity for survival and acts upon it. Naomi assents, now with an intimacy of language absent since Ruth defied her advice. "Go, my daughter," she says.

(2) Ruth goes then by her own choice, and yet another dimension shapes the occasion (vv. 3–17). Since that dimension exists independently of the characters, the narrator reenters to describe it: "she happened to come to the part of the field belonging to Boaz, who was of the family of Elimelech" (v. 3, RSV). It is a felicitous expression, "she happened to come," reporting chance and accident while hinting that chance is caused.[18] Within human luck is divine intentionality. In addition, the latter part of this report stresses again the presence of male life in the family of Elimelech.

Almost immediately Boaz himself appears (v. 4). A man of power and prestige, he surveys the scene, speaking divine amenities to his reapers, and spots the female stranger. He does not know her. "Whose maiden is this?" he asks (v. 5, RSV). Truly a patriarchal question. After all, a young woman must belong to someone; she is possession, not person. Thus Boaz does not ask *her* name but rather the identity of her owner. His question fits his culture, but it does not fit this woman, who is in tension with that culture. Accordingly, the servant cannot answer in the traditional way. He cannot identify Ruth by a (male) lord; she has none. So the servant describes her as the foreign woman "who came back with Naomi from the country of Moab" (v. 6, RSV). Her name he does not give. Her identity he derives from her own strangeness and from another woman.

With that information, Boaz speaks to Ruth (vv. 8–9). He grants her permission to glean; he directs her to the young women in his fields;[19] and he protects her from the young men. Boaz, man of power, assists Ruth, woman of poverty: the male lord grants privileges to the female foreigner; and the older man protects the younger woman. In this last instance, then, he appears as a senior adult, a male counterpart to Naomi.

Ruth's response is appropriately deferential: "Why have I found favor in your eyes, that you should take notice of me, when I am a foreigner?" (v. 10, RSV). It is also ironically subtle. This inferior foreigner, now speaking to a superior, has by choice (and by chance) created this situation. Her deference results from her daring; it is derivative, not determinative. Ruth herself suggests this distinction when to Boaz she repeats a phrase that she has used with her mother-in-law: "to find favor." In other words, Ruth has accomplished here what she set out to do. The favor that Boaz gives her is the favor that she has sought. Therefore, she, not he, is shaping her destiny. That a patriarchal culture restricts her options makes her initiative all the more remarkable. Her decision to "glean among the ears of grain after someone in whose sight I shall find favor" (v. 2, RSV) gives her independence as a human being in the midst of dependence as a needy case.

Boaz himself acknowledges that Ruth is no ordinary individual. Concern for this foreign woman marks him as a true child of Israel, who understands that Israel itself lives as a stranger and sojourner in the world. After all, Israel had its beginning in the foreigners Abraham and Sarah, who journeyed to an alien land to become channels of blessing for all the families of the earth (Gen. 12:1–5). These ancient memories echo now as Boaz speaks to Ruth. He describes her as the one who left her father and her mother and her native land to come to a people whom she did not know (v. 11). This description validates the analogy between Abraham and Ruth that her earlier words to Naomi implied. Moreover, Boaz adds an ingredient—which was both clearly present in the call of Abraham and noticeably absent in the choice of Ruth—the ingredient of divine blessing:

> May Yahweh grant your action due recompense,
>   and may your payment be full from Yahweh the God of Israel
> under whose wings you have come to seek refuge.
>
> (2:12, *AB*)

Boaz's language envelops Ruth within the Abrahamic paradigm of the foreigner who breaks with the past and receives the promise of blessing for the future. But differences remain. Ruth herself chose to abandon the past without call or blessing. The divine blessing extended to her now comes not directly from God but through a human being. Though its content is not specified here, Boaz shall have occasion to remember and make good his prayer. Meanwhile, Ruth responds to him with characteristic deference (v. 13).

If the repeated deference of Ruth results from her own decisions, then the actions of Boaz in her behalf mean reaction and
not initiative. Things are once again not what they seem. Deference is initiative; initiative is reaction. The first meeting of
these two people happens because of a choice and a chance,
neither of which Boaz directs. This powerful male has not
rushed to the rescue of a destitute female. His graciousness has
not sought her out, even though in response it now extends to
her. In truth, Boaz's own words (v. 11) show that he knew already of the plight of Naomi and Ruth; yet until now he,
Naomi's kin, has done nothing to help these women. Again,
although he has been fully told all that Ruth has done for
Naomi, he does not even know Ruth when he sees her in his field
(v. 5). Now the story does not censure Boaz for dereliction of
duty, but it does subordinate him to the women. He has patriarchal power, but he does not have narrative power. He has
authority within the story but not control over it. The story belongs to Ruth and Naomi—and to chance, that code for the
divine.[20]

Mealtime arrives. Boaz continues to show kindness, offering
Ruth more bread and wine than she is able to eat. As she returns
to the field, he instructs his young men to "let her glean even
among the sheaves" and to "pull out some from the bundles for
her" (vv. 15–16, RSV). In this setting, the young men who are
harvesting have their opposites in the young women who are
reaping (vv. 8–9).[21] Ruth has been told to keep close to the
young women; the young men have been told not to molest her.
Thereby an earlier pattern repeats itself. The women signal life;
the men, death. At the same time, however, these young men
draw water for Ruth to drink (v. 9), and they provide sheaves for
her to glean (v. 15). As males opposing females, they threaten
death. As males helping a female, they promise life. Hence, they
mediate opposites.

This episode ends, as it began, with a narrative report: "So she
set forth and went and gleaned in the field after the reapers" (v.
3a, RSV); "so she gleaned in the field until evening" (v. 17a,
RSV). What Ruth determined to do, she has done.

(3) At evening Ruth returns to her mother-in-law with food
for the hungry (vv. 18–22). From the dangers of the field, she

finds security in the city. Naomi is eager to know what happened, even as she invokes blessing upon the one who has helped her daughter-in-law. Their conversation builds on incongruities. Naomi does not know in whose field Ruth has gleaned.[22] Though Ruth knows the name Boaz, she herself does not know in whose field she has gleaned. Each woman has both more and less information than the other. The hearers of the story await full disclosure. A periodic sentence, compounded by redundancy, delays that disclosure: "So she told her mother-in-law with whom she had worked, and said, 'The man's name with whom I worked today is Boaz' " (v. 19e, RSV). When the narrator first introduced Boaz, he or she supplied the name only at the end (v. 1). Similarly now, Ruth withholds the name until the close of her sentence. The suspense of the sentence structure, then, is the emphasis of its revelation. Naomi's reply follows a comparable pattern by delaying the crucial information until last. It commences with a blessing for Yahweh, "whose kindness [*ḥesed*] has not forsaken the living or the dead," and it concludes with the news that Boaz "is a relative of ours, one of our redeemers" (v. 20, RSV*). Slowly the bitterness of an old woman is being transformed.

Yet how very strange is her disclosure. Naomi knows that Boaz is a close relative, but she has not sought his help. Why we do not know. Is it that emptiness has so overpowered her that she forgot his existence, even as earlier she failed to understand that Ruth was with her? Or is it that calamity paralyzed her will to act? Or is Naomi in this instance a woman of her culture who waits for the man to act first? Whatever the reason, she has not sought out Boaz. By the same token, Boaz has not approached her, even though he knew of her plight. Only through the choice of Ruth and through the chance of cause have male relative and female relative acknowledged each other. And with this acknowledgment Naomi now includes Ruth in the family: "The man is a relative of *ours*, one of *our* redeemers." Relinquishing isolation, the mother-in-law embraces the daughter-in-law who has already embraced her.

Immediately after these words of familial inclusion, the narrator juxtaposes the national exclusion of Ruth by calling her a Moabite: "And Ruth the Moabite said, 'Besides, he said to me,

"You shall keep close [*dbq*] by my servants, till they have finished all my harvest" ' " (v. 21, RSV*). This narrative statement, followed by Ruth's concern for providing food, parallels the verse that introduced the entire scene: "And Ruth the Moabite said to Naomi, 'I shall go to the field and glean among the ears of grain . . .' " (v. 2). In both instances the storyteller stresses the alien status of Ruth. On the one hand, how difficult and courageous for a foreign woman to glean in the field (v. 2); on the other, how healing and fulfilling for the empty Naomi to embrace Ruth the Moabite in the language of kinship (v. 20).

Naomi's identification of Boaz as "one of our redeemers" hints at the use that she will make of this relationship later. Certainly she wants Ruth to remarry (cf. 1:9, 11–13), although Ruth herself has not shown a corresponding interest. Her concerns have been loyalty to Naomi and food for the two of them, and her responses here to Naomi's statement bear that out. She does not comment on Boaz as redeemer; after all, she came to his field by chance. She does not comment on herself as relative; long ago she made that decision. Instead, she assures her mother-in-law that, thanks to Boaz, food will be available throughout the harvest. Her first act upon returning home at evening was to give Naomi food (v. 18); now her last words in this encounter return to that act (v. 21). Ruth is faithful to Naomi, and she can provide for the two of them. In other words, Ruth is not looking for a husband.

Naomi answers with words akin to Boaz's: "It is well, my daughter, that you go out with his young women, lest in another field you be molested" (v. 22, RSV*). Boaz and Naomi unite as an older generation concerned for the safety of a young woman in an environment of young men. Male and female mediate life and death.

Ruth began this day by speaking to Naomi (v. 2); now Naomi has concluded it by speaking to Ruth (v. 22). Thus the movement of their day (v. 2 and vv. 18–22) surrounds the movement in the field (v. 3 and v. 17), and this circular design bespeaks a feminist content: the women surround the episode with Boaz. Moreover, design and content yield a feminist interpretation: in their own right the women shape their story. They plan (v. 2); they execute (vv. 3–17); and they evaluate (vv. 18–22). But this symmetry is also asymmetrical. Whereas the young woman takes command at first, the old woman outstrips—not matches—her at last. Much longer than the dialogic introduction, the conclusion moves back and forth between these two females until it stops, where it started, with Naomi.

The structure of this ending parallels the dialogic conclusion of scene one, though its content differs significantly. In both dialogues Naomi has the last word (1:20–21 and 2:10, 22). The first time she perceives herself all alone in bitterness and sorrow. This time she begins to move out of isolation and despair, because Ruth and Boaz have reached her. Accordingly, Naomi hints at a reinterpretation of her past. Shadday who brought calamity (1:21) is now Yahweh "whose kindness has not forsaken the living or the dead" (2:20, RSV). Self-centered sorrow yields to divine blessing through human agents.

C. Conclusion: v. 23. Naomi's speeches are not, however, the final word of scenes one and two; that word belongs to the storyteller. Although he or she struck a note of well-being in scene one with the phrase "the beginning of the barley harvest," here the narrator reverses that sentiment with the phrase "until the end of the barley and wheat harvests" (RSV): "So she [Ruth] kept close [*dbq*] to the women of Boaz, gleaning until the end of the barley and wheat harvests; and she lived with her mother-in-law" (RSV*). The phrase is a warning, since the end of the barley season may mean the return of famine and emptiness. If present kindness has softened past harshness for Ruth and Naomi, their future is still uncertain. At the end of scene one, then, Naomi speaks death; the narrator suggests life. At the end of scene two, Naomi affirms life; the narrator cautions death. And at the conclusion of each scene narration opposes dialogue; the storyteller is in tension with the characters; and the hearers wait in suspense.

SALVATION BY COURAGE ALONE

SCENE THREE: CHAPTER 3

A. Introduction: vv. 1–5. As the last and first to speak, Naomi is the verbal link between scenes two and three. These two scenes are designed similarly, with conversations between the women surrounding a meeting of Ruth and Boaz. Moreover, they share parallel themes: in scene two, women struggle to survive physically, and in scene three, they struggle to survive culturally.

Unlike both preceding scenes, however, scene three has no narrative introduction. From the beginning the characters are in charge, and they dispel any caution of the narrator about their future. Naomi takes over. Aware of the kindness of Boaz, she begins to act upon it. She does not wait for matters to take their course or for God to intervene with a miracle. Instead, she herself moves from being the receiver of calamity to becoming the agent of change and challenge. Once in the land of Moab she urged each of her widowed daughters-in-law to return to her mother's house, with the hope that each of them might find a home in the house of a husband (1:18). On that occasion, Naomi knew their need, as dictated by their culture, but she was powerless to help. Now she returns to that need with the power of a plan: "My daughter, should I not seek a home for you, that it may be well with you?" (3:1b, RSV).

This rhetorical question introduces an outrageous scheme, dangerous and delicate. Ruth is to dress in her finest clothes and go alone at night to the threshing floor where the men are eating and drinking in celebration of the harvest. After Boaz has satisfied himself with food and drink and has lain down to sleep, Ruth will approach him, uncover the lower part of his body, and lie down. Just how much of the lower part of his body she is to uncover remains tantalizingly uncertain in the text.[23] That sexual overtones are present is, however, patently certain. "When you have done this," Naomi concludes, "then Boaz himself will tell you what to do" (v. 4c). Surely at this point the man will take over; that is the least one expects.

Ruth agrees to the plan: "All that you say I will do" (v. 5, RSV). This reply differs from her earlier responses to the topic of a husband. In scene one Ruth's allegiance to Naomi superseded that need; in scene two Ruth's struggle for their physical survival submerged that need; here in scene three Ruth's allegiance to Naomi accords with that need. Loyalty to self and to mother-in-law signifies for Ruth a movement from dissent to perseverance to consent. Her willingness to obey Naomi now means a second meeting between her and Boaz. It contrasts with the first encounter in that circumstances, place, and time reverse. The first meeting was by chance; the second is by choice. The first was in the fields; the second at the threshing floor. The first was public; the second private. The first was work; the second play. The first was by day; the second by night. Yet both of them hold the potential for life and death.

B. *Body: vv. 6–15.* The narrator emphasizes the obedience of Ruth by reporting and repeating the events that Naomi has forecast. Repetition impedes the progress of the story as it heightens suspense. In addition, it both confirms and contradicts the accuracy of Naomi's calculations. "So she [Ruth] went down to the threshing floor and did just as her mother-in-law had told her. And when Boaz had eaten and drunk, and his heart was merry, he went to lie down at the end of the heap of grain" (vv. 6–7a, RSV). "At the end of the heap of grain": a minor detail, yet important for the execution of the plan. The phrase suggests an area separate from the other sleepers and accessible to the waiting woman. Is this detail another hint of that blessed chance which aids these women in their struggles for life? Earlier Ruth happened to come to the field of Boaz (2:3). Does Boaz happen now to lie at the corner of the threshing floor? We cannot be sure. At any rate, Ruth "came quietly and uncovered his lower body and lay down" (v. 7de).[24] How will a patriarch of Israel respond to this bold action by a woman from Moab?

Midnight comes. The man stirs in his sleep, no doubt feeling the chill of the night air upon his exposed body. Groping about in the dark, he discovers the woman lying next to him. "Who are you?" he asks (v. 9, RSV). If their first meeting elicited a question of ownership—"Whose maiden is this?" (2:5, RSV)—the second evokes a question of personal identity: "Who are you?" In both instances, a woman has surprised a man; she has taken initiative to seek life under threat of death.

Thus far the script for this second meeting has happened as Naomi planned. Indeed, the narrator has already said that Ruth "did just as her mother-in-law had told her" (v. 6b, RSV). But now, when Ruth answers the question of this startled man, she changes that script. "I am Ruth, your maidservant," she replies (v. 9, RSV). At this point Naomi said that Boaz would take charge:

"He will tell you what to do" (v. 4c, RSV). That is not the case, however. Ruth herself is in charge; she tells Boaz what to do. "Spread your *wing* [*kānāp*] over your maidservant, for you are a redeemer" (v. 9c; cf. *AB*). By a wordplay Ruth calls upon Boaz to make good on his prayer for her blessing. In the field he wished that a full reward be given her by Yahweh, the God of Israel, "under whose *wings* [*kānāp*] you have come to take refuge" (2:12, RSV). Now at the threshing floor, Ruth recalls and appropriates that language as she challenges Boaz to be the occasion of divine blessing in her life. Marriage is that blessing. And the man who asked it for Ruth is himself capable of fulfilling it. Besides, as redeemer he has an obligation to perform.[25] A foreign woman has called an Israelite man to responsibility.

Ruth's utterance conforms to her portrayal throughout the story as the defier of custom, the maker of decisions, and the worker of salvation. It puts her in tension with her mother-in-law and with the narrator. Furthermore, it confirms the posture of Boaz as re-actor to the initiative of this woman. The suspense of this entire episode—from its conception by Naomi through its description by the narrator, to its altered consummation by Ruth—subsides as Boaz replies (vv. 10–12, RSV). His words are characteristically gracious, recalling his earlier response to Ruth. There is the theme of divine blessing: "May you be blessed by the Lord, my daughter" (RSV; cf. 2:12). Through comparison, there is the theme of *ḥesed* to Naomi: "You have made this last kindness greater than the first . . ." (RSV; cf. 2:11). Through contrast, there is the theme of young men as foils to Boaz: ". . . in that you have not gone after young men, whether poor or rich" (RSV; cf. 2:9b, 15). Finally, there is the theme of assurance and of praise: "And now, my daughter, do not fear, I will do for you all that you ask, for all my fellow townsmen know that you are a woman of worth" (RSV; cf. 2:8, 9, 11, 12). "A woman of worth" (*'ēšet ḥayil*): that description matches precisely the narrator's depiction of Boaz as "a man of worth" (*'îš gibbôr ḥayil*, 2:1). Female and male; foreigner and native; youth and age; poor and wealthy—all these opposites are mediated by human worth. The audience breathes a sigh of relief. A dangerous and delicate scheme on the part of two women has resulted in kindness and blessing from a man. Not one word of censure does Boaz utter or intimate.[26]

But this patriarch has not finished speaking; the audience re-
laxed too soon. "And now it is true that I am a redeemer," he
continues; "yet there is a redeemer nearer than I" (v. 12; cf. *AB*).
This distinction in the order of male redeemers disturbs the
progress of the story. At the same time, it may account for the
failure of Boaz to act thus far, since responsibility belongs to
another man and custom decrees that the proper order be followed. Now that the women have forced the issue, however,
Boaz will respond. His words to Ruth continue in a chiastic pattern. Night surrounds morning; the immediate situation encircles the coming resolution; instruction encompasses condition
and promise:

A   Remain this night, and in the morning,

   B   if he will do the redeemer's part,
        well and good; let him redeem;

   B'   but if he is not willing to do the redeemer's part for
        you,
        then, as Yahweh lives, I will redeem you.

A   Lie down until the morning.

                                        (3:13; cf. *AB*)

"To do the redeemer's part" means to marry Ruth. At the beginning of this scene Naomi herself linked redeemer with marriage (vv. 1–2). Later Ruth makes this same connection when she
tells Boaz to spread his wing over her because he is a redeemer
(v. 9). Boaz understands, but his reply wavers between promise
and postponement. From relief his words return to suspense as
opposites press in and tension mounts. Females and males—
Ruth, who is present, and Naomi, who is absent; Boaz, who is
present, and the unnamed redeemer, who is absent—hover between life and death. Future mediator between Ruth and the
nearer redeemer, Boaz is present intimate of Ruth on the threshing floor. A compromising position occasions a command performance. Consequently, deeds of night both precipitate and
threaten the resolution of morning.

Ruth lies at the "feet" of Boaz, but she rises before daylight in
order that their encounter might remain in the secrecy of the
dark (v. 14a). Boaz also wishes to preserve the privacy of the

occasion. Speaking through an impersonal construction, he distances Ruth from himself and calls her "the woman":[27] "Let it not be known that the woman came to the threshing floor" (v. 14b, RSV). What Boaz's words say, they are. Content and form merge to signal the dissolution of intimacy and the departure of Ruth—yet, not immediately. Just before she leaves, Boaz addresses her directly: "Bring the mantle you are wearing and hold it out" (v. 15, RSV). Into it he measures barley. Once again, then, his action assures fullness over famine to parallel the conclusion of their first meeting (2:14-16). A second parallel is Ruth's success. Potential for life has overcome potential for death. And a third parallel is her return home. From the danger of the threshing floor, she returns to the security of the city.

C. *Conclusion: vv. 16–18.* Alone the two women talk. Naomi asks, "How did you fare, my daughter?" (v. 16, RSV). The answer is an odd mixture of third-person narration and direct discourse, a combination that hides the extraordinary acts of Ruth and highlights the ordinary acts of Boaz. Although Naomi's question is explicitly about Ruth and only implicitly about Boaz, both answers are explicitly about Boaz and only implicitly about Ruth. First the narrator reports: "Then she told her all that the man had done for her" (RSV). Omitted is any report of what Ruth had done, especially of her forthright instructions to Boaz. And yet it was precisely her request that called Boaz to a duty which he did not voluntarily assume. By failing to report specifically, is the narrator covering for Ruth? Would a disclosure of what she said be too much for Naomi to bear? After all, Naomi had expected Boaz to tell Ruth what to do (v. 4c). Or has the radicalness of Ruth's performance escaped the awareness of the narrator? Earlier she or he maintained that at the threshing floor Ruth "did just as her mother-in-law had told her" (v. 6, RSV), when in fact she did more and other than her mother-in-law had told her. Be that as it may, the narrator's reply diverges from Naomi's question.

Ruth's reply does the same. Characteristically, it concentrates upon Naomi and upon food: "These six measures of barley he gave to me, for he said, 'You must not go back empty-handed to your mother-in-law' " (v. 17, RSV). The reply says nothing about marriage and the redeemer's responsibility. Is Ruth reticent to speak openly about this matter? Does she prefer to leave the details of her radical behavior where they occurred—in the darkness of night, at the corner of a grain heap, in whispers between female and male? At any rate, her bold actions for the sake of survival and for the hope of blessing move toward fulfillment. She need say nothing more. And indeed, these are her last words in the entire story. Appropriately, they focus upon the mother-in-law to whom Ruth committed herself for better or for worse, even beyond death.

If Ruth mediates life for Naomi, Naomi mirrors that activity. Her last words advise Ruth: "Wait, my daughter, until you learn how the matter turns out, for the man will not rest, but will settle the matter today" (v. 18, RSV). Ruth is to wait because Boaz will not wait. Thus, opposite actions converge to yield the resolution. "How the matter turns out"—the vagueness of this phrase contrasts with the specificity of its parallel, "the man . . . will settle the matter today." Vagueness invites speculation. Plan is replacing change, but whose plan? Naomi's? Ruth's? Boaz's? They have all participated, but is there something more? Has not Boaz in this very scene both derived blessing from Yahweh (v. 10) and rooted his own resolution in a Yahwistic vow (v. 13)? "How the matter turns out" may be divine plan in, through, and by human agents.[28]

Having introduced scene three by plotting a dangerous mission, Naomi concludes it by counseling a patient wait. Thereby she too completes her speeches in the story; her function is fulfilled. That Ruth may now find a husband satisfies Naomi's original concern. Furthermore, this woman who began as the voice of sorrow and sadness, of bitterness and suffering, of famine and emptiness approaches now the threshold of fulfillment and joy. Through transformation her circle is closing; death is becoming life. So Naomi's voice fades; like Ruth, she steps aside. At this juncture, the drama ceases to be their story and becomes the story about them.

Scene three provides yet another sign of well-being. Unlike the preceding scenes, it has no concluding statement by the narrator. Eliminated is the tension between author and characters, between narration and dialogue. All in all, the story is moving toward its resolution.

ALL'S WELL THAT ENDS WELL

SCENE FOUR: CHAPTER 4

A. Verses. 1–12. The fourth scene begins with a public gathering at the gate of the city where business and legal transactions take place (vv. 1–12). Its setting compares and contrasts with the first meeting of Ruth and Boaz (scene two). Their meeting was a family affair. Although it happened in public, it was not a public happening, since the workers in the field formed only the backdrop. Now that family affair is no longer a chance encounter. Through the insistence of Naomi and Ruth, it has become a public matter that the elders of the city must witness as participants.

This public gathering is entirely a man's world. No women are present, even though their actions alone have made the occasion mandatory. Boaz takes charge. At the gate he meets the redeemer and invites him to sit down. Strikingly, Boaz does not call this man by name: "Turn aside, so-and-so,"[29] he says; "sit down here." Next Boaz summons ten men of the elders of the city to sit down so that he might present the case. Speaking directly to the redeemer (whom the narrator does not name either), Boaz reports:

                      A   B
The portion of the field which belonged to our kinsman Elimelech
            B'   A'
Naomi is selling, she who returned from the field of Moab.
                                                                (v. 3)

Structured chiastically, these words recall early opposites. The native soil of Judah and the foreign soil of Moab surround a dead husband and his living wife. Whereas the husband led in the journey from Judah to Moab, the wife manages the return. If these words echo the past, they surprise the present. Boaz is giving new information. We did not know that Naomi was selling land. Why, we are surprised that she even has land to sell.[30] That fact is itself an incongruity of life and death. Rights over a parcel of land (life) belong to a woman of emptiness (death). Again, the suggestion of direct communication between Boaz and Naomi is surprising, since nowhere do these two meet and talk. Finally, there is the surprise of diversion and suspense. Boaz's statement appears to sidetrack the journey of the tale. Thus he continues speaking: "So I thought I would tell you of it, and say, Buy it in the presence of those sitting here, and in the presence of the elders of my people. If you will redeem it, redeem it; and if you will not redeem it, tell me and then I will know, for there is no one except you to redeem it and I come after you" (v. 4, RSV*).

This I-you language highlights tension between two males. Both living members of the family of Elimelech, one instructs the other. The reply is immediate and firm. "I will redeem," says the unnamed one. Only then does Boaz come to the subject, albeit in a twisted way:

>   A   B
> The day <u>you buy</u> the field from the hand of <u>Naomi</u>,
>   B'   A'
> then <u>Ruth</u> the Moabite, widow of the dead, <u>you "buy"</u>[31]
> to restore the name of the dead to his inheritance.
>   (v. 5, RSV*)

Once more, a chiastic structure presents opposites (see 4:3). Patriarchal duty surrounds two females, and that duty means the revival of life over against death: "to restore the name of the dead to his inheritance." By delaying this information about Ruth until after the redeemer has agreed to redeem the land, Boaz exposes the motive and character of this man. "Then the redeemer said,

> '<u>I am not able to redeem it</u>
>   lest I impair my own inheritance.
> *You* take on my redemption-responsibility
>   for <u>I am not able to redeem it</u>.' "
>   (v. 6; cf. *AB*)

It appears that originally this man agreed to redemption for personal gain, the acquisition of property, rather than for familial restoration. Opposing I and you, his own words show that selfish interest, while they show no interest at all in Ruth. Since he refuses, then, to do the part of a redeemer, the outcome is assured for Ruth and Boaz.

A chance meeting in the fields, followed by a daring meeting on the threshing floor, has worked its way to denouement

through proper and customary channels of patriarchy. Thereupon ensues an ancient ceremony in which the giving of one's
sandal signifies a redemption and exchange transaction. So re-
mote is this custom that the narrator interrupts to explain it
(4:7–8).[32] Upon completion of the ceremony, the redeemer
fades from the story. As a foil to Boaz, he is finished, and he
finishes, as he began, without a name. Now the story provides
ample reason for his anonymity. Since he refused to "restore the
name of the dead to his inheritance," he himself has no name.
Anonymity implies judgment. Moreover, this judgment portrays
the redeemer as the opposite of Elimelech, with Boaz as their
mediator. Unlike Elimelech, the redeemer speaks; unlike the
redeemer, Elimelech has a name. As a result, both men hover
between person (life) and nonperson (death). For Elimelech this
conflict is resolved, on the one hand, by physical death and, on
the other, by narrative life. His name continues to appear in the
story (2:1, 3; 4:3, 9) so that his absence is presence, his death is
life. For the redeemer this conflict is resolved, on the one hand,
by physical life and, on the other, by narrative death. The redeemer dies to the story in order to live to his own inheritance.
Between these two males is Boaz with both name and speech. He
speaks to the redeemer, and he restores the name of Elimelech.
He is totally the life that they are partially.

Next Boaz addresses the elders and all the people:

Witnesses are you this day that

I have bought
   all which belonged to Elimelech and to Chilion
   and to Mahlon from the hand of Naomi
   and also Ruth, the Moabite, the widow of Mahlon,

I have bought
   to be my wife
   to restore the name of the dead in his inheritance
      that the name of the dead may not be cut off from among his
      brothers
      and from the gate of his native place.

Witnesses are you this day.

(vv. 9–10, RSV*)

For the first time since the introduction to scene one (1:2), the entire family that sojourned from Judah to Moab is named. The story begins to complete itself as t⌐e dead live in the living. Ruth is named also—and in a speciai way. The order of verb followed by the object ("I have bought all that belonged to Elimelech," etc.) reverses to emphasize her: "and also Ruth, the Moabite, the widow of Mahlon, I have bought." Of all the characters in scene one, only Orpah is missing. While obvious, the omission is also subtle. Orpah's place at the beginning belongs at the end to the unnamed redeemer. But substitution means dissimilarity. Orpah had both name and speech (1:10). She decided to die to the story oy returning to her own people, and the judgment upon her is favorable (1:15). The unnamed redeemer chooses to die to the story by returning to his own inheritance, and the judgment upon him is adverse. After all, he is not a foreign woman but the nearest male kin. Thus he passes away with the infamy of anonymity.

The public meeting concludes with words of the people and the elders. Addressed to Boaz, these words begin and end with Yahweh and Ruth (though the men do not call her by name). This witness statement stresses fertility, the restoration of a male name, and the continuation of a male line for both the dead and the living.[33]

> May Yahweh make the woman, who is coming into your house [*heth*]
>   like Rachel and Leah who between them built the house of Israel.
>
> May you show fertility in Ephrathah
>   and bestow a name in Bethlehem.
>
> And may your house be like the house of Perez, whom Tamar bore
>   to Judah
>   because of the children Yahweh will give you from this young
>   woman.
>
>   (vv. 11–12· RSV*, cf. *AB*)

Comparison of Ruth to the ancient mothers Rachel, Leah, and Tamar recalls the parallel between Ruth and Abraham, yet with differences. Although the analogy with Abraham exalted Ruth as a model of the radicality of faith, comparison with these women views her in the traditional role of bearer of children. An exclusively female episode suggests the first comparison (1:8–21); an exclusively male occasion asserts the second (4:1–12). Nevertheless, both analogies locate Ruth the foreigner solidly within the traditions of Israel. Recognition of her worth climaxes here a public gathering.

This episode is unique in the story because of its heavy patriarchal cast. Men alone decide the future of women. In addition, Boaz presents the situation of these women quite differently from their own understanding of it. He subordinates both of them to male prerogatives: the buying of land and the restoration of the name of the dead to his inheritance. While the first of these matters does have a feminist slant in that the widow, Naomi, has inherited land which she has the right to sell, that slant is hardly the concern of Boaz. He talks about keeping that land within the family of Elimelech.

The second issue reinforces this male perspective: "to restore the name of the dead to his inheritance" (RSV*). Before the elders, Boaz cites this issue as his reason for marrying Ruth, although alone with her he promised marriage in order to "do the redeemer's part" for *her*. Thus in a private conversation with Ruth, Boaz made her welfare the sole object of his concern, but in a public discussion with men he makes Ruth the means for achieving a male purpose.[34]

The silence of the women on this question of the restoration of the name of the dead suggests that they do not share this male perspective. Conversely, the voice of the women on the question of marriage confirms that they have a different outlook. Often Naomi underscores the need for young widows to remarry, but never does she link this need with the imperative to restore a male name. Indeed, her advice in scene one is precisely the opposite: that Orpah and Ruth should find husbands in Moab. Besides, Naomi describes herself as "too old to have a husband," another indication that she was not oriented to restoring a male name. Even her speculation about a future husband and sons for herself bespeaks concern for her daughters-in-law rather than for the name of her dead husband and sons. Again, the scheme that Naomi proposes (scene three) has as its purpose finding a home for Ruth that it might be well with her. Ruth repeats this theme when she asks Boaz to marry her (3:9c). Nowhere, then, does either woman mention or imply the restoration of a male name. Their emphasis is life for the living.

Altogether the patriarchal cast of scene four is alien to the letter and spirit of the first three scenes, even if it is not alien to the culture of Israel. It alters emphases, and it views Ruth exclusively as a vessel for male progeny. Nevertheless, small ironies abound. If Orpah is a model to be emulated, the unnamed kinsman is a model to be avoided. If Boaz is now the patriarch in charge, it is two women who have summoned him to duty.

B. *Verse 13*. Events move quickly. The privacy of intercourse follows immediately the public transaction. From being an object of discussion, Ruth returns to consummate a marriage.[35] Yet third-person narration distances the intimacy of this occasion.[36] Ruth and Boaz do not speak. The report of the occasion begins with the man acting and the female re-acting: "Boaz took Ruth and she became his wife" (RSV). The pattern continues—"he went in to her"(RSV)—only to be broken when deity intervenes: "but Yahweh gave her conception" (RSV*).[37] The gift of life resides neither in male nor in female, but in God. Only after this perspective is introduced do we read, "she bore a son." Intercourse between Ruth and Boaz is itself divine activity. That equation comes in both the structure and content of the report, and thereby the narrator announces that all is well. Ten years of a childless marriage in Moab (1:4–5) have been quickly redeemed in the union of Ruth and Boaz. Yahweh has given conception; blessing has transformed curse. This announcement of a private union for blessing mediates between public gatherings which, on the one side, legitimate the union and, on the other, celebrate it.

C. *Verses 14–17*. At the celebration, women alone are present. Hence, this episode contrasts with the first in scene four (vv. 1–12), even as it corresponds to scene one (1:6–22). Women of Bethlehem, once excited by Naomi's return from the land of Moab, return themselves both to introduce and to conclude the last event. They commence with a blessing of Yahweh, and they address their words to Naomi, the one who told them that Yahweh brought her back empty. Now they answer her: "Blessed be Yahweh, who has not left you this day without next of kin" (RSV*). The advent of a grandchild transforms death into life, emptiness into fullness:

> May his name be celebrated in Israel.
> He shall be to you a restorer of life
>   and a nourisher of your old age. . . .
> (v. 15a, RSV*)

But the celebration is more than the joy of a male child. The meaning of that child centers in his mother, a foreign woman who has forsaken all to follow Naomi. Thus the blessing climaxes in the exaltation of Ruth, who herself is set above not just a natural child and not just a male child but even above the ideal number of natural sons:

> . . . for your daughter-in-law who loves you bore him,
> she who means more to you than seven sons.
> (v. 15b)

These words of the women converge upon Naomi, and the storyteller reports then that she takes the child, holds him close, and becomes his guardian. The woman of emptiness has become the woman of plenty. And Ruth, the daughter-in-law faithful beyond death, is the mediator of this transformation to life.

Next the women of Bethlehem complete the circle of their words around Naomi as they name the child: "And the women of the neighborhood gave him a name, saying, 'A son has been born to Naomi.' They called his name Obed" (v. 17, RSV*). Their language of naming returns to the theme that Boaz introduced and the elders reinforced: "to restore the name of the dead to his inheritance." By concentrating upon it, the men shifted emphasis from justice for living females to justice for dead males. This shift was jarring in a story of women, even if it was justified in a world of men. But now the women redeem this male theme. They identify the child as the son of Naomi rather than of Elimelech. They perceive this infant as restoring life to the living rather than restoring a name to the dead.[38] They speak of Ruth the bearer rather than of Boaz the begetter. And they themselves name the baby. Repeatedly, these women stand as opposites to the elders. Each group has interpreted according to its kind. Reconciling these opposites is the newborn male child, the symbol of a new beginning with men. Not only does this infant mediate between adult males and females, but he also mediates between the ages. Of that generational function the narrator teaches when, having begun this story in premonarchic Israel, she or he concludes it with the coming of the monarchy. At the beginning we read, "in the days when the judges ruled" (1:1), and, at the end, "a son has been born to Naomi . . . he was the father of Jesse, the father of David" (4:17bc, RSV).

A story beginning in deepest despair has worked its way to wholeness and well-being. Thus, it is a comedy in which the brave and bold decisions of women embody and bring to pass the blessings of God.[39] In the introduction, the curses of famine, exile, and death oppose divine blessing. And yet the storyteller does not attribute these curses to God. Indeed, the very first reference to deity is the narrator's report of blessing: ". . . Yahweh had visited his people and given them food" (1:6, RSV*). Later in scene one, however, Naomi speaks openly of divine affliction. Though she does not fault God for her exile, she does blame the deity for the abundance of death in her life. Shadday has dealt bitterly; Shadday has brought calamity upon her (1:20–21). In the ensuing scenes, this divine curse is gradually removed through hidden and fortuitous means. Ruth "happened to come to the part of the field belonging to Boaz" (2:3, RSV). Conveniently, Boaz lay down "at the end of the heap of grain" (3:7, RSV). Called to duty by a foreign woman, this Israelite patriarch swore by Yahweh to do right for Ruth (3:13). When the matter finally turned out well (cf. 3:18), Yahweh gave conception to Ruth, and the women of Bethlehem blessed this deity in words appropriately addressed to Naomi (4:13–14). From being the agent of death, God has become the giver of life, although at no place has the divine world intruded upon the narrative by speech or by miracles. Clearly, the human struggle itself is divine activity, redeeming curse through blessing.

In scene one, Naomi and Ruth stand alone. They are women without men. They make their own decisions; they work out their own destinies. This posture continues in scene two, though the situation is more complex, since in Boaz a strong male appears. Hence, it is all the more important to discern that the power of the story is not transferred to him. The women continue to shape their tale, as both structure and content confirm. Scene two is their struggle to survive physically even as scene three is their struggle to survive culturally. In both scenes Boaz is reactor to their initiative. Scene four commences with the shock of reminder. After all, it is a man's world, and concerns of women may well be subsumed, perhaps even subverted, by this patriarchal climate. Yet the women of Bethlehem do not permit this transformation to prevail. They reinterpret the language of a man's world to preserve the integrity of a woman's story. Accordingly, scene four concludes with the two themes coming together: a story of women making a new beginning with men. Scene four is, then, the answer to scene one. Having suffered and struggled, the image of God male and female rejoices at last in the goodness of daily life.

As a whole, this human comedy suggests a theological interpretation of feminism: women working out their own salvation with fear and trembling, for it is God who works in them. Naomi works as a bridge between tradition and innovation. Ruth and the females of Bethlehem work as paradigms for radicality. All together they are women in culture, women against culture, and women transforming culture. What they reflect, they challenge. And that challenge is a legacy of faith to this day for all who have ears to hear the stories of women in a man's world.

NOTES

1. On the genre of Ruth, see Edward F. Campbell, Jr., "The Hebrew Short Story: A Study of Ruth," in *A Light Unto My Path: Old Testament Studies in Honor of Jacob M. Myers,* ed. Howard N. Bream, et al. (Philadelphia: Temple University Press, 1974), pp. 83–101; for a detailed exegesis, see also Edward F. Campbell, Jr., *Ruth,* AB (New York: Doubleday, 1975). My debt to this commentary is evident throughout, even where my views differ.

2. Cf. Stephen Bertman, "Symmetrical Design in the Book of Ruth," *JBL* 84 (1965): 165–68; Yehuda T. Radday, "Chiasm in Joshua, Judges and Others," *Linguistica Biblica* 3 (1973): 7–9.

3. Though this language indicates my debt to structuralism, I do not develop a structuralist analysis of Ruth; instead, I explore surface struc-

ture (see Chapter 1, n. 34, above). On Ruth and structuralism, see Hagia Hildegard Witzenrath, *Das Buch Rut: Eine literatur wissenschaftliche Untersuchung*, Studien zum Alten und Neutestament 40 (Munich: Kösel, 1975).

4. Note also that Elimelech is called Naomi's husband in v. 3, in contrast to her being "his wife" in v. 1; thus, the focus of the narrative shifts to the woman.

5. Cf. Edmund Leach, "The Legitimacy of Solomon: Some Structural Aspects of Old Testament History," in *Introduction to Structuralism*, ed. Michael Lane (New York: Basic Books, 1970), pp. 268–77.

6. For attempts to posit poetic antecedents to Ruth, see Jacob M. Myers, *The Linguistic and Literary Form of the Book of Ruth* (Leiden: E. J. Brill, 1955); George S. Glanzman, "The Origin and Date of the Book of Ruth," *CBQ* 21 (1959): 201–7.

7. See SS 3:4; 8:2; also Gen. 24:28.

8. For other interpretations of the phrase "mother's house," see Campbell, *Ruth*, pp. 64–65.

9. *Kindness* is hardly an adequate translation of *ḥesed*; see Nelson Glueck, *Ḥesed in the Bible* (Cincinnati: Hebrew Union College Press, 1967); Katharine D. Sakenfeld, "Studies in the Usage of the Hebrew Word *Ḥesed*" (Ph.D. diss., Harvard University, 1970).

10. On the motif *return*, see Werner Dommershausen, "Leitwortstil in der Ruthrolle," in *Theologie im Wandel* (Munich and Freiburg: Wewel, 1967), pp. 394–407.

11. On the word *me'ay* as "womb," cf. our discussions of Jer. 31:20 (Chapter 2) and of SS 5:4 (Chapter 5).

12. See Phyllis Trible, "The Radical Faith of Ruth," in *To Be a Person of Integrity*, ed. R. James Ogden (Valley Forge: Judson Press, 1975), p. 47; Campbell, *Ruth*, p. 82.

13. The description of Ruth as clinging (*dbq*) to Naomi (1:14), as well as Ruth's words to Naomi, "Entreat me not to abandon ['*zb*] you," recall the primeval man in Gen. 2:24 abandoning ('*zb*) his father and his mother to cleave (*dbq*) to his woman; see Chapter 4, above.

14. On the name *Naomi*, see Campbell, *Ruth*, pp. 52–53.

15. The pattern of emptiness/fullness is explored by D. F. Rauber, "Literary Values in the Bible. The Book of Ruth," *JBL* 89 (1970): 27–37.

16. For the translation "a man of substance," see Campbell, *Ruth*, p. 90.

17. I take this phrase to have an indefinite meaning rather than to be a specific reference to Boaz. In 2:1 the narrator prepares the reader for the eventual link between Boaz and the one in whose sight Ruth will find favor, but the two women themselves do not make this connection until 2:19–20; cf. Campbell, *Ruth*, pp. 92, 109. For the alternative reading, see Jack M. Sasson, "Divine Providence or Human Plan?" (a review of Campbell's *Ruth*), *Int.* 30 (1976): 418.

18. See Ronald M. Hals, *The Theology of the Book of Ruth* (Philadelphia: Fortress Press, 1969), pp. 11ff.

19. Boaz's words to Ruth, "Keep close [*dbq*] to my young women" (2:8c), employ the same verb that described Ruth's clinging to Naomi in 1:14c; also cf. its use in 2:21, 23.

20. Cf. Sasson's resistance to theological interpretation ("Divine Providence or Human Plan?" pp. 417–18).

21. For a different reading, see Campbell, who interprets at least most of the masculine-plural endings on the nouns *harvesters* and *young people* as including both sexes (*Ruth,* p. 97).

22. The question "Where did you glean today?" (2:19b) is perhaps another indication that the reference in 2:2 is indefinite rather than a specific mention of Boaz.

23. The noun *margᵉlōtāw* in 3:4, 7, 8, 14, which is usually translated "feet," probably functions as a euphemism for the genitals; cf. Campbell, *Ruth,* pp. 121, 131–32. I should prefer that Campbell had left intact the ambiguity of this episode in the dark of night rather than conclude "that there was no sexual intercourse at the threshing floor" (p. 134). For the opposite conclusion, see D. R. G. Beattie, "Kethibh and Qere in Ruth IV 5," *VT* 21 (1971): 493.

24. Cf. the woman in the Song of Songs who goes out into the streets at night to find her mate and then brings him home for lovemaking (SS 3:2–4).

25. Discussions about the meaning of *redeemer* in relation to levirate marriage are legion; see, e.g., H. H. Rowley, "The Marriage of Ruth," in *The Servant of the Lord and Other Essays* (London: Lutterworth Press, 1952), pp. 161–86; Thomas and Dorothy Thompson, "Some Legal Problems in the Book of Ruth," *VT* 18 (1968): 79–99 and the bibliography cited there; also Campbell, *Ruth,* pp. 132–37.

26. For a perceptive interpretation of this occasion, see Leszek Kolakowski, "Ruth, or the Dialogue Between Love and Bread," in *The Key to Heaven and Conversations with the Devil* (New York: Grove Press, 1972), pp. 53–56.

27. Cf. in 3:8 the narrator's use of the words "the man" and "a woman" rather than the names Boaz and Ruth. Darkness hides identity. Moreover, after 3:9, this screening of personal identity is maintained throughout the rest of scene three. But, although darkness, privacy, and secrecy hide the names of Boaz, Ruth, and Naomi, these phenomena do not conceal the divine name; see below on 3:10, 13.

28. See Hals, *The Theology of the Book of Ruth,* pp. 13ff.

29. For the translation "so-and-so," see Campbell, *Ruth,* pp. 141–43.

30. On the topic of land and related issues in Ruth 4, see Robert Gordis, "Love, Marriage, and Business in the Book of Ruth: A Chapter in Hebrew Customary Law," in *A Light Unto My Path,* pp. 246–64.

31. I follow the *qere* here rather than the *kethib;* for the opposite reading, see Beattie, "Kethibh and Qere," pp. 490–94; also "The Book of Ruth as Evidence for Israelite Legal Practice," *VT* 24 (1974): 251–67.

32. Note that this interruption is set apart by an inclusion: "this was the [custom] formerly in Israel . . . this was the manner of attesting in Israel" (4:7, RSV*). On the symbolism of the sandal, see Calum M. Carmichael, "A Ceremonial Crux: Removing a Man's Sandal as a Female Gesture of Contempt," *JBL* 96 (1977): 321–36, esp. pp. 332–36.

33. Note the symmetrical arrangement of the proper names in this statement: two women and one man at the beginning; two men and one woman at the end. Cf. "house of Israel" and "house of Perez" with

"mother's house" in 1:8; the last occurs in an episode void of males; the other two in an episode void of females.

34. An alternative interpretation suggests that Boaz is protecting Ruth in public.

35. Cf. the reversal on the theme of exogamy in 1:4: marriage in Moab vs. marriage in Bethlehem.

36. Cf. Gen. 2:24 where third-person narration also distanced the privacy of intercourse.

37. This statement, "Yahweh gave [*ntn*] her conception" (RSV*), corresponds in structure and function to 1:6: ". . . Yahweh had visited his people and given [*ntn*] them food" (RSV*). As the first and last narrative references to the deity, these statements accent two blessings of life: food and posterity.

38. *Contra* Oswald Loretz, "The Theme of the Ruth Story," *CBQ* 22 (1960): 391–99.

39. On comedy, cf. Northrop Frye, *Anatomy of Criticism* (Princeton: Princeton University Press, 1957), pp. 163–86.

The Afterwords

What woman, having ten silver coins, if she loses one coin, does not light a lamp and sweep the house and seek diligently until she finds it? (Luke 15:8, RSV)

Throughout the centuries, interpreters of scripture have explored the male language of faith, full and overflowing. Yet the Bible itself proclaims another dimension that faith has lost—female imagery and motifs. Much as the ancient housekeeper of the New Testament, while possessing nine coins, searched for the tenth which she had lost, so we too, while acknowledging the dominance of male language in scripture, have lit a lamp, swept the house, and sought diligently for that which was lost.

Scripture itself provided the clue for our search:

And God created humankind in his image;
In the image of God created he him;
Male and female created he them.
(Gen. 1:27)

Focusing upon the phrases "male and female" and "in the image of God," we discovered that the formal parallelism between them indicates a semantic correspondence between a better known and a lesser known element. Thus, the parallelism yields a metaphor. "Male and female" is its vehicle; "the image of God," its tenor. At the same time, this tenor becomes itself a vehicle pointing to "God." The repetition of the word *God* establishes similarity between the Creator and the human creatures, while the addition of the word *the-image-of* connotes their difference. Here the lack of any formal parallelism between the two components suggests a semantic disparity. Thus, this latter

200

metaphor saves the former from idolatry by witnessing to the transcendent Creator who is neither male nor female nor a combination of the two. Only in the context of this Otherness can we truly perceive the image of God male *and* female.

This metaphor, the image of God male and female, guided our search in two ways. First, it directed our attention to partial and diverse portrayals of male and female that suggest the image of God. And yet, precisely because our poem presents a balanced image, it provided an impetus to seek out female language for the deity. Accordingly, we swept diligently through scripture to investigate the partial metaphor symbolized by the Hebrew root *rhm*. This semantic journey from the wombs of women to the compassion of God is not a minor theme on the fringes of faith. To the contrary, with persistence and power it saturates scripture. Moreover, along the way, other passages joined this journey to depict Yahweh poetically as a deity who conceived, was pregnant, writhed in labor pains, brought forth a child and nursed it. These many female portrayals expanded, broadened, and deepened our understanding of the biblical God. Thus, our search for "the lost coin" was well under way.

Second, our metaphor directed attention to diverse traditions of scripture that embody male and female within the same context. This context is the goodness of creation, a goodness that fulfills and enhances life (cf. Gen. 1:31). Hence, we lit a lamp to illuminate the tragedy of disobedience in Genesis 2—3, the poetry of eroticism in the Song of Songs, and the struggles of daily existence in the story of Ruth. In Genesis 2 the development of Eros culminates in a poem to sexuality as man and woman become one flesh. Alas, however, this flesh of mutuality and harmony disintegrates through transgression to yield judgment and exile (Gen. 3). The Song of Songs, on the other hand, recovers the love that is bone of bone and flesh of flesh. Belonging neither to a primeval nor to an eschatological setting, this poetry describes joy and ecstasy as realities for life in the present. It knows the grace of sexuality, not the sin of sexism. Narrating a human comedy, the book of Ruth moves from deepest despair to well-being, while challenging and transforming the male culture that it reflects. With these illuminations, our search for "the lost coin" ended, though, perhaps, it is not completed.

Clearly, the patriarchal stamp of scripture is permanent. But just as clearly, interpretation of its content is forever changing, since new occasions teach new duties and contexts alter texts, liberating them from frozen constructions. Moving across cultures and centuries, then, the Bible informed a feminist perspective, and correspondingly, a feminist perspective enlightened the Bible. Shaped by a rhetorical-critical methodology, this interaction resulted in new interpretations of old texts; moreover, it uncovered neglected traditions to reveal countervoices within a patriarchal document. It did not, however, eliminate the male-dominated character of scripture; such a task would have been both impossible and dishonest. And yet, the Bible is a potential witness against *all* our interpretations, for the pilgrim named scripture wanders through history to merge past and present on its way toward the future.

"What woman, having ten silver coins, if she loses one coin, does not light a lamp and sweep the house and seek diligently until she finds it?" My search has also been for the lost token of faith—for the remnant that makes the difference. Now at the end of this search, I join that ancient woman, who, having found the lost coin, called together "her friends and neighbors, saying, 'Rejoice with me, for I have found the coin which I had lost' " (Luke 15:9, RSV).

Scripture Index

204   GOD AND THE RHETORIC OF SEXUALITY